# A Semiotic of Ethnicity

SUNY Series in Italian/American Studies
Fred L. Gardaphe, Editor

# A Semiotic of Ethnicity

## In (Re)cognition of the Italian/American Writer

### Anthony Julian Tamburri

State University of New York Press

*38061637*

PS
153
.I8
T36
1998

The author gratefully acknowledges permission to quote from the following material:

*The Evening News* © 1986 Tony Ardizzone (Atlanta, GA: University of Georgia Press).

*Taking It Home: Stories from the Neighborhood* © 1996 Tony Ardizzone (Urbana and Chicago: University of Illinois Press).

*Umbertina* © 1979 Helen Barolini (New York: Seaview Books).
*Round Trip* © 1991 Luigi Fontanella (Udine: Campanotto Editore).
*Stella Saturnina* © 1989 Luigi Fontanella (Rome: Il ventaglio).
*Simulazione di reato* © 1979 Luigi Fontanella (Manduria: Lacaita).

The poems by Gianna Patriarca are reprinted with the permission of Gianna Patriarca and Guernica Editions Inc. Copyright © Gianna Patriarca and Guernica Editions Inc. (Toronto/Buffalo/Lancaster [UK]) *Italian Women and Other Tragedies*, 1994.

The poems by Giose Rimanelli are reprinted with the permission of Giose Rimanelli and Guernica Editions Inc. Copyright © Giose Rimanelli and Guernica Editions Inc. (Toronto/Buffalo/Lancaster [UK]) *Benedetta in Guysterland*, 1993.

Published by
State University of New York Press, Albany

For information, address State University of New York Press, State University Plaza, Albany, N.Y. 12246

Production by M. R. Mulholland
Marketing by Fran Keneston

Library of Congress Cataloging-in-Publication Data
Tamburri, Anthony Julian.
    A semiotic of ethnicity : in (re) cognition of the Italian/American writer / Anthony Julian Tamburri.
        p. cm. -- (SUNY series in Italian/American studies)
    Includes bibliographical references and index.
    ISBN 0–7914–3915–1 (hc : acid free). -- ISBN 0–7914–3916–X (pb : acid free)
    1. American literature -- Italian American authors -- History and criticism.   2. American literature -- Italian influences.   3. Italian Americans -- Intellectual life.   4. Italian Americans in literature.   5. Semiotics and literature.   6. Ethnicity in literature.
    I. Title.   II. Series.
    PS153.I8T36   1998
    810.9'8951—dc21                                      97-49661
                                                          CIP

10 9 8 7 6 5 4 3 2 1

# Contents

Preface     vii

Acknowledgments     xi

## Part I. New Strategies

1. In (Re)cognition of the Italian/American Writer:
   Definitions and Categories     3

## Part II. New Readings

2. Tony Ardizzone's "Expressive" *Evening News*     23
3. Helen Barolini's "Comparative" *Umbertina:*
   The Italian/American Woman     47
4. Giose Rimanelli's "Synthetic" *Benedetta in Guysterland:*
   A "Liquid" Novel of Questionable Textual Boundaries     65

## Part III. Further Readings

5. Looking Back: The Image of Italy in *Umbertina*     81
6. Gianna Patriarca's "Tragic" Thought: *Italian Women
   and Other Tragedies*     95
7. Italian/American Writer or Italian Poet Abroad?:
   Luigi Fontanella's Poetic Voyage     109

## Part IV. Further Strategies

8. Italian/American Cultural Studies: Looking Forward     121

Notes     133

Select Bibliography     163

Index     171

# Preface

One thing the reader will notice is that I have decided to stay away from a few names that one might readily associate with an ethnic study. I have in mind someone like Richard Alba and his essentialist view of ethnicity—that the melting pot really does exist[1]—or Werner Sollors and his bipolar notion of oppositional discourse.[2] While their work is surely at the heart of a good deal of a certain type of ethnic critical discourse, I had the impression that, because of my own hermeneutico-semiotic perspective, their work would have brought me in a direction that would have clouded my own Peircean lens and moved me to engage in a comparison of strategies that is not the intended focal point of my study.[3] Hence, when it was necessary to deal with sociology, the likes of Herbert Gans, Joseph Lopreato, and Richard Gambino proved equally useful.[4] For a literary discourse, Daniel Aaron and Rose Basile Green, in spite of what some might consider to be slightly dated voices, proved to be insightful and unexpectedly fresh even for a 1990s post-structuralist approach to literature, which indeed informs my study.[5]

This book is divided into four parts. The first offers a specific taxonomy of how we may otherwise consider the Italian/American writer in this age of semiotics, poststructuralism, and the like. The main thrust of my book is therefore to offer another interpretive strategy that may readily accompany and complement, not necessarily cancel out categorically, previous strategies to the reading of Italian/American texts.

As I have chosen to lay out a tripartite paradigm in Part I, I offer in Part II examples of each category in Chapters Two (Tony Ardizzone, expressive writer), Three (Helen Barolini, comparative writer), and Four (Giose Rimanelli, synthetic writer). The third part of this study, Further Readings, is meant to show other considerations—thematic and formalistic—of the Italian/American writer that have either not yet been examined or, if so, dealt with thus far only in a preliminary manner. In Chapter Five, my emphasis is no longer on Barolini the "comparative writer"; rather, I'm interested in reading the Italian/American writer's view of Italy. Barolini is one of the few writers of Italian descent who knows both worlds well enough to be able to offer such a vision. This notion of the view of Italy in writings by Italian Americans has yet to be examined in any great length; this chapter suggests such a study. Chapter Six, dedicated to Patriarca's poetry collection, *Italian Women and Other Tragedies*, speaks to another aspect of Italian Americana I mention briefly in Chapter One: the notion of considering, if only occasionally, Italian Americans and Italian Canadians as members of one larger group, Italian/North Americans. This, too, is a new idea that has yet to be explored.[6] Chapter Seven, which examines Luigi Fontanella's poetry, speaks to the notion of writing in the Italian language within a United States melieu. This chapter also speaks to a more recent notion of a possible reclassification and redefinition of the Italian/American writer. Some work has already been done on this topic in the form of three articles (Paolo Valesio, Peter Carravetta, and Paolo Giordano),[7] an anthology (*Poesaggio*), a special issue (*Gradiva* [SUNY Stony Brook]), and the section dedicated to Italian writing in the United States in the journal *Voices in Italian Americana* (10–40 pages per issue). Finally, Part IV offers a modest proposal of what else we may do in order to help usher into the twenty-first century the study of the North American writer of Italian descent. Through the lens of general notions of cultural studies, we might want to reconsider the Italian/American writer in terms of the multicultural debate. This, too, is an area of Italian Americana that has yet to be explored.[8]

As we shall see at various points throughout this study, much groundwork for a contemporary reading of the Italian/American writer has already been done by the likes of Robert Viscusi, Fred Gardaphé, and Mary Jo Bona, to name a few. Their work has rescued the figure of the writer from the literary ghetto of superficial sociohistorical, thematic criticism and securely placed it within a rhetoric of semiology and, in part, discourse analysis (Viscusi). In addition, we can now explore the dynamics of the various works of these many disparate writers of different generations through other contemporary critical lenses (Gardaphé), thereby discovering that which previous critics did not, could not, or would not bring forth. Further still, we recently became aware of the gender issue that, in the somewhat masculinist culture Italian America seemed to perpetuate, remained hidden both literally and figuratively in the kitchen (Bona). To the work of these three and others, such as William Boelhower, Robert Casillo, Paolo Giordano, Edvige Giunta, Renate Holub, John Paul Russo, Pasquale Verdicchio, Justin Vitiello, we all owe an immense debt.

A final note: On the use of the slash (/) in place of the hyphen (-), I refer the reader to my *To Hyphenate or Not to Hyphenate*, where I considered then, and still do, the use of any diacritical mark in language steeped in ideology in the broadest sense of the terms. It is basically an arbitrary decision that is made according to a systematic set of ideas created by those who have the ability (read, also, power) to do so. In any event, when the *opusculum* first appeared, people asked why I had not just eliminated altogether the diacritical mark and combine both terms. True! But that was not my point. My reasoning in maintaining a diacritical mark—the slash—was to bring further light to the fact that a diacritical mark was, as a manner of speaking, *required*. With regard to the coining of a new term by combining both "Italian" and "American," as had been suggested by some, I would repeat here that it had already been done by Martin Scorsese in the title of his documentary film ITALIANAMERICAN (1974).[9]

# Acknowledgments

Like many books, *A Semiotic of Ethnicity* has its origin in numerous conferences I attended, discussions in which I engaged, and essays I have written.[1] The annual conferences of the American Italian Historical Association and those of the Florida State University Conference on Comparative Literature and Film provided the main outlets where I was first able to try out my ideas in public. Both organizations offered open fora for a type of interpretive experimentation in process and analysis of the various texts I chose to present.

In addition to these public fora for discussion, I also owe a debt to the various journals that published essays that constitute early versions of various parts of this book: *Canadian Journal of Italian Studies, Differentia, MELUS,* and *World Literature Today.* Two other editorial ventures deserve special thanks in this regard. My first essay on Italian/American studies appeared in *The Italian Journal* (3.5 [1989]: 37–42), edited by the late Victor Tesoro. That short, six-page position paper, "To Hyphenate or Not to Hyphenate: The Italian/American Writer and *Italianità,*" I later expanded. The later version saw its light of day in the form of an *opusculum, To Hyphenate or Not to Hyphenate? The Italian/American Writer: An* Other *American,* published by Guernica Editions. These two essays lie at the base of what eventually became the opening essay to this book, whose previous version originally appeared in the special issue of *Differentia* dedicated to Italian/American culture.

Numerous people played different, indispensable roles at various stages throughout the conception and planning of this book. In the past seven years, I have engaged in frequent conversations and debates with various colleagues and friends: Fred Gardaphé and Paolo Giordano heard and read most of what I have had to say. Peter Carravetta underwent a similar aural assault and offered in return valuable comments. Others whose conversations, observations, and comments along the way proved pertinent are Antonio D'Alfonso, Mary Jo Bona, Victoria De Mara, Edvige Giunta, Renate Holub, John T. Kirby, Ben Lawton, Francine Masiello, Mark Pietralunga, Pasquale Verdicchio, Maurizio Viano, Robert Viscusi, Justin Vitiello, and Rebecca West. They have each contributed in their own way to transforming, to some degree, my way of thinking about Italian Americana; I am indebted to all, including the anonymous readers of SUNY Press and its copy editor Scott Duncanson. Finally, Maria Donovan added her own invaluable observations along the way, tolerating also the time absorbed by the various conferences and subsequent work that led to this final product.

This book is dedicated to the Cerulli family.

# Part 1
## New Strategies

# 1

# In (Re)cognition of the Italian/American Writer: Definitions and Categories

Most men do not think things in the way they encounter them, nor do they recognize what they experience, but believe their own opinions.

—Heraclitus

And I thought, "Does this son of a bitch think he is more American than I am?" Where does he think I was brought up? Because my name is Ciardi, he decided to hyphenate the poem. Had it been a Yankee name, he would have thought, "Ah, a scholar who knows about Italy." Sure he made assumptions, but I can't grant for a minute that Lowell is any more American than I am . . .

—John Ciardi, in *Growing Up Italian*

"If every picture I made was about Italian Americans, they'd say, 'That's all he can do.' I'm trying to stretch."

—Martin Scorsese, in *Premiere* (1991)

Part One: A Premise of Sorts

Ethnic studies in any form or manner, for instance, the use of ethnicity as a primary yardstick, do not necessarily constitute the major answer to knowledge gaps with regard to what some may consider ethnic myopia in the United States. Nevertheless, and by now a cliché, we all know that the United States of America was born and developed, at times with tragic results, along lines of diversity.[1] What is important in this regard is that we understand, or a least *try* to understand, the origins of the diversity and difference which characterize the many ethnic and racial groups which constitute the kaleidoscopic nature of this country's population. In accepting literature as, among many things, the mirror of the society in which it is conceived, created, and perceived, we come to understand that one of the many questions ethnic literature addresses is the negative stereotyping of members of ethnic/racial groups which are not part and parcel of the dominant culture. By ethnic literature, I mean that type of writing which deals contextually with customs and behavioral patterns that the North American mind-set may consider different from what it perceives as mainstream. The difference, I might add, may also manifest itself formalistically, i.e., the writer may not follow what have become accepted norms and conventions of literary creation; s/he may not produce what the dominant culture considers *good* literature.

This last point notwithstanding, one of the goals of ethnic literature is, to be sure, the dislodging and debunking of negative stereotypes. In turn, through the natural dynamics of intertextual recall and inference, the reader engages in a process of analytical inquiry and comparison of the ethnic group(s) in question with other ethnic groups as well as with the dominant culture. In fact, it is precisely through a comparative process that one comes to understand how difference and diversity from one group to another may not be as great as they initially seem; indeed, one understands that such difference and diversity can not only co/exist but may even overlap with that which is considered characteristic of the dominant group. This, I believe, is another of the goals/functions of ethnic literature: to impart knowledge of the customs, characteristics, language, etc., of the various racial and ethnic groups in this country. Finally, partial responsibility for the validity, or lack thereof, of *other* literatures also lies with the *critic* or *theorist*.[2] In fact, the theorist's end goal for *other* literatures, perhaps, should not limit itself only to the invention of another mode of reading. Instead, it should become in itself a strategy of reading which extends beyond the limits of textual analysis; it should concomitantly and ultimately aim for the validation of the text(s) in question vis-à-vis those already validated by the dominant culture.

The fortune of Italian/American literature is somewhat reflective of the United States mind-set vis-à-vis ethnic studies. Namely, until recently, ever since the arrival of the immigrants of the 1880s, the major wave of western European emigration, the United States have considered ethnic/racial difference in terms of the melting-pot attitude. The past two decades, however, have constituted a period of transition, if not change, in this attitude. Be it the end of modernism, as some have claimed, or the onslaught of the postmodern, as others may claim, in academic and intellectual circles today one no longer thinks in terms of the melting pot.[3] Instead, as is well known, one now talks in terms of the individual ethnic/racial culture and its relationship—not necessarily in negative terms only—with the longstanding, mainstream cultural paradigm. It is, therefore, with the backdrop of this new attitude of rejecting the melting pot and supplanting it with the notion of Americana as a "kaleidoscopic, socio/cultural mosaic," as I have rehearsed it elsewhere,[4] that I shall consider an attempt to (re)define Italian/American literature and recategorize the notion of the *hyphenate writer.* By using the phrase "kaleidoscopic socio/cultural mosaic," I mean to underscore how the socio/cultural dynamics of the United States reveal a constant flux of changes originating in the very existence of the various differentiated ethnic/racial groups that constitute the overall population of the United States. As an addendum, I would suggest that, as people, we still must come to understand that the population of the United States is indeed similar to a mosaic in that this country consists of various bits and pieces (that is, the various peoples, ethnic and/or racial, of the United States) each one unique unto itself. The kaleidoscopic nature of this aggregate of different and unique peoples is surely descriptive of this constant flux of changes that manifests itself, as the various peoples change physical and ideological position, which ultimately change the ideological colors of the United States mind-set.

Bouncing off notions of *ethnic*—or for that matter any *other*—literature which are immediate to postcolonial literature, we may indeed state that, first of all, such a notion cannot be "constructed as an internally coherent object of theoretical knowledge"; that such a categorization "cannot be resolved . . . without an altogether positivist reductionism."[5] Secondly, *other* "literary traditions [e.g., third world, ethnic, etc.] remain, beyond a few texts here and there, [often] unknown to the *American* literary theorist" (p. 5). While it may be true that Ahmad's use of the adjective *American* refers to the geopolitical notion of the United States of America, I would contend that the situation of ethnic literatures within the United States is analogous to what Ahmad so adroitly describes in his article as, for lack of a better term, "third-world literature." Thus I would suggest that we reconsider Ahmad's *American* within the confines of the geopolitical borders of the United States and thereby reread it as synonymous with *dominant culture.* Thirdly, "[l]iterary texts are produced in highly differentiated, usually overdetermined contexts of competing ideological and cultural *clusters,* so that any particular text of any complexity shall always have to be placed within the *cluster* that gives it its energy and form, before it is totalised into a universal category" (p. 23; my emphasis). Thus, it is also within this ideological framework of cluster specificity that I shall consider further the notion of Italian/American literature as a validifiable category of United States literature and (re)think the significance of the Italian/ American writer within the (re)categorization of the notion of the hyphenate writer.

Finally, I should specify at the outset that which I have in mind for Italian/American writer throughout this essay. Because of language plurality—standard Italian, Italian dialect, and United States English[6]— I believe that there are different types of writers that may fall under the general category of Italian/American writer. They range from the immigrant writer of Italian language to the United States-born writer of Italian descent who writes in English; and in between, of course, one may surely find the many variations of these two extremes.[7] In the pages that follow, therefore, I shall use the phrase "Italian/American writer" in reference to that person—be s/he born in the United States or in Italy—who is significantly involved in creative literary activity in the English language.[8]

## Part Two: Definitions and Categories

The notion for an enterprise of this type is grounded in a slightly unorthodox mode of thought. In this poststructuralist, postmodern society, my study therefore casts by the wayside any notion of universality or absoluteness with regard to the (re)definition of any literary category vis-à-vis national origin, ethnicity, race, or gender. Undoubtedly one can and should readily equate the above-mentioned notion to some general notions associated with the postmodern. Any rejection of the validity of the notion of *hierarchy*, or better, *universality* or *absoluteness*, is characteristic of those who are, to paraphrase Lyotard, "incredul[ous] toward [grand or] metanarratives."[9] Indeed, one of the legitimized *and* legitimizing *grands récits*—metanarrative—is the discourse built around the notion of canon valorization. By implicitly constructing an otherwise nonexistent category, or *sub*set, of American letters, that is, Italian/American literature, the notion of a centered canon of the dominant Anglo/American culture is rattled once more. Rattled *once more* precisely because fortunately there already exist *legitimized*—that is, considering the Academy as the legitimizing institution—similar categories, such as African/American or Jewish/American fiction; one need only peruse the list of graduate courses in American and English literature in the various catalogues of most American universities.[10]

In the past, Italian/American art forms—more precisely, literature and film—have been defined as those constructed mainly by second-generation writers about the experiences of the first and second generations. In a recent essay on Italian/American cinema, for example, Robert Casillo defined it as "works by Italian-American directors who treat Italian-American subjects."[11] In like fashion, Frank Lentricchia had previously defined Italian/American literature as "a report and meditation on first-generation experience, usually from the perspective of a second-generation representative."[12] Indeed, both constitute a valid attempt at constructing neat and clean definitions for works of two art forms—and in a certain sense we can extend this meaning to other art media—that deal explicitly with an Italian/American ethnic quality and/or subject matter.[13] Such definitions, however, essentially halt—though willy-nilly by those who offer them—the progress and limit the impact of those writers who come from later generations. Thus they may result in a monolithic notion of what was or is, and what was not or is not, Italian/American literature. Following a similar mode of thinking, Dana Gioia more recently proposed yet another definition in his brief essay, "What Is Italian-American Poetry?"[14] There, Gioia describes "Italian-American poetry . . . only as a transitional category" for which the "concept of Italian-American poet is therefore most useful to describe first- and second-generation writers raised in the immigrant subculture" (p. 3). Together with his restrictive definition of Italian/American poetry, Gioia also demonstrates a seemingly furtive sociological thought pattern in not distinguishing between ethnicity passed from one generation to the next vis-à-vis a member of the subsequent generation's decision to rid him/herself of or deny his/her ethnicity, when he states that "[s]ome kinds of ethnic or cultural consciousness seem more or less permanent" (p. 3).[15]

One question that arises is: what do we do about those works of art—written and visual—that do not *explicitly* treat Italian/American subject matter and yet seem to exude a certain ethnic Italian/American quality, even if we cannot readily define it? That is, can we speak to the Italian/American qualities of a Frank Capra film? According to Casillo's definition, we would initially have to say no. However, it is Casillo himself who tells us that Capra, indeed, "found his ethnicity troublesome throughout his long career" (p. 374) and obviously dropped it. My question, then, is: can we not see this *absence*, especially in light of documented secondary matter, as an Italian/American sign *in potentia*? I would say yes. And in this regard, I would suggest an alternative perspective on reading and categorizing any Italian/American art form.[16] That is, I believe we should take our cue from Scorsese himself and therefore "stretch" our own reading strategy of Italian/American art forms, whether they be, due to content or form, *explicitly* Italian/ American or not, in order to accommodate other possible, successful

reading strategies. Indeed, recent (re)writings of Italian/American literary history and criticism have transcended a limited concept of
Italian/American literature. New literary and critical publications have
created a need for new definitions and new critical readings, not only of
contemporary work, but of the works of the past. In addition, these new
publications have originated, for the most part, from within an intellectual community of Italian Americans.[17] Therefore, I would propose that
we consider Italian/American literature to be a series of on-going written enterprises which establish a repertoire of signs, at times *sui generis*,
and therefore create verbal variations (visual in the case of film, painting, sculpture, drama, etc.) that represent different versions—dependent,
of course, on one's generation, gender, socio-economic condition—of
what can be perceived as the Italian/American *interpretant*. That is, the
Italian/American experience may indeed be manifested in any art form
in a number of ways and at varying degrees, for which one may readily
speak of the variegated representations of the Italian/American ethos
in literature, for example, in the same fashion in which Daniel Aaron
spoke of the "hyphenate writer."[18]

Within the general discourse of American literature, Daniel Aaron
seems to be one of the first to have dealt with the notion of hyphenation.[19] For him, the hyphen initially represented older North Americans' hesitation to accept the new/comer; it was their way, in Aaron's
words, to "hold him at 'hyphen's length,' so to speak, from the established community" (p. 213). It further "signifies a tentative but unmistakable withdrawal" on the user's part, so that "mere geographical
proximity" denies the newly arrived "full and unqualified national
membership despite . . . legal qualifications and . . . official disclaimers
to the contrary" (p. 213).

Speaking in terms of a passage from "'hyphenation' to 'dehy-
phenation'" (p. 214), Aaron sets up three stages through which a
nonAnglo/American writer might pass.[20] The first-stage writer is the
"pioneer spokesman for the . . . unspoken-for" ethnic, racial, or cultural
group, that is, the marginalized. This person writes about his/her co-
others with the goal of dislodging and debunking negative stereotypes
ensconced in the dominant culture's mind-set. In so doing, this writer
may actually create characters possessing some of the very same stereotypes, with the specific goals, however, of 1) winning over the sympathies of the suspicious members of the dominant group, and
2) humanizing the stereotyped figure and thus "dissipating prejudice."
Successful or not, this writer engages in placating his/her reader by em-
ploying recognizable features the dominant culture associates with specific ethnic, racial, or cultural groups.

Aaron considers this first-stage writer abjectly conciliatory toward the dominant group. He states: "It was as if he were saying to his suspicious and opinionated audience: 'Look,' we have customs and manners that may seem bizarre and uncouth, but we are respectable people nevertheless and our presence adds flavor and variety to American life. Let me convince you that our oddities—no matter how quaint and amusing you find them—do not disqualify us from membership in the national family'" (214). What this writer seems to do, however, is engage in a type of game, a bartering system of sorts that may sometimes downplay, set in the background, or ignore the injustices set forth by the dominant group, asking or instead hoping that the very same dominant group might attempt to change its ideas while accepting the writer's offerings as its final chance to enjoy the stereotype.[21]

Less willing to please, the second-stage writer abandons the use of preconceived ideas in an attempt to demystify negative stereotypes. Whereas the first-stage writer might have adopted some preconceived notions popular among members of the dominant culture, this writer instead presents characters who have already sunk "roots into the native soil." By no means as conciliatory as the first-stage writer, this person readily indicates the disparity and, in some cases, may even engage in militant criticism of the perceived restrictions and oppression set forth by the dominant group. In so doing, according to Aaron, this writer runs the risk of a "double criticism": from the dominant culture offended by the "unflattering or even 'un American' image of American life," and from other members of his/her own marginalized group, who might feel misrepresented, having preferred a more "genteel and uncantankerous spokesman."

The third-stage writer, in turn, travels from the margin to the mainstream, "viewing it no less critically, perhaps, but more knowingly." Having appropriated the dominant group's culture and the tools necessary to succeed in that culture, greater skill in manipulating a language acceptable to the dominant group, for instance, this writer more strongly than his/her predecessors feels entitled to the intellectual and cultural heritage of the dominant group. As such, s/he can also, from a personal viewpoint, "speak out uninhibitedly as an American."[22] This writer, however, as Aaron reminds us, does not renounce or abandon the cultural heritage of his/her marginalized group. Instead, s/he transcends "a mere parochial allegiance" in order to transport "into the province of the [general] imagination," personal experiences which for the first-stage ("local colorist") and second-stage ("militant protester") writer "comprised the very stuff of their literary material" (p. 215).[23]

An excellent analog to Aaron's three stages of the "hyphenate writer" can be found in Fred L. Gardaphé's threefold Vichian division of the history of Italian/American literature. Gardaphé proposes a culturally "specific methodology" for the greater disambiguation of Italian/American contributions to the United States literary scene. In his essay, he reminds us of Vico's "three ages and their corresponding cultural products: the Age of Gods in which primitive society records expression in 'poetry' [*vero narratio,*] the Age of Heroes, in which society records expression in myth, and the Age of Man, in which through self-reflection, expression is recorded in philosophic prose." These three ages, Gardaphé goes on to tell us, have their parallels in modern and "contemporary [socio-]cultural constructions of realism, modernism, and postmodernism" (p. 24). And, ultimately, the evolution of the various literatures of United States ethnic and racial groups can be charted as they "move from the poetic, through the mythic and into the philosophic" (p. 25).

In making such an analogy, it is important to remember, as Aaron had already underscored, that personal experiences "comprised the very stuff of . . . literary material" for both the first-stage ("local colorist") and second-stage ("militant protester") writers; whereas the third-stage writer, on the other hand, travels from the margin to the mainstream without either renouncing or abandoning his/her cultural heritage. For Gardaphé, Vico's three ages (read, Aaron's three stages) constitute the pre modernist (the "poetic" = "realism"), the modernist (the "mythic" = "modernism"), and the postmodernist (the "philosophic" = "postmodernism").

For the first-stage writer, then, a type of self-deprecating barterer with the dominant culture, the *vero narratio* constitutes the base of what s/he writes. S/he no more writes about what s/he *thinks* than what s/he *experiences,* that is, his/her surroundings. His/her art then, in a sense records her/his experiential feelings more than her/his analytical thoughts. This writer is not concerned with an adherence to or the creation of some form of objective, rhetorical literary paradigm. S/he is an expressive writer, not a paradigmatic one; his/her ethnic experiences of the more visceral kind serve more as the foundation of his/her literary signification.

The second-stage writer, the "militant protester," is by no means as conciliatory as was the first-stage writer and belongs to the generation that (re)discovers and/or reinvents his/her ethnicity. While s/he may present characters who have already "sunk roots in the native soil," s/he readily underscores the characters' uniqueness vis-à-vis the expectations of the dominant culture. As Gardaphé reminds us, before this writer can "merge with the present," s/he must recreate—in a *sui generis* manner, I would add—his past; s/he must engage in a "materialization and an articulation of the past" (p. 27).

The use of ethnicity at this second stage shifts from the expressive to the descriptive. As a rhetorical-ideological tool, ethnicity becomes much more functional and quasi descriptive. It is no longer the pre–dominantly expressive element it is in the pre modernist, poetic writer (that is, the bartering, first-stage expressive writer). Whereas in the pre–modernist, poetic writer ethnicity as theme is the expressive conduit, through which s/he communicates his/her immediate sensorial feelings, for the modernist, mythic writer ethnicity becomes more the tool with which s/he communicates his/her ideology. In this second case, the ethnic signs constitute the individual pieces of the ethnic paradigm this second-stage writer so consciously and willingly seeks to construct.

While this modernist, mythic second-stage writer may engage in militant criticism of the perceived restrictions and oppression set forth by the dominant group as an *expressive* residue of the evolution from the pre modernist to the modernist stage, the third-stage writer (Gardaphé's postmodernist, philosophic writer) may seem at first glance to rid him/herself of his/her ethnicity.[24] This writer, as Aaron reminds us, will often view the dominant culture "less critically" than the previous writers, but indeed "more knowingly." This should not come as any surprise, however, since, as Gardaphé later tells us, this writer finds him/herself in a decisively self-reflexive stage in which s/he can decide to transcend the experiential expressivity of the first two stages by either engaging in a parodic tour de force through his/her art or by relegating any vestige of his/her ethnicity to the background of his/her artistic inventions.[25] In both cases, the writer has come to terms with his/her personal (read, ethnic) history without totally or explicitly renouncing or abandoning cultural heritage. This writer therefore transcends "mere parochial allegiance" and passes completely out of the *expressive* and *descriptive* stages into a third—and final—reflexive stage in which everything becomes fair game. All this is due to the "postmodern prerogative" of all artists, be they the parodic, the localizers, or others simply in search of rules for what will have been done.

What can we finally make of these writers who seem to evolve into different animals from one generation to the next? Indeed, both Aaron and Gardaphé look at these writers from the perspective of time, and their analyses are generationally based, and rightfully so. However, we would not err to look at these three stages from another perspective, a cognitive Peircean perspective of firstness, secondness, and thirdness as rehearsed in his *Principles of Philosophy*.[26] All three stages, for Peirce, represent different modes of being dependent on different levels of consciousness. They progress from a state of non rationality ("feeling")[27] to practicality ("experience")[28] and on to pure rationality ("thought")[29]— or potentiality, actuality, and futuribility.

If firstness is the isolated, *sui generis* mode of possibly being Peirce tells us it is, we may see an analog in the first-stage writer's *vero narratio*. For it is here, Gardaphé tells us, that primitive society records expression in poetry, in unmitigated realism, by which I mean that which the writer experiences only.[30] In this sense, the writer's sensorial experiences, his/her "feelings," as Peirce calls them, constitute the "very stuff of [his/her] literary material." Namely, those recordings of what s/he simply experiences, without the benefit of any "analysis, comparison or any [other] process whatsoever . . . by which one stretch of consciousness is distinguished from another."

As the second-stage writer shifts from the expressive—"that kind of consciousness which involves no analysis," Peirce would tell us—to the descriptive, s/he now engages in some form of analysis and comparison, two processes fundamental to Peirce's secondness. This writer therefore becomes aware of the dominant culture—"how a second object is"—and does not repeat the conciliatory acts of the first-stage writer; s/he undergoes a "forcible modification of . . . thinking [which is] the influence of the world of fact or *experience*."

The third-stage writer transcends the first two stages of experiential expressivity either through parody or diminution of significance of his/her expressivity, because s/he has seen "both sides of the shield" and can therefore "contemplate them from the outside only." That "element of cognition [thirdness, according to Peirce] which is neither feeling [firstness] nor the polar sense [secondness], is the consciousness of a process, and this in the form of the sense of learning, of acquiring, mental growth is eminently characteristic of cognition" (1.381). Peirce goes on to tell us that this third mode of being is timely, not immediate; it is the progressive "consciousness of synthesis" (1.381), which is precisely what this third-stage, postmodern writer does. S/he can transcend the intellectual experiences of the first two stages because of all that has preceded him/her both temporally (Aaron, Gardaphé) and cognitively (Peirce).[31]

What we now witness after at least three generations of writers is a progression from a stage of visceral realism to that of incredulous postmodernism, with passage through a secondary stage of mythic modernism in which this monolithic modernist writer believes to have found all the solutions to what s/he has perceived as the previous generation's *problems*. In light of what was stated above, we may now speak in terms of a twofold evolution—a both temporal and intellectual process—that bears three distinct writers to whom we may now attach more precise labels. The *expressive* writer embodies the poetic realist who writes more from "feelings." Through the process of analysis, on the other hand, the second is a *comparative* writer who sets up a distinct polarity between his/her cultural heritage and the dominant culture in that s/he attempts to construct a *sui generis* ethnic paradigm. The third writer instead, through "mental growth," as Peirce states, can embrace a consciousness of process (that is, self-reflexivity) and consequently engage in a process of synthesis and "bind . . . life together" (1.381). This I would consider to be the *synthetic* writer. The following graph charts my use of the above-mentioned terminology in what I have proposed as three possible categories of the Italian/American writer or, for that matter, any ethnic/racial writer:

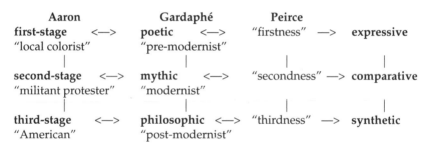

| **Aaron** | | **Gardaphé** | | **Peirce** | | |
|---|---|---|---|---|---|---|
| **first-stage** | <—> | **poetic** | <—> | "firstness" | —> | **expressive** |
| "local colorist" | | "pre-modernist" | | | | |
| \| | | \| | | \| | | \| |
| **second-stage** | <—> | **mythic** | <—> | "secondness" | —> | **comparative** |
| "militant protester" | | "modernist" | | | | |
| \| | | \| | | \| | | \| |
| **third-stage** | <—> | **philosophic** | <—> | "thirdness" | —> | **synthetic** |
| "American" | | "post-modernist" | | | | |

Having proposed such a reclassification, I believe it is important to reiterate some of what was stated before and underscore its significance to the above-mentioned categories. First and foremost, it is important to emphasize that the three different general categories, while generationally based for Aaron and Gardaphé and cognitively based for Peirce, should not by any means represent a hierarchy—they are, simply, different. For in a manner similar to Peirce's three stages, these three general categories also represent different modes of being dependent on different levels of consciousness. The key word here, of course, is *different*. These categories are different precisely because, as Ahmad reminded us, just as literary texts in general "are produced in highly differentiated, usually over-determined contexts of competing ideological and cultural clusters," so too do each of the three categories constitute specific cognitive and ideological clusters that ultimately provide the energy and form to the texts of those writers of the three different stages.

Second, these stages do not necessarily possess any form of monolithic valence. What I am suggesting is that writers should not be considered with respect to one stage only. It is possible, I would contend, that a writer's opus may, in fact, reflect more than one, if not all three, of these stages.[32] In this respect, we should remind ourselves that pertinent to any discourse on ethnic art forms is the notion that ethnicity is not a fixed essence passed down from one generation to the next. Rather, "ethnicity is something reinvented and reinterpreted in each generation by each individual,"[33] which, in the end, is a way of "finding a voice or style that does not violate one's *several components of identity*" (my emphasis) constituting the specificities of each individual. Thus, ethnicity—and more specifically in this case, *italianità*[34]—is redefined and reinterpreted on the basis of each individual's time and place, and is therefore always new and different with respect to his/her own historical specificities vis-à-vis the dominant culture.

This said, then, we should also keep in mind that we may now think in terms of a twofold evolutionary process—both temporal and cognitive—which may or may not be mutually inclusive. The temporal may not parallel the cognitive and vice versa. Hence, we may have, sociologically speaking, a second- or third-generation writer—according to Aaron's distinction, s/he would have to be a "second-" or "third-stage" writer—who finds a voice or style in his/her recent rediscovery and reinvention of his/her ethnicity. This writer, though a member of the second or third generation, may actually produce what we may now expect from the *expressive* or *comparative* writer, namely, the first- or second-generation writer. Conversely, we may actually find a member of the immigrant generation—undoubtedly, a "first-stage" writer from a temporal point of view—whose work exudes everything but that which we would expect from the work of a first- or even a second-generation writer (that is, Aaron's "first-" or "second-stage" writer). This immigrant writer may indeed fall more easily into the category of the *synthetic* writer rather than that of the *comparative* or *expressive* writer. For my first hypothesis, then, I have in mind a writer like Tony Ardizzone, a third-generation Italian American whose work fits much better the category of the *expressive* and/or *comparative* writer. My second hypothesis is borne out by the example of Giose Rimanelli, an Italian born, raised, and educated in Italy, who has spent the past four decades in the United States. His first work in English, *Benedetta in Guysterland,* is anything but the typical novel one would expect from a writer of his migratory background.

## Part Three: Some General Considerations

An analogous discourse of one's own cultural and historical specificities may indeed be constructed around the notion of the reader. The manner in which texts are interpreted today, that is, the theoretical underpinnings of a reader's act of disambiguation, is much more broad and, for the most part, tolerant of what may once have seemed to be *incorrect* or *inadequate* interpretations. Today the reader has as many rights as the author in the semiotic process. In some cases, in fact, the reader may even seem to have more rights than the writer. Lest we forget what Italo Calvino had to say about literature and the interpretation thereof: the reader, for Calvino, relies on a form of semiosis which places him/her in an interpretive position of superiority vis-à-vis the author.[35] In "Cybernetics and Ghosts" Calvino considers "the decisive moment of literary life [to be] reading (p. 15)," by which "literature will continue to be a 'place' of privilege within the human consciousness, a way of exercising the potentialities within the system of signs belonging to all societies at all times. The work will continue to be born, to be judged, to be distorted or constantly renewed on contact with the eye of the reader" (p. 16). In like manner, he states in "Whom Do We Write For" that the writer should not merely satisfy the reader; rather, he should be ready "to assume a reader who does not yet exist, or a change in the reader" (p. 82), a reader who would be *"more cultured than the writer himself"* (p. 85; Calvino's emphasis).[36]

In making such an analogy between reader and viewer I do not ignore the validity of the writer. For while it is true that the act of semiosis relies on the individual's time and place and is therefore always new and different with respect to its own historical specificities vis-à-vis the dominant culture, that is, the canon, it is also true that the writer may willy-nilly create for the reader greater difficulties in interpretation. Namely, if we accept the premise that language—verbal or visual—is an ideological medium that can become restrictive and oppressive when its sign system is arbitrarily invested with meanings by the dominant culture, i.e., the canon-makers, so too can it become empowering for the purpose of privileging one coding correlation over another by rejecting the canonical sign system and, ultimately, denying validity to this sign system vis-à-vis the interpretive act of a noncanonical text.[37] Then, certain ideological constructs are deprivileged and subsequently awarded an unfixed status; they no longer take on a patina of *natural facts.* Rather, they figure as the *arbitrary categories* they truly are.

All this results in a pluralistic notion of artistic invention and interpretation which, by its very nature, cannot exclude the individual artist and reader/viewer who has found "a voice or style that does not violate [his/her] several components of identity" (Fischer, p. 195) and who has thus "recreated," ideologically speaking, a different repertoire of signs. In this sense, then, the emergence and subsequent acceptance of certain *other* literatures, due in great part to the postmodern influence of the breakdown of boundaries and the mistrust in absolutes, has contributed to the construction of a more recent heteroglossic culture in which the "correct language" is deunified and decentralized. In this instance, then, all "languages" are shown to be "masks [and no language can consequently] claim to be an authentic and incontestable face." The result is a "heteroglossia consciously opposed to [the dominant] literary language," for which marginalizing and thus the silencing the *other* writer becomes more difficult and thus less likely to occur.[38]

Turning now to a few writers, we see that their work represents to one degree or another the general notions and ideas outlined above. Two fiction writers, John Fante and Pietro di Donato, and a poet, Joseph Tusiani, have produced a corpus of writing heavily informed by their Italian heritage. Their works celebrate their ethnicity and cultural origin, as each weaves tales and creates verses which tell of the trials and tribulations of the Italian immigrants and their children. Fante and Di Donato confronted both the ethnic dilemma and the writer's task of communicating this dilemma in narrative form. Tusiani, on the other hand, invites his reader, through the medium of poetry, to understand better, as Giordano points out, the "cynical and somber awareness of what it means to be an immigrant" and to experience the "alienation and realization that the new world is not the 'land of hospitality' he/she believed it was."[39] Tusiani's "riddle of [his] day" indeed figures as the riddle of many of his generation, be it the novelist Di Donato, or the short-story writer Fante, as it may continue to sound a familiar chord for those of subsequent generations: "Two languages, two lands, perhaps two souls . . . / Am I a man or two strange halves of one?"[40]

In a cultural/literary sense, it becomes clear that these and other writers of their generation belong to what Aaron considers stage one of the *hyphenate writer.* They are, from the perspective of what is stated above, the *expressive* writers, for this type of writer is indeed bent on disproving the suspicions and prejudices his/her stereotyped figure seems to arouse and, at the same time, win over the sympathies of the suspicious members of the dominant culture. Fante, Di Donato, Tusiani, and their *co–ethnics* indeed both examined in a *sui generis* way their status in the new world and, insofar as possible, presented a positive image of the Italian in America.

Writers who have securely passed from the first to the second stage of hyphenation may include the likes of Mario Puzo and Helen Barolini. Each writer has dealt with his/her cultural heritage as differently from each other as from those who preceded them. No longer feeling the urge to please the dominant culture, these writers adopted the thematics of their Italian heritage insofar as it coincided with their personal development as writers. In his second novel, *A Fortunate Pilgrim* (1964), recounting the trials and tribulations of a first-generation immigrant family, Mario Puzo figures as a fine example of the *comparative* writer. Ethnically centered around Lucia, the matriarch of the Corbo family, the novel examines the myth of the American dream and the real possibility that the *outsider* might succeed in realizing it. As he does later in *The Godfather,* Puzo does not always paint a positive picture of the Italian American in this novel. Yet, considered from the perspective of a greater social criticism, Puzo may indeed engage in a form of "militant criticism." His use of a sometimes sleazy Italian/American character, especially those involved in the stereotypical organized crime associations, may readily figure as an indictment of the social dynamism of the dominant culture which refuses access to the *outsider*.[41] The novel's expansive themes of survival and the desire to better one's situation lie at the base of the variegated, kaleidoscopic view of a series of tragedies which the family, as a whole, seems to overcome.

Helen Barolini's *Umbertina* (1979) could not be more Italian/American. As the author of a novel which spans four generations of an Italian/American family, she undoubtedly is acutely aware of her ethnicity and hyphenation.[42] Her main characters are all women, and each represents a different generation. In a general sense, they reflect the development of the Italian/American mind-set as it evolved and changed from one generation to the next. Yet, with this novel, it becomes increasingly clear that Barolini has gone one step further than both the men and the women who preceded her. She is now able to reconcile her ethnic/cultural heritage with her own personal specificities of gender and generational differences in order to transport these personal experiences, as Aaron stated, closer to the province of the general imagination. As a more advanced *comparative* writer, Barolini in *Umbertina* combines her historical awareness of the Italian and Italian American's plight with her own strong sense of feminism, and the reader ultimately becomes aware of what it meant to be not just an Italian American but indeed an Italian/American woman.[43]

In a different vein, yet also "bind[ing] life together," as Peirce would state, Gilbert Sorrentino could easily represent the *synthetic* writer. His poetry attempts to fuse his inherited immigrant culture—represented by terms of nature—with his artistic concern, as John Paul Russo has demonstrated.[44] Yet references to Italian/American culture are most infrequent throughout his *opus*. In his own words, Sorrentino surely "knew the reality of [his] generation that had to be written,"[45] as he too contributed to this cultural and literary chronicle. However, he took one step further than his *co-ethnics* (Italian Americans) and, so to speak, dropped the hyphen. Yet the dropping of the hyphen, according to Aaron, does not necessarily eliminate a writer's marginality. Aaron states that the writer " . . . has detached himself, to be sure, from one cultural environment without becoming a completely naturalized member of the official environment. It is not so much that he retains a divided allegiance but that as a writer, if not necessarily as a private citizen, he has transcended a mere parochial allegiance and can now operate freely in the republic of the spirit." In Sorrentino's case, while he was keenly aware of the American literary tradition that preceded him, in dropping the ethnic hyphen he appropriated yet another form of marginality; with the likes of Kerouac and Ferlinghetti as immediate predecessors, Sorrentino chose the poetics of late Modernism over that of mainstream literary America.[46]

In dealing with his/her Italian/American inheritance, each writer picks up something different as s/he may perceive and interpret his/her cultural heritage filtered through personal experiences. Yet there resounds a familiar ring, an echo that connects them all. Undoubtedly, Italian/American writers have slowly but surely built their niche in the body of American literature. Collectively their work can be viewed as a written expression par excellence of Italian/American culture; individually each writer has enabled American literature to sound a slightly different tone, thus bringing to the fore another voice of the great kaleidoscopic, socio/cultural mosaic we may call Americana—*kaleidoscopic mosaic* precisely because the socio/cultural dynamics of the United States reveal a constant flux of changes originating in the very existence of the various differentiated ethnic/racial groups that constitute the overall population of the United States. What emerges, as Fischer has stated, "is not simply that parallel processes operate across American ethnic identities, but a sense that these ethnic identities constitute only a *family of resemblances,* that ethnicity cannot be reduced to identical sociological functions, that ethnicity is a process of *inter-reference* between two or more cultural traditions (my emphasis)" and, I would add, between two or more generations of the same ethnic/racial group.

An appropriate way to close perhaps would be to borrow from Marshall Grossman and, again, from Lyotard. If the "power of the [hy-

phen] lies in its openness to history [or better still] in the way it records
and then reifies contingent events," (Grossman) and since the "ideology
of a particular hyphen may be read only by supplying a plausible history to its use,"[47] then the person who opts to eliminate it, to use something else in its place, or, as I have suggested elsewhere,[48] turn it on its
side, does so in the search "for new presentations," (Lyotard). In this
manner, the text the writer creates and the work s/he "produces are not
in principle governed by pre-established rules [of canon formation],
and they cannot be judged according to a determining judgment by applying familiar categories to the text or to the work. Those rules and categories are what the work of art is looking for. The artist and the writer,
then, are working without rules in order to formulate the rules of what
*will have been done*" (p. 81; emphasis textual).

In an analogous manner, so does the reader of these texts work
without rules, establishing as s/he proceeds similar interpretive rules of
what *will have been read*. Such is the case with the reader of ethnic texts,
who proceeds to recodify and reinterpret the seemingly arbitrary noncanonical (read, ethnic) signs in order to reconstruct a mutual correlation of the expressive and content functives, which, in the end, do not
violate his/her intertextual knowledge. Moreover, such an act of semiosis relies on the individual's time and place, and is therefore always
new and different with respect to its own historical specificities vis-à-
vis the dominant culture—the canon.

In final analysis, it is the dynamics of the conglomeration and agglutination of different voices and reading strategies which, contrary to
the hegemony of the dominant culture, cannot be fully integrated into
any strict semblance of a monocultural voice or process of interpretation. The utterance will always be polyvalent, its combination will always be rooted in heteroglossia and dialogism,[49] and the interpretive
strategies for decoding it will always depend on the specificities of the
reader's intertextual reservoir. For the modernist reader, therefore, one
rooted in the search for existing absolutes, an Italian/American sign
system may appear inadequate, perhaps even contemptuous. For the
postmodernist reader, who is open to, if not in search of, new coding
correlations, an Italian/American sign system may appear significantly
intriguing, if not on occasion rejuvenating, as these texts indeed may
present a sign system consisting of manipulated sign functions which
ultimately (re)define the sign. In defense of a sustained but fluctuating
Italian/American category of creative works, one may recall Lyotard's
"incredulity toward metanarratives" (xiv) and the late twentieth century's increasing suspicion of narrative's universal validity, for which
artistic invention is no longer considered a depiction of life. Stated in

more ideological terms, artistic creation is no longer executed/performed according to established rules and regulations.[50] Rather, it is a depiction of life as it is represented by ideology,[51] since ideology presents as *inherent* in what is represented that which, in actuality, is *constructed* meaning.[52]

# Part II
## New Readings

# 2

# Tony Ardizzone's "Expressive" Evening News

Details *are* significant. Literally they can be matters of life and death.

—Tony Ardizzone, "My Mother's Stories"

Tony Ardizzone's *The Evening News*[1] is a collection of short stories that won the 1986 Flannery O'Connor Award for Short Fiction.[2] This collection of eleven stories offers its reader a portrait, for the most part, of the neighborhood where Ardizzone spent his childhood. He presents his reader with both working- and middle-class citizens of all ages, men and women, mostly of Italian descent. Except for a few stories about college, Ardizzone's characters are the so-called "hyphenated" Americans who occupy a world seemingly different from what one might expect; they are very much ensconced in a world of memory and recollection that keeps them ineluctably tied to their past, either in search of some form of understanding their present situation or, in certain cases, in an attempt to escape from their present situation.

In articulating a sense of empathy for his characters, Ardizzone is also, to paraphrase Daniel Aaron, a sort of pioneer spokesperson—similar to Aaron's "first-stage" writer—for the unspoken-for, marginalized Italian/American citizen of, in his case, Chicago's North Side. Undoubtedly, he offers portraits of his co-ethnics with the goal of dislodging and debunking negative stereotypes ensconced in the dominant culture's mind-set. In so doing, he also creates characters possessing at times some of the very same stereotypes that some sensitive types, such as thin-skinned Italian Americans, would rather see debunked.[3] In this manner, he surely succeeds in humanizing the stereotyped figure. At the same time, he does not necessarily engage directly in militant criticism of any preconceptions, restrictions, or oppression of ethnicity set forth by the dominant group. As a result, demystification of negative stereotypes is, at best, left for the reader to infer.[4] Thus the general reader's strategy for and interpretation of "dissipating prejudice" is called to the fore, and the semiotic responsibility for any sort of finalized act of signification is shifted from the author to being a more complicit act between author and reader. What I thus propose here is a reading of some of Ardizzone's stories as an example of his *expressivity*, as it pertains to what I have outlined earlier in Chapter One of my re–consideration and re–definition of the Italian/American writer.

## Rewriting Ethnicity

In Ardizzone's opening tale, "My Mother's Stories," the narrator clearly speaks in his own, personal voice, offering us a moving tribute to his ill mother of German descent married to his Italian/American father. The story opens with a brief description of how his mother was born frail and sickly. In fact, we read that "they were going to throw her away when she was a baby. The doctors said she was too tiny, too frail, that she wouldn't live" (p. 1). What becomes significant here at the outset is that this is also the opening of the entire collection, for which the frailty of the narrator's ethnic mother is also, I would contend, a signal of the frailty of the immigrant and his/her progeny. Such frailty of one's existential condition, I suggest, will reappear at the end of the collection in the figure of "Nonna."

All this is couched in a more intimate rapport between the narrator and his reader when Ardizzone passes to direct discourse with his reader, in a Calvinian sense, by adopting the "You" in "You can well imagine the rest."[5] Such a shift, immediately placing the relationship between narrator and reader on a personal level, transforms the reader semiotically into a type of listener and emotionally into a type of confidant. Thus, from the viewpoint of both representation and content, a shift in modality also occurs. Such a shift in levels between narrator and reader—or for that matter, any transformation in one's narrative technique—is part and parcel of the author/narrator's sense of self-awareness that informs much of this story, signaled here at the beginning: " . . . my mother and her stories. For now the sounds and pictures are *my* sounds and pictures. Her memory, my memory" (p. 1). Such self-awareness first of all puts the narrator on the same level as his mother, and, in a certain sense, his storytelling replicates that of his mother, which he now recounts. Thus, we become witness to a type of circularity between who tells and what is being told. The narrator thus engages in an act of identification with what and about whom he recounts. This identification becomes more significant precisely because the person in the narrator's story is indeed a storyteller. The act of narration is underscored both by the fact that the narrator alludes to his narrating as well as to his mother, the storyteller as protagonist, and her previous storytelling to him and his family.

Such a layered narrative situation might be mapped out by a curious set of graphs. First, in modifying slightly Seymour Chatman's 1978 schemata,[6] we may chart the overall narrative communication act in the following manner:

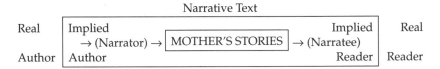

What we see is that Ardizzone sets up a multilayered narrative text that has embedded in his narrative communication act a second text—his mother's stories—that includes him as a character. Second, in charting further the relationship between our narrator (N) and his narrated protagonist, his mother (M), we see the circularity of identification between who narrates (N) and what/whom is being narrated (M):

$$N \rightarrow M = M/N \text{ (mother} \Leftrightarrow \text{narrator)} \Leftarrow N$$

The narrator (N), we see, discusses ( $\rightarrow$ ) his mother who soon becomes ($\Leftrightarrow$) for us also the mother/narrator (M/N) with whom our narrator eventually identifies ( $\Leftarrow$ ), as we saw above: " For now the sounds and pictures are *my* sounds and pictures. Her memory, my memory."

A secondary level of identification becomes equally significant, this time in relation to the theme of ethnicity. Whereas above, on the one level, the narrator becomes a storyteller like his mother, the protagonist of his story, on another level, the narrator also becomes a (metaphoric) first-generation hyphenate that is also his mother. The storyteller's story thus replicates the life of his character. We therefore see the polysemy of the above-cited act of identification insofar as the storyteller, that is, Narrator (read, Ardizzone?) as both raconteur and ethnic, becomes his character the storyteller, i.e., his mother. In so doing, he signals to us that, like his mother, he is a first-generation storyteller. It is in this framework that I suggest we read Ardizzone's *The Evening News*. Namely, in spite of his actual ethnic status of second or third generation, Tony Ardizzone's stories may often appear as examples of that type of narrative a first-generation writer might readily offer.

This story has everything in it necessary for examination. Along with the author's self-consciousness, we see that ethnicity is not limited to Italian Americans only; the character's mother is in fact German. Second, the difference in immigrant groups is underscored with colors; the Germans are light, the Italians are dark—"dark Sicilians" as is her girlfriend and sister of her future husband who, in turn, is "finely muscled, dark, deeply tanned" (p. 2). Thus we have the usual light-versus-dark binary opposition between ethnic groups. Indeed, lest we forget, Italians were considered people of color by some sociologists in the early years of the twentieth century.[7] The initial description of the character, in fact, is presented from the young woman's perspective, the narrator's frightened young mother:

> Perhaps our Mary, being young, is somewhat frightened. The boy behind the dark fence is older than she, is in high school, is *finely muscled, dark, deeply tanned*. Around his neck hang golden things glistening on a thin chain. He wears a sleeveless shirt—his undershirt. Mary doesn't know whether to stay with her young friend or to continue walking. She stays, but she looks away from the boy's dark eyes and gazes instead at *the worn belt* around his *thin waist*. (p. 2; emphasis added)

We see above that the father, as a young man, is an Adonis-like individual, a handsome replica of a Greek statue, who nevertheless readily recalls an image representative of the stereotype of the working-class Italian and/or Italian American of long ago as well as of today. Tony, the multireferential irony of which should not be lost on us, wears a sleeveless shirt, the classic "guinea t-shirt," as it was often called years ago, and sports, again according to what we might consider a classic Italian/American semiotic, a golden chain laden with what can only be easily recognizable amulets—indeed, so recognizable that it isn't necessary to specify and enumerate them. The Italian/American sign system is further employed in the physical description of the narrator's young father. Both his physical attributes of corporal muscularity and his olive complexion, dark and deeply tanned, are presented as integral parts of one another; for he is "finely muscled, dark, [and] deeply tanned," as we read. In addition, his working-class status is signaled at the end of this brief description together with his physical attributes, as Mary, too shy from her proper raising, does not look him in the eyes, but instead "gazes . . . at the worn belt around his thin waist." This portrait of the narrator's young father thus figures as a most reminiscent interpretant of the Italian or Italian American of a certain social class of the early and mid-twentieth century. The good-looking, athletic type often ended up in professional sports if not, on those rare occasions, in the movies.[8]

As one might suspect, the father in this story is also a positively framed character. Different from some father figures in the writings of some other Italian Americans,[9] Tony is a good husband and father, a sensitive man. Toward the end of this story, in fact, his sensitivity comes to the fore in discussing his wife's terminal illness with his son, the narrator. We are witness to his serious demeanor as we are told he was "not a man given to unnecessary talk" (p. 12). Tony's ability to communicate his feelings of imminent loss and seeming desperation belie any notion of the stereotypical macho, emotionally hard-nosed—paralyzed—Italian or Italian/American male. For the father now confides in his son, seeking obvious comfort and reassurance, as is evident from the following conversation:

> I don't know what I'd do without her, he says. I say nothing, for I can think of nothing to say. We've been together for over thirty years, he says. He pauses. For nearly thirty-four years. Thirty-four years this October. And, you know, you wouldn't think it, but I love her so much more now. He hesitates, and I look at him. He shakes his head and smiles. You know what I mean? he says. I say yes and we walk for a while in silence, and I think of what it must be like to live with someone for thirty-four years, but I cannot imagine it, and then I hear my father begin to talk about that afternoon's ball game—he describes at length and in comic detail a misjudged fly ball lost in apathy or ineptitude or simply in the sun—and for the rest of our walk home we discuss what's right and wrong with our favorite baseball team, our thorn-in-the-side Chicago Cubs. (p. 12)

As we look further, we find other dynamics at work in the above-cited passage. While it is true that the son cannot identify with his father's thirty-four years with his mother, an identification process between father and narrating son, analogous to what we saw between mother and son, is also at work. We see, first of all, that the dialogue recounted in an indirect format does not immediately distinguish between the *I* of the father and the *I* of the son: "*I* don't know what *I'd* do without her, he says. *I* say nothing, for *I* can think of nothing to say." But if this initial amalgamation of the two *I*s seems to be belied by the narrator's admitted inability to empathize and/or comprehend his father's feelings—"I cannot imagine it"—such inability is further countered by the transformation of the first-person singular pronouns (*I*) into the first-person plural adjectives (*our*) and pronouns (*we*). Such transformation, I would further add, takes place on two occasions. Immediately after the first two ambiguous *I*s we have a *we:* "*I* don't know what *I*'d do without her, he says. *I* say nothing, for *I* can think of nothing to say. *We*'ve been . . . " The second occurrence can be found in the final complete sentence of the paragraph, as the son responds to his father's question, "You know what I mean? he says":

> *I* say yes and *we* walk for a while in silence, and *I* think of what it must be like to live with someone for thirty-four years, but *I* cannot imagine it, and then *I* hear my father begin to talk about that afternoon's ball game—he describes at length and in comic detail a misjudged fly ball lost in apathy or ineptitude or simply in the sun—and for the rest of *our* walk home *we* discuss what's right and wrong with *our* favorite baseball team, *our* thorn-in-the-side Chicago Cubs. (emphasis added)

What starts out as an inability to understand his father's sentiments vis-à-vis his wife transforms itself into a total amalgamation of the two men as they now discuss something they both know intimately: "*our* thorn-in-the-side Chicago Cubs."[10]

## Caught in the Middle

Other stories in this collection underscore much of the mind-set of the immigrant and ethnic world that occupies much of Ardizzone's work. We find the interweaving of Old World values into the New World of the United States; we witness the cultural clash of the ethnic world with the greater world of the non-ethnic, the non-Italian American. This clash could be no more apparent than in the world of Gino, the protagonist of "The Eyes of Children," a story that offers a view of Catholic school education before Vatican II and an altar boy's crisis of faith. The story opens with a dichotomy of color similar to that which we saw in "My Mother's Stories." Gino is a "dark, seventh grader" who is smitten with a girl he does not know, an eighth-grader, "light-haired . . . blond girl." However, since eighth–graders did not talk with seventh–graders unless they were on the basketball team, Gino finds himself up against the incommunicability with his "light-haired" wonder, a problem of difference that is accompanied by the added quality of his darkness and her lightness.

Gino, however, has other characteristics that seem peculiar to his other schoolmates. In fact, he has to work and go to church, and because of this he is virtually unknown to them:

Gino had wanted to be on the team, but his father insisted he work after school, to learn responsibility, the value of a dollar. His mother insisted he serve God by being an altar boy. He had to obey. But no one knew him. The pretty girl didn't look at him. . . . (p. 15)

We find values here that echo those the immigrant and first-generation Italian Americans, as well as other ethnics, upheld as primary. In addition, the issues of class which abound in this collection, as we saw in the previous story, are underscored in the above-cited passage. Gino could not interact with the other children insofar as playing basketball was considered of little significance, since his family, his father especially, believed in the work ethic above all else for his children. Gino had to "learn responsibility, the value of a dollar" precisely because economics was considered the primary source of amelioration for many Italian Americans.[11]

In addition to Gino's socio-economic restrictions are his commitments to the Catholic church. At his mother's insistence, we see that he is an altar boy who serves early morning masses and ends up tired by mid-afternoon. We also see that Gino's experience with his religion— the church and its nuns and priests—becomes the vessel through which he eventually comes to know the real world. When the two girls Donna Pietro and Maureen Ostrowski, representatives of two major ethnic groups of Chicago, come running and screaming about a mystery man bleeding in the church, they are so upset that they, in a similar vein, are mysteriously sent home. Gino's reaction was to assume immediately that there must be some sort of miracle at hand, that the bleeding man no one saw could have, indeed must have, been Christ. But, to his chagrin, there was no news in the newspaper, and his parents didn't believe him later that evening. The next day, "the day after the miracle," Gino went to church to serve mass, assuming that he would find some evidence of Christ's visit, and he only found signs of vandalism. When he then saw his idol Father Manning, Gino understood the priest's sudden concern, not for the vandalism but for Gino's having found the priest smoking. Gino to his great dismay finally realizes that what he had thought was a special event—the apparition of the bleeding man—was nothing more than an incident of vandalism perpetrated by a drunkard:

No miracle. A flush as burning as the flame washed over him. *Fool.* To try to be *special.* To *believe.* For a moment he stood quietly at the altar, holding the flame to the tall candle, feeling the tears drip from his cheeks to the altar cloth. Then a sudden sorrow fell over him. All at once the world seemed *very dark and very big.* (p. 24; emphasis added)

Feeling foolish and childish at this point, we see that in an instant Gino loses his innocence as a child when he comes to realize that the man he thought could possibly be Christ is nothing but a petty-thieving wino. In addition, however, he also loses his belief in the institution of the Church, as Father Manning's main concern is with being discovered as the closet smoker he is, not with the vandalism to the church or, for that matter, his seemingly unintentional insensitivity to the young boy's innocent belief in Roman Catholicism that comes to a screeching halt. In constructing a compelling and overwhelming world ("very dark and very big"), Ardizzone thus combines innocent fantasy and brute reality in representing Gino's introduction into the so-called *real* world of adults.

Paul, the protagonist of the title story "The Evening News," is another fine example of the dichotomous world that informs much of Ardizzone's work. Here, we find Paul sitting in front of the television watching the evening news; it is in fact the news broadcast that forms the foundation for this story's narrative. Paul, Italian American, and Maria, of Hispanic roots, are expecting a baby and, in reminiscing about their university days of idealistic protest, now discuss with significant delusion the world into which they are soon to bring their child. Paul is a university professor. In fact, he is a sociology professor. Such a field is pertinent both to Paul's idealistic period of adolescent protests as a university student and metanarratively to the overall thematics of Ardizzone's fictional world of the ethnic. In both cases sociology proves significant: 1) It is the intellectual world in which he believes he can make a difference; 2) It is also the epistemological world that will allow him to understand better, perhaps, his own world experience as an Italian American.

That sociology in every sense of the word is important to Paul is evident from the beginning of the story. Paul is very much involved in his ethnicity as an individual. We soon read that he is not too comfortable in his new world, even though he has been able to climb the socioethnic ladder, now that he is a university professor. Two incidents underscore Paul's strong sense of ethnicity and, to the contrary, his wife's quasi-indifference to her ethnicity:

> Paul drinks a lot of wine, mostly imported, now that they can afford it. None of the expensive wine is as good as what he remembers drinking. *He thinks of himself as ethnic.* At a Sociology Department party he joked that America was a Wonder Bread culture, soft and white, slightly packaged with pictures of *colorful* bal-

loons. You think you're holding something of integrity and sub-stance, but when you squeeze it you have mostly preservatives and air. Maria doesn't know what to think of herself. Her Spanish isn't fluent, and she has never been to Mexico, where her grand-parents were born. She always feels peculiar checking the box next to Hispanic on the equal opportunity forms. *Paul is much less American than she, and he has no box to check.* (p. 26; emphasis added)

A number of things come to the fore in this passage. First, Paul is obvi-ously engaging in a moment of ethnic nostalgia as he sips expensive im-ported wine, something we have to assume is very good, and thinks back instead to the homemade wine as something much better. Indeed, I would submit, the homemade wine was good and had its certain charm, especially through reminiscence; but good imported wine, we must admit, may often be hard to supersede. Thus, we might think of Paul's nostalgia as a form of ethnic re–discovery, which Fischer intends, as we saw in the last chapter, when he states that one finds "a voice or style that does not violate [his/her] several components of identity" and thus (re)creates an ethnic sign system. Maria, on the other hand, places little significance on her ethnicity in her everyday life. We see that, while she checks the box on the EEOC forms, she gives it little importance to her "American" daily life. She accepts her roots, we find out later, "mat-ter of factly" (p. 37), whereas a disconcerted Paul, we see above, has no box to check. The difference between these two persons' relationship to their ethnic origins is, again, symptomatic of Fischer's notion of ethnic-ity as individualistic. What emerges, as we saw in Chapter One, "is not simply that parallel processes operate across American ethnic identities, but a sense that these ethnic identities constitute only a family of *resem-blances*, that ethnicity cannot be reduced to identical sociological func-tions, that ethnicity is a process of *inter-reference* between two or more cultural traditions" (p. 195; my emphasis).

A second set of sentences in this passage is also indicative of the clash of cultures that society at large would prefer not to discuss—that the melting part has lost all significance as the ultimate metaphor of United States culture. And, here, we may read this into Paul's use of the USA icon par excellence of Wonder Bread when he "joked that America was a Wonder Bread culture, soft and white, slightly packaged with pic-tures of colorful balloons. You think you're holding something of in-tegrity and substance, but when you squeeze it you have mostly preservatives and air." The sense of cultural difference and colors should not be lost on Paul's statement of the package's "colorful bal-loons." Paul's concern with color, in fact, was already underscored at the story's very opening, just before the above-cited passage, as he tried to adjust the television's color. Now, in retrospect, we should not lose the metaphoric irony in this scene. Paul wanted to be sure he could "always return the colors to where they were supposed to be, . . . bright and true," whereas Maria, we read, didn't "care about the color" (p. 26).

### The Old Vis-à-Vis the New

The following two stories pick up the theme of Catholicism that appeared, early on, in the forefront of the narrative of "The Eyes of Children." There we saw an innocent young boy, still very much ensconced in the Catholic belief of miracles and visitations, harshly introduced to the more skeptical, grown-up Catholic world of adults, where religion, nevertheless, still reigns. In a similar vein, the two stories examined here provoke analogous readings. Catholicism plainly rules the lives of those who chose to believe or are taught to do so.

"World without End" recounts the story about a suicidal son's move to the South from Chicago and his mother's subsequent disappointment in the outcome. Together with his parents on a visit, Peter searches through Norfolk, Virginia, for a Catholic church for his mother, Lena, the strong archetype that domineers over the ethnic family. Gus, Peter's father, is more the hen-pecked husband whose feet are, perhaps, too tied to the ground. In pointing out these great differences, Ardizzone resorts to what has been characterized as Neil Simonish[12] in his construction of a dialogue between them.

As many of the themes we saw in the previous stories reappear here intertwined into the religious theme, Peter's ethnicity is also in the forefront. Whereas before, however, it seemed that the characters' Italian/Americanness was put into question, here Peter's mother becomes a spokesperson for the defense of, for lack of a better phrase, ethnic purity. She refuses, for example, to accept the fact that Peter's former non-Italian/American girlfriend, Lorraine, could have had any positive qualities. Indeed, the implications are that she, a flight attendant, was indeed, as Peter's mother would say, a fallen woman. This is further reinforced for Lena by the fact that Lorraine later moved in with Peter:

"Your son throws away his good money on an opium den in South Halsted and you don't think his mother sees? Then he met that girl—That stewardess—That hussy"

"Lorraine wasn't a hussy, Mamma."

> She moved in with you didn't she? You didn't marry her, did you? What do you think, I was born yesterday? I don't want to open old wounds, but you had only one bed in that apartment, Petie." (p. 121)

A number of things come to the fore in this passage that reflect a generalized notion of the Italian American. First, we see that Lena could not accept her son's desire for independence. His taking an apartment in an inexpensive, questionable neighborhood can only be considered a move to "an opium den," since drugs and poverty are often unfairly coupled. Second, Lena is incapable of accepting Lorraine's job and her moving in with Peter as valid; she can only be a "hussy" in Lena's eyes, a typical notion that permeated much of the Italian immigrant and early Italian/American communities, where a number of professions were not deemed worthy for morally upright Italian/American women.

As the conversation continues between mother and son, we see other old-world notions arise. Lena proceeds to discuss, though ever so euphemistically, Peter's and Lorraine's love life:

> "What's the difference?" Lena asked. "You gave her some thrills, and the hussy packed her bags. So you had some fun, a little pleasure, a little enjoyment."
>
> "Lena," Gus said, "it's Sunday. Don't describe."
>
> "It's only natural, Augusto. We raised a healthy boy. His blood is red like everyone else's. Just as long as he doesn't get disease. Don't pretend to be such an innocent." (p. 121)

Lena continues to underscore old-world values and contradictions, as she now turns to her son's part in the relationship. While Lorraine is a "hussy," according to Lena, Peter "had some fun, a little pleasure, a little enjoyment." Contrary to Lorraine the "hussy," he is a "healthy boy [whose] blood is red like everyone else's." Lena, that is, engages willy-nilly in a boldface act of double standards.[13] After she virtually condemns to the stake Peter's former live-in girlfriend, except for Peter possibly being taken in by Lorraine, Lena sees her son's part in the relationship as a healthy, normal thing—for after all, he is a "healthy boy." Her only worry is that he "doesn't get disease." Any sense of questioning Peter's moral rectitude doesn't even seem to enter her mind. What is also curious is that Lena engages in a type of self-destructive behavior insofar as she, a woman, defends that very double standard that both keeps her down and that she ironically is unable to comprehend.[14]

Catholicism is ever-present from the story's very first words: "*Gloria in excelsis Deo.*" In fact, the entire opening page and one half are peppered with Latin phrases from the liturgy that Peter obviously knew from his previous altar-boy days.[15] While Peter is clearly engaging in ironic or sarcastic behavior, Lena's reactions seem to be of a different tone:

> "I'm glad my boy still knows his prayers," Lena said, patting Peter's bony knee. (p. 117)
>
> [ . . . ]
>
> "My Petie," Lena laughed. "He's giving us the whole mass." She turned from her husband's frown and faced her son. "So you're a regular parishioner at this church, Petie?" (p. 118)

Although it may not initially seem clear if Lena's reactions are totally serious, we can, I contend, assume they are. Her later conversations about religion in general, as well as the specifics about Peter's old parish, underscore such an impression. Lena's religious beliefs are literal; she seems to take everything at face value, without any ability to penetrate the surface. While it is now "legal" for lay people to give out communion, Lena cannot accept this new practice. In extolling her husband's occasional reading of the Gospel, in the same breath she agrees with his not wanting to give out communion, as we read: "He gets up and reads the Gospel sometimes, but he doesn't want to give out Communion. Why should he, *he's no priest*" (p. 119; emphasis added).

Lena, we see, is totally ensconced in old-world thinking that permeates, in the guise of her religion, her entire world view. Everything is seen in terms of her religion, or better, Catholicism. Lena first tries to coax her son back to Chicago by recounting a supposed conversation between her and Father Luigi. In so doing, she also tries to make Peter feel guilty for his decision to move away: "[Father Luigi] says, 'And how is Petie, good old Petie, my favorite altar boy, how's Petie now that he's left his good parents and moved down to the South all because he didn't look hard enough for a job in Chicago or maybe because he just wanted to get away from his *poor mamma*—'" (p. 119; emphasis added). Lena's supposed quotation of Father Luigi is significant here because the words could easily be attributed to either type of person: the generalized notion of the guilt-laying, over-protective, Italian or Italian/American mother who does not want to see her children move away; or the not so subtle, reproachful priest accusing independent offspring of not being loyal to their parents. Both cases, we see from the story, could easily fit Peter's situation.

Another significant aspect of this story is that *Catholic* becomes synonymous with *Italian*. We should emphasize that their religion is *Roman* Catholicism, the adjective *Roman* underscoring to one degree or another some form of Italian semiotic to their beliefs. Though not explicitly articulated, we might assume that another of Lena's objections to Lorraine was her supposed non-Italian/Americanness. This becomes suspicion in retrospect when we witness Lena's conversation with her son about Rosamaria D'Agostino: "'What you need is to come back to Chicago where you could meet a good clean Catholic girl. Somebody like Rosamaria D'Agostino.' 'Mamma, Rosamaria D'Agostino joined the Carmelites. She teaches kindergarten in South Bend.'" (p. 122) Rosamaria D'Agostino, the "good clean Catholic girl," proves to be the complete opposite of Lorraine who, by living with Peter while not married (not good), is a "hussy" (not clean), and, further, is most likely not of Italian origin (not Catholic). This is all underscored by the formula that Ardizzone provides for us here:

a good clean Catholic girl = Rosamaria D'Agostino.

Lena, in fact, is so entrenched in her old-world thinking that even the church they eventually find to attend mass has to be a more traditional one. Like the old, traditional Catholicism, the actual structure of the church in which she worships has to be old: "It's a nice church, Petie, not one of those *new* ugly ones?" (p. 127; emphasis added).

But Lena, we see toward the story's end, softens a bit in her previous opinion of Lorraine, as well as her more recent opinion of Peter's job as a messenger. All this comes about when Peter, in finally confessing his emotional breakdown, also communicates his need for his mother's love. This moment of weakness on Peter's part actually strengthens his mother's sense of self as she now feels more an integral part of her son's life. That is to say, she is now once more the mother of old, of the family of long ago when Peter was in fact Petie the altar boy:

"Walk on this side of me, August."

"Coming, Lena."

[ . . . ]

"And you walk on this side, Peter." Lena was smiling. The bright morning sunshine spilled their long shadows across the sidewalk. "I want us to enter the church together, like one big happy family." (p. 127)

Lena, that is, becomes the matriarch she once was. She is literally in the center of her family once again. Thus flanked by her husband and son, she believes that by entering the church together in this manner they are one big happy family, precisely because for her the form—"together, *like* one big happy family"—equals/becomes the substance, which should read, "together *as* one big happy family."

"Nonna" is a story about an old immigrant woman in a state of confusion and disconnection, seemingly senile, who is no longer able to cope with the changes taking place around her. We see how these changes effect the elderly in general when they find themselves in a state of confusion and/or conflict with change. In Nonna's specific case, her confusion and resultant indecision manifest themselves in the very beginning in her movements, as the first full paragraph signals:

> Follow her now as she *slowly* walks down Loomis toward Taylor, her heavy *black* purse dangling at her side. Though it is the middle of summer she wears her *black* overcoat. The air conditioning is too cold inside the stores, *she thinks*. . . . (p. 144; emphasis added)

The adverb "slowly" ("slowly walks") and the seemingly contrary-to-fact "she thinks" prefigure what throughout this story is to be her constant conflict with the actual, changing reality around her and her own version of what it was and should still be. The conflict is further prefigured by Nonna's wearing an overcoat in the midst of summer because of the stores' air conditioning. Finally, her elderly, female, widowed Italianness is also prefigured not only by her name but by the color of her purse and coat—black—a color that has, by this point in the collection, acquired a semiotic value of Italianness in Ardizzone's aesthetic sign system.

The story's second full paragraph continues the thematics of the first in emphasizing Nonna's disconnection and perceptual conflict with the reality around her and in prefiguring the perennial conflict between old-world and new-world values, as well as the sometimes not so respectful reception of the former by the latter:

> She hesitates, the taste of *aglio* on her tongue. Perhaps she is outside this afternoon to shop. She cannot decide. The children of the neighborhood call out to her as she passes them. *Na-na!* The sound used to call in goats from feeding. Or, sometimes, to tease. Or is it *Nonna*, grandmother, that they call? It makes no difference, the woman thinks. (p. 144; emphasis textual)

We see that both her actions as well as her impression of the boys' speech underscore her confusion and disconnection. As we saw in the previous paragraph, her hesitation and initial unawareness of being inside or outside indicate Nonna's vacillation vis-à-vis the world around her. This oscillation continues in that Nonna cannot decide whether the children of the neighborhood are calling out to her in a respectful or disrespectful manner: "*Na-na!* The sound used to call in goats from feeding. Or, sometimes, to tease. Or is it *Nonna,* grandmother, that they call?"

We already saw in Ardizzone's previous stories, especially the first, how he purposefully constructs his narratives with multiple layers. Such a technique is apparent here also. What is intriguing in this regard is Ardizzone's use of the verb "decide," almost as if it were Nonna's choice whether reality should be one way or the other. I make this point because it not only seems to put Nonna in a position of personal enfranchisement, however limited it may be, but on a more grand scale it underscores the general semiotic notion of reality as a quasi-individual entity. Namely, inside or outside, respectful or disrespectful, Nonna as a sign source offers up to the reader multireferential signs, for which s/he has the interpretive privilege of reconstructing a reality more similar to his/her own ideological sign system.[16]

Such semiotic freedom allows for the interpretive reconstruction of the Italian aspect of the story "Nonna" that is signaled here in a number of ways. First, the Italian sign, "aglio," anticipates its linguistic counterpart "Na-na" which, in turn, anticipates its homonymous "Nonna." Second, while the Italian word "aglio" is inserted in an American sentence with one reference only, garlic, the second Italian word, "Na-na," conjures up a multiplicity of meanings that all prove significant to some degree in this story. In its own right, as we read, *Na-na* can refer both to the calling of sheep or to a teasing sound. On the other hand, *Na-na,* as just stated, can also be a homonym for the Italian noun *Nonna.* As all this underscores the Italian aspect of the story, it also brings to the fore cultural dualism and its various consequences, here prefigured by the positive and negative, as the children call to her or tease her. Finally, Nonna's initial oscillation is punctuated at the end of the paragraph with its closing sentence: "It makes no difference, the woman thinks."

Nonna's experience in her bicultural world of Chicago's old Italian neighborhood that we witness here is one of dealing with difference, her state of difference that is, first of all, immigrant. Such a state is represented in a number of ways. Her being ignored on the street by the people whom she does not recognize, but who she assumes are sons of people she once knew, makes her wonder if they speak the "old language"; after all, this is Chicago's original Italian neighborhood. She also assumes that these young men are Catholic since they wear "cornicelli" around their neck. All this provokes her to wonder about the non-Italian names she sees on the storefronts and to reminisce about her dead husband and their Italian origins. In the first case, she assumes that these people, like many Italian immigrants, have shortened their names; she also wonders if they are still in touch with their culture of origin: " . . . what part of the boot [Mr. Swanks's] family came from, and does he still speak the old language" (p. 149). Like the first part of this sentence alluding to Italy, the adjective "old" here also appears on a number of other occasions in this story with the distinct feature of underscoring the dichotomy of Nonna's bicultural experience—the difference between the "old" and "new" worlds.

In the case of Nonna reminiscing about hers and Vincenzo's Italian origins, Ardizzone informs his text with a number of significant, multireferential signs:

> She pictures Padova on the worn, tired boot. Vincenzo called Italy that. Nonna remembers that Padova sits far up in the north, west of Venezia. She looks down at her black shoes. Italia. She was from the south, from Napoli, and Vincenzo, her husband, may he rest, came from the town of Altofonte, near Palermo, in Sicilia. The good strong second son of *contadini.* (p. 149: emphasis textual)

Italy is the "worn, tired boot" that obviously could not accommodate Nonna's and Vincenzo's needs, personal and professional, enough for them to stay and live in their own country. The dichotomy of the two worlds, Italy and USA, in which Nonna has lived for so long is now replicated in the north/south dichotomy to which she alludes in her thoughts. Padova and Venezia stand as the northern counterpart to hers and Vincenzo's southern cities of Napoli and Altofonte. Nonna's dilemma is amplified through this north/south dichotomy, punctuated by the phrase, "She *looks down* at her *black* shoes." The geography of north/south is signaled by Nonna's bowing of her head, and the Italy that cannot offer them the sustenance they need is signaled by the color "black" of her shoes. Third, we see that Vincenzo, like many immigrants of their generation who come to the United States, was one of many farmers who, in New York and other United States metropolitan areas, were often considered unskilled laborers. Finally, we should not ignore another example of Ardizzone's subtle choice and use of language, here signaled by the contrasting use of *Italy* for the country from which they came for economic reasons and *Italia* for the area of the country about which she reminisces and obviously misses.

Having examined its Italian theme, we may now look toward the story's two other major themes, Nonna's Catholicism and her gender dilemma. In fact, these two themes, we shall see, are often intertwined. With regard to her Catholicism, we saw early on that while Nonna now finds herself in a differently evolved neighborhood, where she no longer recognizes the faces of the sons of grandsons of those she once knew, she is, as we saw above, relieved to see that they are still Catholics:[17] "Well, at least they are still Catholics, she thinks, and her lips move as she says *They are still Catholics,* and her hand begins to form the sign of the cross" (p. 148; emphasis textual).

As Nonna's state of mental disconnection continues to manifest itself during her walk down Taylor street, her state of confusion consists of mental shifts back to her youth in the States, and she notices a young girl in the bookstore window:

> She looks inside the bookstore window and sees a long-haired girl behind the counter. Her head is bent. She is reading. Nonna smiles. It is what a young girl should do when she is in a bookstore. When she is in church she should pray for a *good husband,* someone young, with a job, who will not hit her. Then when she is older, she should pray to the Madonna for some *children.* To have one. To have enough. (p. 150–51; emphasis added)

Nonna immediately consents to the young women's behavior of reading a book, for, after all, that is what one should do in a bookstore. In like fashion, Nonna's simplicity of logic manifests itself as she suddenly shifts from the bookstore scene to a church, where we find our first intertwining of the gender and religious themes. As Nonna turns to thinking about church, we see that the young woman should not only pray while she is in church, but she should in fact pray for "a good husband, someone young, with a job, who will not hit her." She should, we see, immediately relegate herself to the role of wife, as old-world values would require. In addition, we see two basic requirements to this desired relationship: 1) The man should have a good job, that is, pure and basic economic amelioration is the end goal. It is not important, as we are *not* told, what her husband's profession may be, for it is only important that he have a good job—that it pay well, we should understand. 2) He should not hit her. This reference to the violent male is all too frequent in Italian/American literature, and here it figures as a basic tenet of marriage. We shall see in some of the other writers we discuss, especially in Gianna Patriarca's poetry, that male violence in the Italian/American community was omnipresent.[18]

But the old-world influence does not stop here. We also see that this young woman must also "pray to the Madonna for some children. To have one. To have enough." Along with relegating herself to the role of homemaker, she must also be a mother. In order to find fulfillment, according to Nonna's semiotic, this young women must become both a wife and a mother. This traditional role is something we shall find in other works we examine later. This is especially true with the plight of women in Helen Barolini's novel, *Umbertina*, and Patriarca's poetry, fittingly entitled *Italian Women and Other Tragedies.*

Nonna's disconnection is further manifested in her confusion as to where her sons are and what happened to them, when she associates the young girl in the bookstore with her imaginary Mrs. Swanks who cannot have children. At this point in the narration, two things occur. First, she momentarily realizes that Mrs. Swanks's husband's problem of infertility is actually the problem her husband Vincenzo had; this was the reason she and Vincenzo never had children. Nonna's reaction proves equally significant for the discussion at hand:

> Poor Mrs. Swanks, Nonna thinks. Her Antonio must not be good for her. It is often *the fault of the man.* The doctors in New Jersey had told her that. Not once, but many times. That was so long ago. But do you think I listened? Nonna says to herself. For one moment? For all those years? My ears were deaf! Nonna is gesturing angrily with her hands. She strikes the store's glass window. It was part of *Heaven's test,* she is saying, to see if I would *stop believing....* Inside the bookstore the manager closes his book and comes to the window. Nonna watches her close her book and stand, then raise her head. *She* wears a mustache. It is a *boy.* (p. 152; emphasis added)

Nonna, we discover at this point, took on the responsibility of not having had children even though it was her husband who was infertile. In addition, we see that she has associated hers and Vincenzo's misfortune as a test of her faith, that it was part of the Catholic experience to endure misfortune as part of one's faith. At this point in the story we also realize that Nonna is, in fact, engaged in creating her own little world as, we see here, she has re-constructed the reality around her into one that suits her own emotional needs. Mrs. Swanks, we now realize, is a re-creation of Nonna's own misfortune of long ago, and the only way for Nonna to confront her situation so many years later is to create a fictional character who reflects her own experience. This re-creation, as Ardizzone informs his text, is underscored by an impersonal narrative interspersed with Nonna's thoughts of Mrs. Swanks and her perceptions of the book-store manager: "Inside the bookstore the manager closes *his* book and comes to the window." She sees a young woman who is really a male: "Nonna watches *her* close *her* book and stand, then raise *her* head. *She* wears a mustache. It is a *boy.*"

Nonna's gender dilemma comes to the fore when she overhears her downstairs neighbor, young Lucia, and her boyfriend. At this point we see the intermingling of religion and gender, and more specifically the sexual, as Nonna thinks back to the first time she and Vincenzo made love:

The night was hot, and that brought back to her the thin face of Vincenzo, and she was suddenly young again and back in New Jersey, in her parents' house, with young Vincenzo in the stuffed chair opposite her and the around them the soft sound of her mother's tranquil snoring. Nonna shakes her head. She knows what she must feel about that night. She was trusting, and Vincenzo was so handsome—his black curls lay so delicately across his forehead, and his smile was so wet and so white, bright—and she allowed the young boy to sit next to her on the sofa, and she did not protest when he took her hand, and then, when he kissed her, she even opened her mouth and let his wet tongue touch hers. Oh, she was so frightened. Her mouth had been so dry. On the street now she is trembling. She is too terrified to remember the rest. But the memory spills across her mind with the sound of the girls' easy laughter, and she moves back on the pink sofa and does not put up her hands as Vincenzo strokes her cheek and then touches her, gently, on the front of her green dress. And then she turns to the boy and quickly kisses him. The light from the oil lamp flickers. The snoring stops. She looks at Vincenzo, and then she blushes with the shame of her mortal sin, and now if Vincenzo does not say they will marry she knows she will have to kill her-self, and that in God's eyes she has already died.

Nonna is still, silent, standing in her guilt on the street, afraid even now to cross herself for fear she will be struck down. She feels the stifling weight of her sin. Vincenzo then moved back to the stuffed chair, coughing. Neither spoke. She began to cry. The next morning Vincenzo spoke to her father. (p. 156)

We see that Nonna has been socialized to feel the way she does, for she "knows what she must feel about that night," even though, as we continue to read, she felt comfortable with Vincenzo and was indeed complicit in bringing their first experience to fruition: "She was trusting, . . . and she allowed the young boy to sit next to her . . . she did not protest when he took her hand, . . . she even opened her mouth and let his wet tongue touch hers." In addition, we see that Nonna's desire of that time to make love with Vincenzo is now counterpoised to her current fear of the consequences as she now thinks back to what they had done. Ardizzone, we see here, adroitly sets up another dichotomy that represents the difference between Nonna's personal wishes as a young woman and the restrictions placed on her by her Catholicism and the society in which she lived then and still does now: "Oh, she was so frightened. Her mouth had been so dry. On the street now she is trembling. She is too terrified to remember the rest." Nonna's fear of the moment was that she was not ready to receive Vincenzo's kiss, for "her mouth had been so dry."[19] Now, to the contrary, her fear is a different one, as she now, old, stands "trembling . . . too terrified to remember the rest," for she, we can safely assume, lived with an overwhelming sense of guilt all of her life.

Again, the difference between then and now is underscored in the second half of Ardizzone's narrative of the event. Nonna, we see, is a willing participant: "she moves back on the pink sofa and does not put up her hands as Vincenzo strokes her cheek and then touches her, gently, on the front of her green dress. And then she turns to the boy and quickly kisses him." She welcomes his caresses and, in fact, becomes an active co participant as she "turns . . . and . . . kisses him." Yet she cannot live with what others consider "her mortal sin," where the adjective "mortal" for Nonna indeed proves to be multireferential. For she now sees in her act with Vincenzo the consequences of both the death of her soul—"in God's eyes she has already died"—and her own potential physical death if Vincenzo does not now agree to marry her—"if Vincenzo does not say they will marry she knows she will have to kill herself." Nonna, we see again, suffers from the pressures visited on her from both her religious association and social position. As a young *Catholic woman*, she should remain a virgin until her wedding; otherwise, she runs the threat of the consequences of her "sin" in the death of her soul and a general ostracism from society, because if "everyone, even the old priests here in Chicago, will know, [she'll] have to move to another neighborhood" (p. 157).

Nonna has remained locked up in an emotional state of guilt that, while she has in one sense created it in her own mind, has been thrust upon her by society. From one act early in her life, an act of sentiment and affection in which she was a co-participant, Nonna still suffers the consequences, as we saw in the above-cited paragraphs: "Nonna is still, silent, *standing in her guilt* on the street, *afraid even now to cross herself for fear she will be struck down.* She feels the *stifling weight of her sin.*" In fact, we also realize that she has blamed herself for the fact that she and Vincenzo never had children, in spite of the fact that he was physically incapable; she nevertheless feels compelled to bear the brunt of the guilt, as the following paragraph underscores:

> Vincenzo understood why she could bear no children; it was because of their sin. Perhaps now that everyone knows, she thinks, she would not have to move anymore. Maybe since the whole world knows, I can finally rest where I am now and be finished with my punishment. And then I'll die, Nonna says. And then, if I have been punished enough, I will be once again with Vincenzo. (p. 157)

The last and surely one of the most effective stories of the collection,[20] "Nonna" eulogizes the passing of the old world and, at the same time, welcomes in a new world of new values and new immigrants. The Italian neighborhood, it becomes apparent throughout, has been transformed into a mixed ethnic locale where a Mexican population has superseded the Italian. And in a sense, the change in the neighborhood accompanies the change that may still take place in Nonna's value system, as this story, as well as the collection, now comes to a close:

> What she needs is next to the counter. In plastic bags. Nonna is so happy that tears come to her eyes. So this is why she was outside, she thinks, why she is now inside this *strange* store. She had wanted to try the freckled *Mexican flat breads.* Hadn't someone before been telling her about them? Nonna holds the package in her hands and thinks. . . . Someone who explained that her punishment would be over, that soon she would be with her Vincenzo. That these were the breads that were *too simple* to have been baked with yeast, that these *did not rise, round and golden,* like other breads, like women fortunate enough to feel *their bellies swell,* their breasts grow heavy with the promise of milk, but instead these stayed in one shape, *simple, flat.*

> The dark man behind the counter nods and smiles.

> Perhaps, Nonna thinks as her fingers unclasp her purse and search for the coins her eyes no longer clearly see, perhaps bread *is just as good* this way. (p. 160–61; emphasis added)

The "strange store" in which she now finds herself is such because of what it no longer is, because it is *not* Italian. Things have changed around Nonna, and she has not been able, cognitively, to process it all, chiefly because she has been consumed most of her life by her overwhelming sense of guilt from her one love-act with Vincenzo. In fact, we see that Nonna now connects this "simple" bread to her own personal situation of being a woman who did not bear children.

As we saw elsewhere, Ardizzone informs his text with multireferential signs for his reader to decode. As a counterpoint to Nonna's lifelong dilemma of sin and guilt, Ardizzone uses the simple motif of food, and more precisely, bread, to make his closing point. Something so basic and so simple as bread becomes a type of prism though which Nonna can finally begin to consider a different way of thinking. In so doing, Ardizzone inserts the ambiguous sign of consent on the part of the Mexican store owner—ambiguous since we as readers are not sure to what he concurs with his nod and smile.[21] The immediate antecedent is Nonna's comparison of bread to childbearing women. Looking forward, we may assume that the store owner welcomes what we are about to see as Nonna's new propensity to change. Namely, Nonna, we can infer, is—albeit at a late age—now open to change. It is a change that is not just the transformation of the Italian neighborhood into a Mexican one, or the substitution for yeast bread by unleavened bread. Instead, it is a more fundamental change in her way of thinking about her own personal gender position in society, as well as that of other women.

## General Considerations

As is apparent from a number of stories in *The Evening News*, Ardizzone's characters, occupy a "big dark world," as Gino the young altar boy in "The Eyes of Children" tells us, one which in effect is metonymous of the world of the ethnics that inhabit Ardizzone's world.[22] The estrangement that they experience is an easy metaphor for the more general ethnic estrangement that the immigrant and, in some cases the first generations, especially feel. Like Ardizzone's characters, the members of these generations are caught between two worlds. They are neither the *Americans* they traveled to be nor are they any longer members of the world from which they emigrated.

Part of what marks this and other stories in the collection as "expressive" is the so-called time warp in which many of Ardizzone's characters seem to be fixed.[23] Some of the male characters, for instance, are most sentimental, often thinking back to their old girlfriends or mothers. Needy to know what has touched them, as the reviewer for *Booklist* stated, they are reluctant to let go of these old emotional bonds in order to move on, and so they remain in a most modernist framework, undesirous of the somewhat detached postmodern.

Ardizzone's style and narration vary with each story. Simple on the surface, Ardizzone at the same time challenges his reader to delve deep below that surface in order to grapple with some sort of existential unease, if not despair and hopelessness, often present in his stories. Equally significant is Ardizzone's self-awareness as a storyteller and crafty builder of tales. As he tends to lie outside his stories as omniscient narrator, he also inserts himself in stories masked as one of the characters, usually as the story-teller. In fact, to echo the long-forgotten Wayne Booth, in our theoretical, critical, sometimes narrow-minded world of poststructuralism,[24] the narrator of "My Mother's Stories" tells us how writers engage in what I would label *narrative irresponsibility:*

> I stand here, not used to speaking about things that are so close to me. I am used to veiling things in my stories, to making things wear masks, to telling my stories through masks. (p. 12)

The *here* where our narrator stands is an ambiguous place. This paragraph, which appears at the end of Ardizzone's opening story, is set apart from the main text by spaces inserted before and after the preceding and subsequent paragraphs. Thus, as involved readers we must look for whatever bits of evidence lying beneath the surface, like "veil[ed in] masks," as Ardizzone's narrator would tell us, might lead us down one or the other interpretive path. For we should not forget what Ardizzone's narrator tells us at the end of his first story: " . . . but [my mother] never said what it was that she saw from the front windows. A good storyteller, she leaves what she has all too clearly seen to our imaginations" (p. 13). We may surely borrow our initial narrator's words and, in considering Ardizzone's storytelling, state that, like his narrator's mother, Ardizzone the "good storyteller, . . . leaves what [he] has all too clearly [crafted] to our imaginations."

Indeed, as his characters seem to inhabit a certain time period or possess characteristics of a period long gone, in his own way Ardizzone inhabits, in a thematic sense, an ethnic warp. To cite one of his reviewers, he "can't seem to cut himself free [from working-class, ethnic, city life]. And that's good, because his book not only entertains, it fills a void."[25] He does not engage in the militant criticism we would expect of a *comparative* writer; nor does he go beyond the ethnic in an attempt to *synthesize* his stories and characters with irony and/or ethnic dispassion. He succeeds, like those who (re)turn to their ethnicity and (re)invent it through their craft, while filling in the above-mentioned void. It is, in fact, this filling of such a void—an ethnic void—that, in one sense, makes Ardizzone the expressive writer that I suggest he is with *The Evening News*. The characters he presents are still very much tied to individuals with the vicissitudes of those whom Aaron outlined in his essay. Ardizzone, that is, writes from the heart of the North Side of Chicago, a socio-economic milieu where ethnicity is still very much alive and well, and class issues are up front and personal.

# 3

## Helen Barolini's "Comparative" Umbertina: The Italian/American Woman

David Riesman once stated that "the Italian immigrant has to go through a gastronomically bleached and bland period before he can publicly eat garlic and spaghetti."[1] Helen Barolini's first novel, *Umbertina* (1979), deals directly with the Italian immigrant's assimilation process in the United States. She presents the lives of three women of the Longobardi family: Umbertina, the immigrant; Marguerite, and Tina, Marguerite's daughter. Each, in fact, represents a different stage of the Italian and Italian/American assimilation process to American culture. Yet Barolini's novel goes one step further than that experience to which Riesman refers in the above-cited statement, and it is thus more appropriate to change the *he* to a *she*. Indeed, as the theme of ethnic identity develops throughout the novel, there also emerges concurrently the theme of gender identity, as each woman must contend with a male-oriented social structure in their struggle for personal fulfillment. In this chapter, we shall see how these two apparently parallel themes are instead intertwining factors of each woman's experience depicted in the novel.

*Umbertina* is a fictionalized account of the social changes and conflicts within the Italian/American family as it grew and developed from one generation to the next—those generations Joseph Lopreato describes and analyzes in his study *Italian Americans* (1970): "peasant," "first-," "second-," and "third-generation."[2] His "peasant" family comes to life in the figure of Umbertina, a shepherd-girl from a small mountain village in Calabria who tended goats in the burned-out hills near her birthplace until she married. After her marriage to Serafino, a marriage of convenience rather than one of love, they acquired a parcel of secularized land and gave it their best at farming. However, their attempts at making a better life for themselves were futile because of the barrenness of the land and the exorbitant taxes. It was, then, soon decided that they would go to the United States, where Serafino had spent a good part of his youth. Their subsequent move to the United States and the hardships of the trip and of their initial years in New York City are representative of those experienced by most southern Italians who made the journey during the great wave of immigration at the turn of the century. Their later years of life also correspond to the general pattern of behavior among their *paesani* in the new country: the father was considered the head of the family; the "boys" enjoyed more freedom than the "girls."

Barolini does not deal directly with the second-generation family. Instead, the members of this type of family are presented intermittently, as part of the life stories of the three women who make up the book. Yet, even here, some classic stereotypes are presented.[3] What stands out most significantly in this generation is the "apathetic individual," who tends to see things from an economic perspective and avoids the conflict of cultural duality by de-emphasizing and "de-emotionalizing" national origin (Lopreato, 42), if not at times rejecting it and proclaiming him/herself American *rather than* Italian.

This second-generation characteristic is portrayed in various parts of the novel by the reactions of Marguerite's parents (Carla, Umbertina's daughter, and Sam) to their daughter and granddaughter. At the beginning of Marguerite's story we learn of her parents' (especially her father's) attitude toward Italians:

Marguerite learned that it was not nice to look too Italian and to speak bad English the way Uncle Nunzio did. Italians were not a serious people, her father would say—look at Jimmy Durante and Al Capone; Sacco and Vanzetti. Italians were buffoons, anarchists and gangsters, womanizers. "What are we, Dad, aren't we Italian?" she would ask. "We're Americans," he'd say firmly, making her wonder about all the people in the shadows who came before him. Grandmother Umbertina was exempt, even though she didn't speak good English, because she had made good. (*Umbertina*, p. 150; hereafter only page numbers will appear in parentheses.)[4]

What Marguerite's father alludes to is the fact that Umbertina was a successful businesswoman. She had started out making sandwiches for her husband's coworkers, and, in time, opened a neighborhood "groceria" that continued to thrive. Eventually the business went completely wholesale, and the entire family achieved social status according to the norms of social mobility in the Old Country: hard work, regular saving, and secure but gradual success.[5] But Umbertina, though successful fi-

nancially, did not actually enjoy a complete sense of personal fulfillment, as we shall see later on. A similar denial of natural origin is re-
peated toward the end of the novel in a conversation between Tina and
her grandfather, Sam:

> "Now let me ask you, Tina," her grandfather said, . . . "What
> are your plans for the future?"
>
> "Gramp," she said patiently, "I'm getting a Ph.D. in Italian. I
> want to be a scholar."
>
> "But why Italian?" he said in real consternation, his face
> frowning in bewilderment. "What will that fit you for?"
>
> "I can teach or write. . . . "
>
> "I don't understand this infatuation with Italy!" her grand-
> father was saying, rattling his newspaper and looking agitated.
> "Where will that get you? Italy has no future. What has Italy ever
> done for the world?"
>
> "Civilization, Gramp." She thought with sad resignation of
> this useless old argument, and of how, paradoxically, non-Italians
> like the Jowers family were so Italophile. (p. 397)

The significant aspect of her grandfather's reaction to his granddaughter's subject matter is that he is both bewildered and agitated by her
choice. Twice Tina mentions the occupation: "I want to be a scholar. . . .
I can teach or write." Twice the grandfather objects to her choice of subject matter: "But why Italian? . . . What has Italy ever done for the
world?" His disdain for Italian as a subject matter of study is just another way in which he denies, his Italianness.

Sam is not alone in his ethnic denial. Carla, Marguerite's mother,
also engaged in denial of her Italian ethnicity. Only with the marriage
of her son to Betty Burke did she include her in-laws, whom she had not,
for many years, invited into her home. Furthermore, with the excuse of
tradition—since it was the same baker for her wedding—she suggested
that the Italian North Side Bakery furnish the cake. But, as the narrator
interjects, "it was not tradition, but firm assurance that the old times
could never again touch her" (p. 155). Sam and Carla had moved out of
the Italian neighborhood into a much more residential and *American*
one. Sam's relatives, instead, remained in the old place.

Marguerite is prototypical of Lopreato's "second-generation"
(that is, third-generation) family, which he considers to be the first "to

make the big cultural break between the old society and the new" (Lopreato, p. 74). He goes on to describe three different types of individuals who make up this group: the "rebel," the "apathetic individual," and
the "in-grouper." Of the three, Marguerite best represents the "rebel,"
whose "impatience [and] intensity of [her] negative attitude toward the
ways of the old folks" (Lopreato, p. 76) were her dominant characteristics at an early age. She rebelled against middle-class malaise: the reli-
giosity of the traditional family and her mother's middle-class civility.
In fact, we read:

> At school, where all the daughters of the top Irish families went,
> including the mayor's daughter, she got to be known as Mad Mar-
> guerite—because she read books that no one else had heard of
> (Voltaire, Spengler, T. S. Eliot, Ivy Compton-Burnett) and because
> she defied convent ways. She wore her uniform too tight, she stud-
> ied too hard, her answers were delivered in a deprecating way,
> and for religion class she had written a notorious answer on a test
> that the Virgin birth could be explained by *coitus ante portam*—"in-
> tercourse outside the door," i.e., without penetration. (p. 152)

Indeed, we see that her defiance was unlimited in scope: she rebelled
against everything her parents' generation, and some of her own, considered proper and sacred. Her contempt for imposed roles is represented by her mode of dress and behavior at school. More significantly,
we find a great deal of contempt for the specific role of the female, as her
uniform was too tight—most *unladylike*—and her answers were offered
in a deprecating manner. In addition, she studied too hard: this also was
unladylike, since education was usually reserved for the male, who,
having finished, believed he would enjoy economic success. Marguerite's contempt for an imposed female role is manifested as well in
her attitude toward religion. In reference to the most holy of Catholic
beliefs, she describes it with what may be considered by some, a most
desecrating and *vulgar* description.

Along with Marguerite's defiant efforts to break away from the
old-world ways, we also see in the above-cited passage the second generation's attempt at shedding its Italianness: her parents sent her to a
school "where all the daughters of the top Irish families went, including the mayor's daughter." Implied here is the belief that economic success leads to individual amelioration. Indeed, it was at this school,
according to her mother, where Marguerite could meet "worthwhile
girls" whom she could invite over because her family had "a nice home
now" (p. 153).

In her rebellion, Marguerite disagreed with the old-world idea that children *owed* their parents respect. She saw, to her dismay, the parent-child relationship of the Italian family set in economic terms: children *owed, paid back, bore dividends* for having done good deeds. Thus for her, the family motto could have been "Money Talks," as it was also the motto for their concept of social mobility and individual development. But Marguerite believed there was more to life than material well being; she turned to literature and other arts as a means of achieving some sort of personal fulfillment. Thus, her rebellion was aimed at the traditional form of education, more specifically, the overall ideological viewpoint of the parochial school, which is "person-oriented [since it] teaches children rules of behavior appropriate to the adult peer group society, and it stresses discipline." The public school, on the other hand, is "object-oriented and teaches [children] aspirations and skill for work, play, family life and community participation."[6]

With regard to her Italianness, as both a child and an adult Marguerite found herself in a "confusion of roles." And it was precisely this confusion that seemed to spark her rebellious acts. Her desire to break away from first- and second-generation (that is, ethnic) bonds and her belief in freedom and spontaneity are evidenced by both her "quickie marriage" to Lennert Norenson, "the Nordic" (as her cousin labeled him), and her later trip to England, where she strikes up an affair with a self-exiled literary type. Her subsequent marriage to Alberto, a wise and philosophical older Italian writer, and her later trips to Italy reveal, on the other hand, the extent to which she accepts her ethnicity. Yet her marriage is, at best, an ambivalent one for both personal and cultural reasons, and she is reluctant to stay in Italy for long. Thus she seems to exhibit signs of confusion indicative of the third-generation Italian. Namely, while this individual seems to be more self-confident and secure about her life's trajectory, there still remains some cultural residue from the previous generation.

In his study of the Italian/American family in the United States, Campisi found that there was indeed more security fostered in the third-generation individual than in the second-generation. However, he also found what he calls "conflict lags", and because of these lags, this third-generation family many times reflects a "confused American situation" (Campisi, p. 446). In Marguerite's case, her initial breaking away demonstrates her desire to live a life different from her parents'. Yet she also feels a strong tie to Italy, and it is precisely her oscillation between America and Italy, between American culture and Italian culture, that perpetuates her identity confusion.

This antagonism between Americanness and Italianness is a major theme both in Marguerite's story and in the novel itself. In the prologue to the novel, which takes place in her analyst's office, he interprets her dream as an expression of her "feeling of alienation . . . anxiety as to whether she is American, Italian, or Italo-American" (p. 17). Soon after, recalling a picture of her father, she describes him in a manner similar to that in which her analyst described her:

> I remember a picture of him in our album, at eighteen on his motorcycle when he had already organized the business but was still just a kid full of God knows what kind of dreams of an exciting future. I thought of him separating himself from the Italians of the North Side to make himself into a real American. He turned reactionary to do it, but he started courageously. He was caught in a terrible trap; he couldn't be either Italian like his father and mother or American like his models without feeling guilty toward one or the other side. And even now he doesn't know how to be American while accepting his Italianness because it's still painful to him. So there's conflict and bitterness. (p. 19)

The conflict and bitterness she sees in her father are equally strong in her, for she too was *caught in a trap*. Marguerite was an intellectually curious child of a culturally unsophisticated family, who was often chided for having her "nose in a book," something deemed ever "so impractical."[7] Throughout her life, she was constantly trying to live according to "everyone else's idea of what [her] life should be" (p. 19). This included her parents, her husband Alberto, and even her Italian lover. In the first case, she lay victim to her parents' shame in their Italianness which they tried not to pass on to her. In the second and third cases especially, while her Italianness was partially satisfied, she was nevertheless dependent upon them because of her gender. Consequently, she felt personally unfulfilled because she was not her own person but rather a part of everyone else.

Tina's story may seem slightly different from the usual fourth-generation experience, because she is the child of an Italian/American mother and Italian father. Yet, her father's situation notwithstanding, she stills reflects those characteristics that, according to Lopreato, the fourth-generation individual may possess. She is introduced to us as a young American feminist of the 1960s generation, completely unidentifiable as Italian. Yet, she too struggles with the Italian/American dilemma. Like her mother, she experiences a love/hate relationship with Italy and with America. When in Italy, she is enamored of the "natural, human life," but she also realizes that as an individual, or better yet, as a woman, "it won't get [her] anyplace and that [she has] got to go back [to the United States] and plug into the system" (p. 298).[8]

Tina's experience, however, differs greatly from that of her mother and from her great-grandmother's as well. Two major reasons come to the fore with regard to this distinction. Tina is, first of all, a member of a generation that initiated a cultural and sexual revolution, and thereby challenged an entire set of norms that had trapped women, especially, of previous generations. Secondly, she is a fourth-generation Italian who was, like most members of this group, according to Lopreato, "deliberately educated in the ways of the middle-class, [according to which] education is highly valued" (p. 86). Education is highly valued precisely because it becomes an end in itself, "used to maximize individual development of the person" (Gans, p. 247).[9]

Tina, in fact, wants to be a "scholar who teaches for a living"; she does not want to end up both emotionally and financially dependent on marriage. Indeed, she adamantly refuses to repeat the experiences of both her mother and great-grandmother;[10] she decides to define herself as an autonomous individual before becoming permanently involved with a man. Thus, she places her college degree over her love for Jason, even at the risk of losing him, because she firmly believes that there would not exist between them a relationship "in which individuals seeking to maximize their own development as persons come together on the basis of common interests" (Gans, p. 247). It is therefore through education that she achieves not only material well being but also self-expression, self-fulfillment, and empathy for the behavior of others. It is precisely this last characteristic that eventually helps her understand and ultimately resolve her ethnic (if not also gender) dilemma.[11]

At the beginning of this chapter, I stated that *Umbertina* can be considered a fictionalized account of the social changes and ethnic conflicts Italian immigrants and their progeny experience in America. Early in the novel, Barolini introduces ethnic identity as a dilemma; even earlier, however, she introduces the theme of gender identity as a dilemma. In the prologue, during Marguerite's session with her analyst, the problem of stereotyping women arises. When Marguerite tells her doctor of her occasional desire to sleep with her husband despite her wish to divorce him, he responds in the following manner:

"Then do it, do what you feel," he said energetically.

"But I can't! Don't you understand that if I do he'll never agree to the divorce and I haven't even gotten him to sign the separation agreement. ( . . . )"

"There's a typical female wile for that. You get him to sign first and then go to bed. This is something all women understand."

"I . . . I never thought of that," she stammered, confused.

"It's something women have always been able to do. It's a classic strategem, no?" (pp. 5–6)

She was, in fact, offended by his masculine arrogance, by his presumption that the female role was not only different from the male role but inferior as well. The last thing Marguerite wanted was to live on the margin of a man's existence; she wanted to be her own person, autonomous to the extent of being able to make her own decisions. But her struggle for a sense of fulfillment was impeded not only by her own lack of vision, but also by the male-oriented society in which she lived.[12] It was in fact her awareness of a new feminism which induced her to seek analysis, yet her analyst proved himself to be a perpetuator of female stereotypes.

It is significant that at this point in the novel Barolini deals with male chauvinism in a general context. Not just Marguerite, but all the women in the novel encounter and must confront the problem of living within a patriarchal culture. Their struggle is thus twofold: not only are they fighting against the ethnic barriers set up by the predominant culture in America—specifically in the United States—but they must also contend with gender oppression. With regard to their gender dilemma, the Italian and Italian/American women we encounter in the novel have a double-layered struggle to fight. They must first contend with the prejudices within their own ethnic group, only to deal a second time with similar sexist attitudes once they break the bonds of ethnicity and gain some semblance of autonomy as an individual. Thus, these women are denied a sense of personal achievement and are relegated to a "second-class citizen" status as well.

Turning our attention first to Umbertina, we see that hers was a financial Cinderella story; not only her immediate family, but likewise the generations to follow, benefit from her hard work and astute business sense. Nevertheless, in spite of her many victories over various economic hardships, she seemed destined to lie victim to social norms concerning the male-female relationship. In Italy, when she once interfered in the bargaining process at the market, her brother scolded her harshly even though she saved the family money and him a tongue-lashing from their father: "I'm the man, [he told her . . . ] Men have to deal with these things not women" (pp. 30–31). Indeed, however independent she may seem at times throughout her story, she most always defers to what is "customary." In fact, Barolini presents Umbertina—as was the case with many Italian women of her generation both in Italy and in the United States—as a woman conscious of her *place in society*, that "she was bound by men's notions of what women must be" (p. 34).[13] When, as a young woman in Italy, it seemed she was secretly meeting Giosuè (the young charcoal maker) in the hills outside her village, her father decided it was time *for him* to find her a husband. Once he announced Serafino's offer of marriage, she readily accepted: first, because Serafino represented something new in her life; second, because it was her father's wish that she do so.

It was Umbertina's decision that they emigrate to America, as it was also she who started the sandwich business which eventually turned into a major wholesale company. Yet, in spite of all her time and energy devoted to the family business, the future of it was in her sons' names, not in her daughters', and the sign out front read, "S. Longobardi and Sons." Thus, she adhered to family conventionality, and when Serafino died, the wholesale company was at its zenith, and *he* was credited, "as was customary," with having left his family "secure, its fortune started." His obituary read: "Serafino Longobardi knew how, with his honest and untiring work, to launch his sons into business and open for them that excellent place in everyone's esteem that the Longobardi family enjoys today" (p. 128). The irony, if not injustice to be more precise, lies in the fact that Serafino did not work in the store for most of his life; he was instead a railroad worker. When the time came for him to retire, it was Umbertina who told him he should do so. Thus, when he finally did join the family in the store, he would do "odd jobs," or roast chestnuts on the potbellied stove in bad weather.

Umbertina's incomplete sense of fulfillment—as that of any woman who compromises her position as an individual because of family conventionality or other social norms—poignantly manifests itself toward the end of her story. She realized how, as a *business woman,* she received very little if any credit at all. She thought it indeed strange that it was Serafino's "name which triumphed and . . . his presence, *as a man,* which had been necessary to give her the standing from which to command" (p. 134; emphasis added). She now realized that a woman could not be a whole person in a male-dominated society. In one way or another, in fact, the female of her generation was almost always subservient to the male, whereas an "increase in the freedom and family influence of the woman" began to manifest itself in the following generations (Gans, p. 207).

That Marguerite may have lacked her own sense of direction by no means discounts the fact that she too was a victim of a male-oriented social structure. Her marriage to Lennert was a rebellious reaction to her family's insistence that "girls" should be married. That it was a "quickie marriage" to a non-Italian is also significant, because it figured also as a means of an escape from her family's dominance over her life. She hoped it would bring greater possibilities in her life for self-fulfillment. Soon to be disappointed, she opted for other means. Her marriage to Alberto and the family they started left her, however, with a sense of unfulfillment, as she still yearned for professional completeness. After many attempts at various pursuits, only one seemed to have any success: *she* translating *his* poetry. Thus, life centered around him: he prospered professionally and personally, and she took care of the family.

Notwithstanding Marguerite's vague and undefined goals, Barolini poignantly demonstrates how even Alberto, consciously or not, contributed to her gender dilemma. His initial promise, "I'll make a real human being out of you" (p. 177), is indicative of the masculine presumption that a woman needs a man for her personal development. When she was truly depressed, he would address her as his *"bambina mia,"* telling her that she did love him and was happy but resisted seeing it. Finally, when she insisted on divorce, his response was that *she* was tired of too much sun, that *she* should see a psychiatrist once they returned to Rome, since *she* was still upset over the death of their son. We see, then, that Marguerite was relegated to the "homemaker role," and unhappily so.[14]

Apologetic about her work of translating Alberto's poetry, she once stated to her secret lover, Massimo, that she really wanted to be a photographer: "'Why don't you? That's a beautiful thing to do, you know' [Massimo]. 'I have a family,' she said. They fell silent. She tried to retrieve things." Not possessing any autonomy as an individual, Marguerite remains trapped in the traditional female role and is thus subordinate to her husband (and lover). She is thereby unable to realize any of her desired goals. Indeed, the traditional role sometimes acts as a "brake on [the female's] aspirations and[, more specifically in Marguerite's case,] as an accelerator on her frustrations" (Gans, p. 216). This is the case with Marguerite, as it had also been with Carla and Umbertina.

These antithetical feelings Marguerite experiences with regard to her femaleness are, in a certain sense, analogous to those concerning her Italianness, as was evidenced earlier. She finds herself in a confused situation, at times opting for the more traditional role while at other times wanting to break free and be her own person. It is important to keep in mind that traditional roles, especially female, were passed on from one generation to the next, and among Italian immigrants it was considered "'normal' [for adolescent females] to expect and to want children when they married";[15] furthermore, they were expected to live out their lives as mothers and housewives, and consequently they were relegated to limited personal development as integral individuals. It is also important to remember that Marguerite's gender dilemma was complicated by the fact that she married an older, conservative Italian who was a defender of the traditional female role and, consequently, of a male-oriented social structure.[16] Thus, these two seemingly distinct problems of ethnicity and gender actually prove to be separate parts of a whole: namely, the Italian/Amercian female dilemma.

Marguerite never resolves her gender conflict. Although she remained with Alberto, she struck up an affair, as mentioned above, with a writer, younger than her husband, named Massimo. He was to be her "bridge to a new reality." Instead, however, it was she who became his bridge to a possible literary award: she was his contact to Alberto, then editor of a literary review. She could also spread his fame by translating his prose, and she filled the sexual and emotional void between Massimo and his wife, who had, with the years, become his "domestic," serving and seconding him in everything. Thus, once again, Marguerite had become another man's woman, and when Massimo lost the award, Marguerite lost Massimo.

After the fatal car crash during her return from their summer home during a rain storm, Marguerite's life is summed up by the last two entries in her diary. The first reinforces her ethnic dilemma:

> All those snooty, shining girls. They know who they are and where they're going. ( . . . ) I'm the only Italian name here. They're all saying they're going to be writers or doctors. . . . Whoever told me I could do any of that? (p. 310)

The second entry heightens her gender identity dilemma:

> Is this the bill for happiness? Is this paying the goddam fiddler? Now I'm pregnant and it's Massimo's child and who else but me is going to pay? Now what? Ask him to leave his wife? ( . . . ) A backroom abortion? A quick trip to England or Switzerland? And where would the money come from? What could I tell A.? What do women do in Italy . . . or anyplace? (p. 312; elisions textual)

One of the implications in the first passage is that the stifling of aspirations is not necessarily unidirectional. While it is true that Marguerite is the only Italian, this impediment does not originate solely from the dominant, non-Italian culture. Someone (their parents) has told these "snooty, shining girls" that they can be doctors, writers, or whatever else they might aspire to be. Education for the dominant culture figures as a primary tool, if not an end in itself, for individual development. The Italian American, on the other hand, did not consider education to be a primary source for personal well being. This was especially true with regard to the female, an obvious inheritance from the first generation, according to whom "girls should get married" and raise a family. It is only with the third and fourth generations that education becomes a highly valued asset.

Marguerite's second entry underscores the female's dilemma, which significantly is no longer restricted to the Italian or Italian American but concerns women in general: "What do women do in Italy . . . *or anyplace?*" Briefly, Marguerite alone would have had to bear the burden and responsibility of her unplanned pregnancy. The illegality of abortion limits its availability and contributes to exorbitant fees, which, for her, having been primarily a homemaker and thus financially dependent on her husband, seemed virtually impossible.

Barolini's implication of female victimization becomes more complex at this point in the novel. Taken together, both entries sum up the problems of the Italian/American females of Marguerite's generation. Indeed, the gender dilemma is no longer limited just to the woman's right to study, opt for a professional career, and therefore decide her own destiny. Up to this point in the novel, in fact, the woman's struggle was primarily ethno-cultural and psychological: she had to fight the barriers imposed by her parents in order to escape the prison-house of ethnicity and eventually reconcile any cultural residue in her attempt at greater assimilation into the dominant culture. Now, however, an unwanted pregnancy brings to the fore the problem of physiological victimization.[17] In a male-dominated society in which the female, as in Marguerite's case, is financially dependent upon the male, abortion— an operation which undoubtedly effects the female's life more directly than the male's—is considered illegal. Someone in Marguerite's predicament must therefore resort to an illegal, backroom abortion, which, besides being beyond her financial means, may also prove to be dangerous to her physical well being.

Notwithstanding her lack of success in achieving some semblance of personal fulfillment, Marguerite, as victim of a patriarchal system, remained throughout intellectually curious and unwilling to bend com-

pletely to tradition. In so doing, she helped pave the way for the following generation of females, here represented by Tina.

Although Tina's situation is relatively different from her mother's
and great-grandmother's, she too must confront the question of gender
identity. Barolini skillfully presents the difficulties Tina, as a woman,
faces in her search for independence and personal fulfillment. Because
of the emerging feminism of the 1960s, Tina is much more aware of the
inequities in all realms of the professional world. In fact, we have already seen in Marguerite's story how Tina grew increasingly aware of
her mother's plight. Specifically, Tina realizes that a woman is not a
good investment, according to the professional world, because she will
"quit and get married." She also understands how her father's suggestion that she could credit her career by translating his new novel would,
as it did in Marguerite's case, make her "part of his success," and
thereby deny her the opportunity of her own self-realization.

Jason, her seemingly sensitive and understanding future husband,
also exhibits signs of (unconscious?) male pride when he tells her she
does "all the essentials so well—( . . . ) cook, make love, go with guys on
trips, swim—and yet, [has a] hang-up about getting married" (p. 360).
The essentials she does so well, according to him, are in fact male-
directed, especially "cook, make love, go with guys on trips," and characteristic of the traditional female role, which this is precisely what Tina
rejects. What is a hang-up according to Jason is for Tina, at this point in
her life, freedom from the "dependency on any man who would keep
her from the fulness of her own life and expectations" (p. 337).

Barolini offers in Tina's story other examples of indoctrination into
the traditional female role and of gender oppression. In a brief exchange
between Tina and her grandmother Carla, we see how the latter figures
as a staunch defender of the old-world concepts of marriage, as the major priority for women, and professional success, conversely, as the major priority for men:

"Do you have any boyfriends?" her grandmother asked,
standing back to appraise Tina. . . .

"I can't bear it!" she retorted. "Is that all you want to hear
about me, *nonna*?"

"I wish you would find someone . . . a beautiful girl like you.
You should be able to do very well."

"*Nonna*! Such ideas—how can you do well by marrying if
you haven't got your own personal life together first? No one's

rushing into marriage these days. It's much better to concentrate on one's work and have other interests."

"That's not natural," Carla went on shaking her head. "I saw Ron Peters, who used to like your mother—he's doing so well. But she pretended she was never interested either. Now he drives a Rolls Royce, has a yacht, a house in Florida, one son in Harvard, and a daughter in Paris." (pp. 396–97)

Significant at this point is that Carla, here a seemingly staunch defender of old-world concepts, was herself a victim of those very same prejudices. For Carla, as a young woman, once entertained ideas of finishing high school and going on to college. But because of the family business, she was pulled out of high school before she could graduate and put to work in the store. Her rewards were "charge accounts to all the stores downtown, . . . two fur coats and several Paris gowns before she was married" (p. 135). In reality, it was not just the family business which impeded Carla's education; it was also the family's strong conviction that "girls" should not go "off to sleep out of town under strange roofs. Girls should be married" (p. 135). The notion that a woman is happy with shopping, fur coats, Paris gowns, and other material goods of the sort is indeed a masculine stereotype of the female. In the novel, the male-presumption of such a notion is heightened by the fact that the offer was made to Carla by her brothers.

Barolini presents Tina's abortion not as a moral issue, but rather as a political statement concerning the social structure of male vis-à-vis female: namely, the power and control the former may exert over the latter. Briefly, it is an illegal, expensive, backroom operation performed by a male doctor. Once it is done, Tina thinks back to her former lover:

> . . . that poor, sweet, easygoing Duke who would have been the last guy in the world to bring her pain. And yet he had because he was a man, and she, no matter what she did to her brain and willpower, was still inhabiting a female body. Just one night that she forgot a pill, and this was what happened. She thought about her mother's jokes about "Who pays the fiddler? The girl pays the fiddler." (p. 345)

In her review essay on literature dedicated to abortion over a ten-year span, Barbara Hayler has demonstrated how many feminists argue that opposition to abortion is only one aspect of a greater opposition to female autonomy within a patriarchal society.[18] According to Mary

Daly, who considers such opposition as part of a larger system that she calls "gynocide," this contributes to the "domestication and deprivation of female vitality, both physical and spiritual, [and] the 'cutting to pieces' of women's autonomous wills."[19] More directly, she also states that the male-oriented social structure functions "to keep women supine, objectified and degraded—a condition ritually symbolized by the gynocologist's stirrups and the psychiatrist's couch" (pp. 229–30). For Daly, *gynocology* includes the practice of both medicine and psychiatry; accordingly, she distinguishes between "mind-gynocologists" [psychiatrists] and "body-gynocologists" [gynocologists] (p. 228). In *Umbertina*, symbols similar to Mary Daly's are indeed present. One need only to think back to Marguerite's analyst for an example of the mind-gynocologist. However, the more forcefully described socio-political issue of the two is abortion. Barolini presents this issue to her reader in three different doses, culminating in Tina's experience. In the last entry of Marguerite's diary, we saw that it was the woman who was responsible for the unwanted pregnancy; in fact, Marguerite was to pay the consequences. The second case involves a four-months-pregnant woman who was beaten to death by her husband because she wanted an abortion. It is with this case that the stereotypes and injustices of a patriarchal system rise to the surface. Angela, the woman of whom Tina asked help in procuring an abortion, recounts:

> She was twenty years old and already had two small children. *Naturally* she was viewed as the monster, while the husband, who beat her to death, was looked upon as acting within *his rights*. At her funeral service the priest said, "She was a mother who gave two lives into the world. She was also a wife. In the next life she will still be a wife and mother." (p. 340; emphasis added)

The relegation of the female exclusively to the role of wife and mother indeed describes this twenty-year-old woman's life. A similar role had been imposed on Marguerite, as was apparent in the story. Also imposed here, however, is the gender dilemma of a woman's right to self-determination. In the above-cited passage, we find that the husband was considered to have been within his rights to kill his wife because she had decided to abort. With this scene, Barolini also makes it clear that a woman's lack of self-determination is felt in all facets of society, even in the Church. In fact, the priest's eulogy implies that this young woman's lack of self-determination even extends beyond her natural life to her afterlife: "She was mother [ . . . and] wife. In the next life she will still be a wife and mother." In its own way, then, the Church appears to be both highly complicit in the oppression of women and arrogant to the point of attributing its own judgment on women to *God, the father.*

Barolini reiterates this notion in Tina's visit to the male doctor who will perform her abortion. It is, in fact, with Tina's abortion that Barolini movingly describes the oppression and powerlessness the female experiences in a patriarchal society:

> She slipped off her sandals, got onto the table, and following his directions, put her feet into the steel stirrups, uselessly trying to keep her knees together.
>
> "Relax," he said, quickly forcing her knees apart and lifting her skirt up around her waist. She felt like one of the half-clothed dummies she used to see in storefronts . . . and she tried . . . to keep her feelings at dummy level.
>
> He was not a bad person; and he was quite unaware of the revulsion and anger he stirred in her as he patted and looked. By telling her to have courage he was, in his way, trying to keep her spirits up. Still, she hated him—as much as she hated the pope in his long unsullied skirts, or the fat-bellied old priests who told women they sinned, or the pigs in Parliament who daydreamed about women to fuck as they deliberated on laws that violated their bodies.
>
> No matter how cordial, the doctor was a profiteer and a butcher, and she thought of herself, legs apart, as one of those carcasses hanging in all the meat markets of Rome—revoltingly explicit with their hairy bodies intact but split up the middle. . . .
>
> Tina thought of Mussolini hanging like a pig by his feet and his mistress hanging alongside him, her crime having been that of loving him. But even in that bad time, someone had had pity enough to pin Clara's skirt together as she hung upside-down at the gas station in Milan. . . .
>
> Now as she lay, stiff with fear, she thought again of her mother who had willed her to life and whose death might have come because she was pregnant, just as Tina was. She was sharing with her mother for the first time the communion of motherhood. (pp. 343–44)

We see the male doctor, who is seemingly cordial yet basically unsympathetic to his patient's needs during the operation; he is, according to Tina, a "profiteer and a butcher" whose sole concern is not to get caught by the authorities. His exorbitant fee largely is due to the attitude of two other patriarchal groups: the "fat-bellied priests" and the "pigs in Parliament [who decided on] laws that violated [women's] bodies." Yet, more than a violation of bodies, such an experience proves to be a violation of the entire person: body *and* spirit. The psychological degradation is evidenced by Tina's initial feeling of intrusion as the doctor lifted her skirt; by the comparison of herself to one of the carcasses hanging in the meat markets; and by her recollection that even for Mussolini's mistress, someone had had enough pity to pin her skirt together as she hung upside-down. Finally, the denial of control to women, in this specific instance, of their reproductive capabilities, and, in more general terms, of their destiny, is summed up in the final sentence of the above-cited passage; for the first time, Tina "was sharing with her mother . . . the *communion of motherhood.*"

There are other examples of gender oppression which Tina confronts. Yet, in spite of these and other obstacles, she does succeed in gaining the "license to be a woman professional in a man's world" (p. 389)[20]. Tina, in fact, wants to be a "scholar who teaches for a living"; she does not want to end up emotionally and financially dependent on marriage, repeating the experiences of both her mother and great-grandmother. Because she firmly believes that there would not exist between them a relationship "in which individuals seeking to maximize their own development as persons come together on the basis of common interests" (Gans p. 247) she places her degree over her love for Jason, even at the risk of losing him. Thus, as we saw earlier, through education she achieves not only material well being but also self-expression, self-fulfillment, and empathy for the behavior of others which eventually help her understand and ultimately resolve both her ethnic *and* gender dilemmas.

As witness to the Italian ethnic dilemma, Barolini indeed succeeds in creating experiences similar to those reported by sociologists such as Gambino, Gans, and Lopreato. Likewise, she succeeds in portraying those experiences and difficulties of the Italian/American female which have been recorded by Winsey, Yans-McLaughlin, and those who have contributed to the volume *The Italian Immigrant Woman in North America*. Yet, *Umbertina* is more than just a fictionalized account of those experiences. For while it is enhanced by this documentary quality, it also enjoys an unsparing true-to-life characterization of the protagonists and thus proves to be extremely intriguing and, at times, provocative.

Of the three stages we saw in Chapter One, Barolini represents the second-stage writer, that "militant protester" who, by no means conciliatory, belongs to the generation that rediscovers or reinvents his/her ethnicity. Barolini, that is, presents characters who have already "sunk roots in the native soil" and readily underscores the characters' uniqueness vis-à-vis the expectations of the dominant culture. Indeed, as Gardaphé reminds us, before a writer like Barolini can "merge with the present," she must recreate—and I add, in a *sui generis* manner—her past: she engages in a "materialization and an articulation of the past" as we saw above. Umbertina, for example, is not the stereotypical, dominated Italian female the mainstream culture might readily expect. Instead, and in a certain sense in spite of her inner strength, she is one of the strongest characters of the novel. She is the catalyst and, obviously, business acumen behind the Longobardi family's success. She is also the catalyst that eventually leads to the success of female independence manifested in Tina, her own namesake to appear three generations later.

Therefore, as the use of ethnicity at this second stage shifts from the expressive to the descriptive as a rhetoric-ideological tool, it becomes much more functional. No longer the predominantly expressive element it is in the pre–modernist writer, for the modernist, mythic writer ethnicity becomes more the tool with which she communicates her ideology. In Barolini's ethnic/gender case, the ethnic signs constitute the individual pieces to the ethnic paradigm she so consciously and willingly seeks to construct.

Finally, it is important to remember that the figure of the woman in Italian/American literature has been portrayed, for the most part, in a traditional female role by a male author. Even in those few exceptions written by women, the female has still occupied a fixed role—that of the central position in the family.[21] The novelty of *Umbertina* lies precisely in Barolini's treatment of women as individuals, who, at one point or another in their lives, become aware of their true plight—the duality of gender and ethnic oppression—and, especially with regard to Marguerite and Tina, attempt to free themselves from the prison house of patriarchy.

# 4

## Giose Rimanelli's "Synthetic" *Benedetta in Guysterland*: A "Liquid" Novel of Questionable Textual Boundaries[1]

Certo è un azzardo un po' forte,
scrivere delle cose così,
che ci son professori oggidì
a tutte le porte.

—Aldo Palazzeschi, "E lasciatemi divertire"[2]

*Benedetta in Guysterland. A Liquid Novel* is Giose Rimanelli's first book-length prose fiction in English. Written well over twenty years ago, conceived, processed, and finally drafted into manuscript form during the 1961–1972 decade, it was published only recently by Guernica Editions of Montréal (March 1993). While it may not be ironic that this work is published only now in this decade—for Rimanelli tells us that he wrote it for love, not money—it does seem a bit ironic for two diametrically opposed reasons that it be published by a Canadian house: 1) Rimanelli spent most of his adult life outside Italy in the United States; 2) perhaps a sweeter irony, Rimanelli was born in Italy of a Canadian mother and a United States grandfather. He thus returns not to one or the other of the two North American English-speaking countries, that is, the United States or Canada, but indeed to the two non-Italian countries that contributed in different ways to his adult cultural specificity. *Benedetta in Guysterland. A Liquid Novel*, in this sense, represents the amalgamation of two socio-cultural experiences—the Italian and the North American—which, in turn, constitute Rimanelli's status as a truly bicultural (as well as bicontinental) writer.

One premise discussed earlier that crosses generations with regard to the image of Italy and Italian America in Italian/American art is the general notion of cultural specificity: that literature and film, as is the case with any other artistic form, are conceived and produced in highly differentiated contexts of culturally specific ideological clusters, and that any particular work will have to be viewed against the backdrop of that specific cluster in which it was produced, as well as the viewer's intertextual cultural reservoir. Another premise, analogous to the general notion of cultural specificity and more specific to the Italian/American experience, that links many Italian/American art forms is the notion of ethnogenesis: as we saw in chapter one, that ethnicity is not a fixed element or unchanging form that is passed down from one generation to the next. Rather, ethnicity is continuously regenerated through the following generation's discovery of it, and hence reinvented according to this new generation's ideological specificities.[3]

Also pertinent to an understanding of the Italian American's relationship to Italy and Italian America is the notion of the hyphenated individual. With regard to literature, people have already spoken of the "hyphenate" writer; I remind the reader of Aaron and Gardaphé, as discussed in Chapter One. Sociologists have likewise spoken of the hyphenated ethnic, and I remind the reader of Lopreato and Campisi. In both cases, the characteristics of each group overlap, and the progression from one generation to the next follows a similar trajectory.

The hyphen, as Aaron told us, initially represented older North Americans' hesitation to accept the newcomer; it was their way to "hold him at 'hyphen's length,' so to speak, from the established community" (p. 213). It further "signifies a tentative but unmistakable withdrawal" on the user's part, so that "mere geographical proximity" denies the newly arrived "full and unqualified national membership despite . . . legal qualifications and . . . official disclaimers to the contrary" (p. 213).

Of the different stages of the hyphenate writer, Giose Rimanelli represents the third-stage writer, who travels from the margin to the mainstream "viewing it (that is, mainstream = dominant culture) no less critically, perhaps, but more knowingly" than the previous first- and second-stage writer. This writer, moreover, as Aaron reminds us, does not renounce or abandon the cultural heritage of his/her marginalized group. Instead, s/he transcends "a mere parochial allegiance" in order to transport "into the province of the [general] imagination," personal experiences which for the first-stage ("local colorist") and second-stage ("militant protester") writer "comprised the very stuff of their literary material" (p. 215). This, in fact, is precisely the case with Giose Rimanelli's *Benedetta*. His novel is chock full of all that is Italian and Italian/American to the extent that it could not exist without the "stuff" of ethnic experiences with which Rimanelli informs his text.

To be sure, Rimanelli's Italian/American cultural specificity is an important component of *Benedetta in Guysterland.* Nevertheless, there are other aspects of the novel that also need to be considered. In what follows, I shall deal with the questions of text and textual boundaries as they relate to the structural division of *Benedetta in Guysterland. A Liquid Novel.* If we consider, in a general sense, a text to be a series of signs transmitted through a verbal or visual medium with the intent of comunicating a message of any sort, regardless of how easy or difficult it may be to decode such a message, then the notion of text is not so significant a matter; *Guysterland* surely satisfies this general definition.[4] What is more significant here, I would contend, is the notion of textual boundaries. Looking at the book's table of contents, we find the following:

Prefaces

Preface by Fred Gardaphé          11

For-a-word                        27

Benedetta in Guysterland          31

Post-word                         205

Appendix                          211

As is evident from the graph, we find a preface by Fred Gardaphé and four other sections; three are written by Giose Rimanelli, and the fourth is a collaborative effort. What we may normally consider the narrative text, that is, a succession of events which constitute the "story," is the second and longest section, "Benedetta in Guysterland." But there is also a "For-a-word" and a "Post-word" written by Rimanelli, or, as he refers to himself, "the Author," that special construct that is/may be Rimanelli, in this instance. What concludes this succession of internal texts—or better, "microtexts," to borrow from Maria Corti[5]—is an "Appendix" consisting of a series of responses to "Benedetta in Guysterland" by Rimanelli's friends and colleagues of the early 1970s, capped by two mini-sections—responses and thanks—written by Rimanelli himself.

To be sure, Gardaphé's preface is precisely that, an outsider's view of the book intended to lay some foundation for any reader's encounter with the narrative text. Some poststructuralist critics, however, might want to see this, too, as part of the overall text. Indeed, from a hermeneutico-semiotic point of view, the idea is not too far-fetched;

after all, any information the reader may gather from Gardaphé's preface will influence her/his reading of Rimanelli's novel.[6] Yet, even if, for argument's sake, we decide to eliminate Gardaphé's preface, we find ourselves nevertheless with four other microtexts, not just Benedetta in Guysterland, for which the question of textual boundaries persists. Namely, we still have a similar textual lineup of a For-a-word, Benedetta in Guysterland, Post-word, and an Appendix. The reader, whoever s/he may be, will most likely consider, at least at his/her first encounter with the book, the central microtext Benedetta in Guysterland to be the *novel*. In what follows, I shall limit myself to a discussion of the three central microtexts penned exclusively by Giose Rimanelli: the opening For-a-word, the central Benedetta in Guysterland, and the concluding Post-word.[7]

What further complicates the matter is that the narrating voices of each of these three microtexts is a different one. The narrator of the For-a-word may readily be identified with the actual pen-holder, or, as we might say today, wordprocessor user, whom we know as Giose Rimanelli, "emigré," as he readily defines himself here (" . . . when the Author was still an emigré in U.S.A." [p. 29]), to the United States in 1961. Here, in a somewhat personal way,[8] Rimanelli offers a few interpretive keys to his reader. We find out that Benedetta in Guysterland is, in a very Gozzanoan and Palazzeschian way, "made up by the careful use of famous and infamous quotations, scraps of personal *co co rico co co rico* lyrics, confessions of country girls with kitsch and poetry pap, advertisements" (p. 28), and so on, as he continues to tell us.[9] We also come to know that the Author is a lover of words and sees himself here as a

> free collector of paper joy and paper anguish instead of a producer of them—in order to attempt a new experiment on verbs and syntax, speech, writing, and paranoia. I stretched my hands out and found what we usually produce: dreams, love, murder, golden charades, lampoons. (pp. 28–29)

Two things stand out in the above-cited quotation. First, we see that the Author's intent is to experiment as free collector—again, Gozzanoan / Palazzeschian reverberations come to the fore—not as producer, for which the production of the "paper joy and paper anguish," what we may consider a metaphor for meaning/signification, becomes an act of coproduction. Second, such coproduction is implicit, I would suggest, in his shift from a singular first-person pronoun to the plural form: "*I* stretched my hands out and found what *we* usually produce: dreams, love, murder, golden charades, lampoons." This desire for coproduction—the connection between author and reader—is underscored by the physical act of stretching, the Author's literal reaching out to his reader. We see, in fact, that as the *I* of "I stretch" transforms into the *we* of "we usually produce," coproduction takes place; and what follows— those "dreams, love, murder, golden charades, lampoons"—may easily constitute thematics of an author's work as well as those of a reader's list of desired motifs.

Another allusion to interpretive strategies in the For-a-word can be found in the opening sentences. We have already seen how the Author wants to reach out to his reader. What we also see in his opening sentences is an allusion to the notion of individual cognitive and interpretive specificities. Rimanelli opens his For-a-word in the following manner:

> Just after finishing this, I went out in the open and read, on a billboard: *As dada rock gets worse, outdoor micro-boppers get better.* True, but I don't understand. Probably because I never belonged to a Band. . . .
>
> Well, I guess that when everything is questionable each person must choose for himself what he wants. (p. 27; emphasis textual)

In the first sentences of the opening paragraph we find allusions to a reader's intertextuality. The narrator, here as reader, cannot understand the billboard because his intertextual reservoir does not possess the (acquired) knowledge necessary to reconcile the information he sees on the billboard, as he himself tells us; for he "never belonged to a Band." In a similar manner, the opening sentence of the second paragraph refers to a person's decision (to "choose"), metaphorically speaking, to affix value (significance) to something (words).

But this second paragraph also announces another significant aspect of the novel. We saw earlier that the Author wants to be a "free collector" and "not a producer" of signification. The notion of coproduction mentioned above is first alluded to in this second paragraph of Rimanelli's For-a-word, in the phrase, "when everything is questionable," the implication being that everything is indeed questionable and that any notion of an absolute is called into question. This said, it clears the path for Rimanelli's desire for experimentation, which, in turn, affords him the opportunity to create a text—or a series thereof—that calls into question all of that which is representative of tradition. Indeed, Rimanelli tells us in this same text that he was once "in another country . . . sick with language and style" (p. 29), and his only way out of the "inherited malaise" (p. 29) of tradition, or the hegemony of the canon was to write a novel that is free of tradition, therefore without a narrative, and lacking any sense of logical plot or story line. Rimanelli's For-a-word is, to be sure, a for[e]word to the reader in order to help him/her through, among other things, the "golden charades and lampoons" that constitute his fictive prose piece, Benedetta in Guysterland.[10]

Rimanelli's second microtext, herein labeled above as the novel, "Benedetta in Guysterland," is the long fictive narrative that constitutes the major part of the book. As in the For-a-word, here too the narrating voice is in the first person singular. But here it is not just a fictive voice that constitutes the difference between this and the previous text's narrator; here, we encounter a female narrator who tells her own story.[11] And what a story it is! Or, better, what [kind of?] story is it?

Benedetta's story is not an easy one to recount or, for that matter, to follow and understand.[12] Born Clarence Ashfield, she gets her name Benedetta from the mobsters she meets once she enters the underworld. They meet her as Benie, a nickname bestowed upon her by mob lawyer Willie "Holiday Inn" Sinclair, from the Italian adverb *bene*. However, they believe the nickname is a shortened form of Benedetta, whence she gets her name, thus becoming the blessed among "guysters," Rimanelli's idiosyncratic sign for *gangster*. Leaving her home town of New Wye, in Nabokov County, in Appalachia, U.S.A., Benedetta becomes intricately involved in the underworld of organized crime, falling in love with and, eventually, yearning for the exiled Joe Adonis, Santo "Zip the Thunder" Tristano's nemesis. Through a series of episodes, events, and adventures (some more realistic, others more fantastical), Benedetta does not actually tell her story as we might expect from traditional first-person narrative; rather, in her dialogue with her beloved exiled mobster, Joe Adonis, Benedetta's story unfolds.

The novel begins in the present, so it seems, with Benedetta, in the first person, directly addressing Joe Adonis: "I love you, Joe Adonis" (p. 33). But we soon find out that she is not actually *talking* to him; instead, she is *writing* to him, as we find out in Chapter Two: "I am now pounding on the typewriter" (p. 40). Benedetta's letter writing is an obvious act of any author's, and indeed of Rimanelli's, self-reflexivity. But it is not just Benedetta's act of writing that reflects Rimanelli's writing; it is also how and what she writes that reflect the Rimanelli we encountered in the For-a-word. There we saw Rimanelli's desire for experimentation, his wish to write a novel free of tradition, without a narrative, lacking any sense of logical plot or story-line. Benedetta, in her letters to Joe Adonis, reflects similar hermeneutico-semiotic actions and creative desires in the first two chapters. In Chapter One we see that she misses "sharing nonsenses" (p. 34) with Joe Adonis. In Chapter Two, where we find out that she is actually writing to Joe, Rimanelli's "free collector" status is mirrored in Benedetta's description of her own writing:

> These thoughts live in my mind as they appear on the paper, muddled and, as I know only too well, unorganized. I feel that if I organize them, they will seem like an essay to me and I would not be writing for myself if I spent time arranging ideas into neat little compartments. Do you understand me, Joe? While I am writing, I am far away; and when I come back, I have already left. I am now pounding on the typewriter, talking to myself and at the same time listening to Zip and the band downstairs . . . (p. 40)

*Muddled* and *unorganized,* the adjectives that describe Benedetta's thoughts, figure as logical metaphors for that which does not adhere to tradition, since tradition is, as implied immediately above, organized and essayistic, in the form of ideas and emotions arranged "into neat little compartments" according to, we might add, neat little rules. Binary oppositions of this sort, the sensical versus the nonsensical and the organized versus the unorganized, constantly reappear in Benedetta's story both on a formalistic and a contextual level. More significantly, the three central texts—For-a-word, Benedetta in Guysterland, and Post-word—rely on a strong dose of irony, be it directed inward, in self-parody as writer, thinker, Italian American, or outward, in parody of cultural phenomena such as the mafia, sexual liberation, and both popular and high cultures of various societies and countries of the western world.[13] All of this distinguishes Rimanelli as a synthetic writer, in this case having opted for parody and irony, as opposed to the militancy of the comparative writer or the sensorial experientiality of the expressive writer.

"Benedetta in Guysterland" also has a certain frame to it. The story opens with Benedetta in an unidentified place, upstairs (we really do not know where, but we may assume it is *La Gaia Scienza, Scienza,*[14] or the "Club" as it is called, where the Band plays), listening to Zip and the other members of the band playing downstairs. After a few chapters that serve to introduce us to Benedetta and offer some other basic information about what and whom we will eventually encounter, we begin to follow Benedetta through her many adventures, some phantasmagorical and therefore puzzling to the reader, with the many

guysters from New York and New Jersey, the latter being the more desired of the two places. At the end of her story, she finds herself in a similar physical situation. She returns to the "joint" (p. 200), as she refers to
it, and is upstairs, as in the beginning of the novel, in earshot of music
coming from somewhere downstairs, where "the Fish was singing
on his banjo something like an invitation to freedom and discovery"
(p. 202).

Another frame marker at the beginning of Benedetta's story is the
newspaper article about Joe Adonis's exile to Italy. Brought up to her
with a note attached, the article tells of Joe Adonis's exile: who he is,
where he is, and when he was exiled back to Italy. In mirrorlike fashion,
the same situation of with a second newspaper article occurs at the end
of Benedetta's story. There, too, she is brought an article accompanied
by a note that speaks this time of Joe Adonis's death. Regardless of differences in the content of the articles, the similarities, I suggest, are too
blatant to ignore. In Chapter Two, in fact, we read: "They send me a
newspaper, upstairs. With the note: 'Is this one your lover?' " (p. 38).
Likewise, in Chapter Twenty-eight, we read: "Once again, they send me
a newspaper, upstairs. With the note: *Well, isn't this one your lover?*"
(pp. 200–201; emphasis textual). The appearance of this second article at
the end of Benedetta's story is intriguing indeed. What adds to any
reader's interest are the similarities of how the article arrives to
Benedetta, where she is, and the fact that the topic of both articles is Joe
Adonis, the first announcing his exile and the second announcing his
death. But there are two other intriguing aspects of these frame markers that stand out. First, the albeit brief introduction of the second article mirrors, with slight changes, the first incident of almost two hundred
pages earlier. Second, the slight changes that take place seem merely to
signal a reoccurrence: "Once again . . ." and *"Well, isn't . . . "* But more
than signaling a mere reoccurrence, the second article's appearance,
along with its similarities to the first, actually raises a few other questions for the reader: Where is she now? Has she returned to the same
place? Or is she, or has she remained, in the very same place where we
met her at the beginning of her story?[15]

In Rimanelli's third microtext, the Post-word, we have another
first-person narration. Just as the narrator changed from the construct
*Author* of the For-a-word, seemingly external to the novel, to Benedetta
of Benedetta in Guysterland, the main protagonist of the novel, we witness a change from Benedetta to a narrating *I* who seems to be initially
part of Benedetta's story, a sort of protagonist *post-quem*. However, after
reading the first four pages, we realize that this narrating *I* is not really

part of Benedetta's fictive world; rather, it figures as the construct *Author* we had already met in the For-a-word.

As should be apparent from what has been stated thus far, the question of signs and sign-functions is constantly problematized beginning with the For-a-word. As we begin reading the Post-word, questions of signification and the semiotic act of interpretation rise again to the surface. The very opening of the Post-word ("Was it good zook? Boy, was I turned on! Is this the truth? Boy, I don't know" [p. 205].) brings to the fore a number of issues. First, we are confronted with the problems of signification and interpretation. The initial interrogative poses such issues by the introduction of the unfamiliar and unexpected verbal sign *zook,* which nevertheless resembles very much a well-known and expected verbal sign, *book,* since the reader has just finished that which one readily considers a book. That *zook* be a mere substitution for *book* in Rimanelli's idiosyncratic yet serious word-game world is not easily acceptable. Indeed, the requisite indefinite article *a* is missing, for which one is forced to read *zook,* I would suggest, as something other than *book* whatever that may be. It is, in fact, this something other that the reader must (re)construct.[16] Such (re)construction calls into question, among other things, the stability of both cognitive and semantic value, or truth, as posed by the second question: "Is this the truth? Boy, I don't know."

Truth, to be sure, is not the stable, objective, accurate, factual, and, last but not least, monolithic notion it is generally considered to be when we find it, or so we believe, in Rimanelli's "liquid" world of *Bendetta in Guysterland.* Everything, especially within the general realm of signification, depends on one's semiotic interaction with the subject matter at hand. In fact, in continuing our metaphorical reading of Benedetta, this becomes quite clear in the second paragraph of the "Post-word":

> She [Benedetta] was a *Beautiful* Person, an *enigmatic* femme fatale. No man who was seeking to know how the wind blows could afford to ignore Benedetta, the *intellectual's pinup.* And she was good at *manipulating* the very rich and the very famous. She was a *mirror* that gave a man back the *image of himself* he wanted to see. (p. 205; emphasis added)

Since there are two sides to a text—first the author's rendition, which we consider the work of art, and second the reader's rendition, which s/he draws from the work of art—Benedetta as text may be viewed from these two different angles in the above-cited passage. As author's rendition, we find a "beautiful" text that should hold the reader's attention; indeed, Rimanelli's Benedetta does hold the reader's atten-

attention; indeed, Rimanelli's Benedetta does hold the reader's attention. Yet, we also see that Benedetta is not an easy text to decipher; it is an "enigmatic" text, perhaps because it is so chock full of the author's cultural inheritance that in his "manipulating" it so, a reader would need a certain cultural background to understand more fully the textual references. After all, as text, Benedetta is the "intellectual's pinup."

As the reader's rendition, on the other hand, we see that Benedetta as text is a "mirror." But we see that it is not a mirror of what one sees; such a statement would imply an objective valence of signification, which, on the contrary, is constantly and consistently undermined throughtout the three texts. Instead, Benedetta as text is what one "want[s] to see"; her existence, so to speak, who/what she is, depends on the reader's hermeneutico-semiotic makeup which, in itself, is an integral part of the creation of any text. As Italo Calvino, Rimanelli's conational and coeval, stated years ago in his essay, "Cybernetics and Ghosts,"[17] "the decisive moment of literary life [is] that of reading (p. 15)," by which "literature will continue to be a 'place' of privilege within the human consciousness, a way of exercising the potentialities within the system of signs belonging to all societies at all times. The work will continue to be born, to be judged, to be distorted or constantly renewed on contact with the eye of the reader" (p. 16). The author, therefore, no longer holds a privileged position for Calvino, since "literature is a combinatorial game that pursues the possibilities implicit in its own material" (p. 22).[18] That is, "writing," for Calvino, "is purely and simply a process of combination among given elements" (p. 17), while reading, or better, "the spirit in which one reads is decisive: it is up to the reader to see to it that literature exerts its critical force, and this can occur independently of the author's intentions" (p. 26).[19]

There is one more aspect of the third text that stands out. We saw earlier a certain framing structure in Benedetta in Guysterland articulated by the two articles dedicated, respectively, to Adonis's exile and death. In a significant and analogous manner, we now find a second framing structure that this time has its origin not at the beginning of the third text, but at the very beginning of the first text, the For-a-word. As in the internal frame of Benedetta in Guysterland where we found a reappearance of an article, here we find a reappearance of a billboard; and there is a second set of similarities too blatant to ignore. The For-a-word opens in the following manner:

Just after finishing this, I went out in the open and read, on a billboard: *As dada rock gets worse, outdoor micro-boppers get better.* True, but I don't understand. Probably because I never belonged to a Band. . . . (p. 27; emphasis textual)

The Post-word, conversely, closes in the following manner:

. . . I went out in the open and read, on a billboard: *As traffic gets worse, advertising gets better.* True. So, I thought, allow the poet to strive to be modest in his lines. And I walked away.

Let's hope there's no monsoon Thursday. (p. 209–10; emphasis textual)

One notices, first of all, a change in the narrating I's thought process: he (Rimanelli, the Author) is now able to comprehend the billboard, notwithstanding a different message, a change due perhaps to a growth (greater abundance of information) in the narrating I's intertextual reservoir. After all, the narrating I, in each particular situation, is a reader. The second significant aspect to this ending is the reference to "the poet." In a blatantly self-reflexive way that curiously echoes Palazzeschi, Rimanelli exhorts his readers to allow the poet to do as s/he pleases, with the hope, metaphorically speaking, that no negative criticism rain down on him/her.[20]

I opened my discussion of Rimanelli's *Benedetta in Guysterland. A Liquid Novel* with an allusion to the table of contents and the question of textual boundaries. Having examined the book's three microtexts, I would contend that there exists a certain textual layering that clearly involves all three texts and as a result influences the reading process. Indeed, the interrelation of writer and reader and *their* respective, *concretized* texts problematize the layering of texts and the subsequent complexities vis-à-vis textual interpretation. Namely, at the end of the Post-word, as readers of *Guysterland* we ultimately witness a return to, and therefore a connection with, the For-a-word. All three texts are interrelated, as the one provides information for a more complete understanding of the other(s), especially, I would add, a greater decodification of Benedetta in Guysterland. As a result we may now answer the earlier implied question as to where the textual boundaries (ext)end. In light of what we saw above, I would suggest that the layering of texts includes the three microtexts examined above, and the *novel*, which I had initially considered to be Benedetta in Guysterland, should now be extended to include all three of Rimanelli's microtexts. Our new novel's graph should read as follows, clearly indicating the different textual layers of the overall text, or, in continuing to adopt Corti's nomenclature, the macrotext:

| *Benedetta in Guysterland. A Liquid Novel* | | macrotext |
|---|---|---|
| For-a-word | 27 | microtext 1 |
| Benedetta in Guysterland | 31 | microtext 2 |
| Post-word | 205 | microtext 3 |

In closing my discussion of *Benedetta in Guysterland. A Liquid Novel*, I would remind the reader of one of Rimanelli's autobiographical references:

At one time in my life, as a *master-builder-producer* in another country I was sick with language and style. My body was covered with sentences, words, newspaper print. Then I took a shower. The tattoo's still showing, because I was not at all convinced that one can free himself at once of the inherited malaise. (p. 29; emphasis added)

We already discussed the last sentence of this passage, "the inherited malaise," as a metaphor for the Author's disenchantment with tradition and his desire to free himself of it. What is significant here is his self-description as "master-builder-producer."[21] Such a label immediately recalls Lyotard's previously seen notion of "incredulity toward meta-narratives" (p. xiv), the late twentieth century's increasing suspicion of the notion of master narratives, narrative's universal validity, for which literature, as was stated in Chapter One, is no longer considered merely a depiction of life. Instead, it is a depiction of life as it is represented by ideology, which ideology presents as *inherent* in what is represented, that which in reality is *constructed* meaning.

Ultimately, the act of semiosis involved in Rimanelli's *Benedetta in Guysterland* is a restructured and redefined act of sign interpretation dependent on a sign repertoire no longer consonant with that of the literary canon, that is, the dominant culture. What occurs concomitantly is Bakhtin's previously noted concept of the decentralization of the "verbal-ideological world." More specifically, along the lines of sign-functions, one sees that the two functives of expression and content are no longer in mutual correlation. At this point in time with regard to a noncanonical literature, the content is different from that of the canon. The sign-function realized in this new process of semiosis is now in discord with the dominant culture's expectation of the coding correlation.[22] Another important consideration here is the interpreter's fore-understanding "drawn from [his/her] own anterior relation to the subject" (Gadamer p. 262). This notion of fore-understanding is surely a basis for both the sender's and the addressee's use and interpretation of signs. That is to say, the sign (or sign-function) is not ideologically neutral. Rather, its use and interpretation are dependent on *both* the sender's and the addressee's prejudgments.[23] In a general sense, language, that is, sign systems, cannot but be ideologically invested. As an ideological medium, language can become restrictive and oppressive when its sign system is arbitrarily invested with meanings by those who are empowered to do so, that is, the dominant culture; so can it become empowering for the purpose of privileging one coding correlation over another, by rejecting the canonical sign system and ultimately denying validity to this sign system vis-à-vis the interpretive act of a noncanonical text.[24] Then certain ideological constructs are deprivileged and subsequently awarded an unfixed status; they no longer take on a patina of *natural facts.* Rather, they figure as the *arbitrary categories* they truly are. All this results in a pluralistic notion of literary invention and interpretation which, by its very nature, cannot exclude the individual—author and reader—who has (re)created and developed a different repertoire of signs.

The resultant noncanonical text that arises from such an unorthodox creative act as Rimanelli's may initially problematize and frustrate a reader's interpretive act. But more than an attempt to frustrate or block his reader's semiotic *iter,* I would contend that such problematics in textual boundaries and framing constitute Rimanelli's desire to involve his reader intimately in the coproduction of textual signification. The purpose of Rimanelli's sign system is not to elicit, simply, pleasant or unpleasant memories and imagery in his reader's mind. Rather, he attempts to render his reader complicit in an emotional and sensorial state as expressed through his prose. Indeed, it is both expression and description, infused with a good dose of irony and parody, that define Rimanelli's prose, and his reader, in his/her complicity in this polysensorial state, becomes a coparticipant in Rimanelli's sign production and signification. Hence, his *liquid* novel, precisely because it acquires its signifying shape from, metaphorically speaking, the form of its reader's hands, is like any liquid that takes the shape of the container in which it is situated.[25]

The emergence and subsequent acceptance of this and other valid acts of semiosis, due in great part to the postmodern tendency toward the breakdown of boundaries and the mistrust of absolutes, has contributed and can continue to contribute to the construction of a more recent heteroglossic reading (and creative) culture in which the "correct language" (Bakhtin p. 270), and therefore *correct process of interpretation,* is disunified and decentralized. In this instance, if all "languages" are "masks [and no language can] claim to be an authentic and incontestable face," so no one reading process is "incontestable," and many can be considered valid. The result is a "heteroglossia consciously opposed to [the dominant] literary language" (p. 273), for which marginalization and subsequent invalidation of other *readers* become more difficult to impose and thus less likely to occur.[26]

An appropriate way to close would be to borrow again from Lyotard, for if the text a writer creates and the work s/he "produces are not in principle governed by preestablished rules [of canon formation], and they cannot be judged according to a determining judgement, by applying familiar categories to the text or to the work," as does Rimanelli in *Benedetta in Guysterland,* then, one must look elsewhere for interpretive strategies, precisely because, as Lyotard continues, "[t]hose rules and categories are what the work of art is looking for. The artist and the writer, then, are working without rules in order to formulate the rules for what *will have been done"* (p. 81: emphasis textual). In an analogous manner, so does the reader of these same texts work without rules, establishing as s/he proceeds similar interpretive rules of what *will have been read.*

Moving now from the particular (the reader of Rimanelli's *Benedetta in Guysterland*) to the universal (any reader of any text), such an act—or any act—of semiosis relies on the individual's time and place and is therefore always new and different with respect to its own historical specificities vis-à-vis the dominant culture, that is, the canon. In final analysis it is a dynamics of the conglomeration and agglutination of different voices and reading strategies which, contrary to the hegemony of the dominant culture, cannot be fully integrated into any strict semblance of a monocultural process. The utterance, therefore, will always be polyvalent, its combination will always be rooted in heteroglossia and dialogism, and the interpretive strategies for decoding it will always depend on the specificities of the reader's intertextual reservoir.[27]

# Part III
## Further Readings

# 5

# Looking Back: The Image of Italy in Umbertina

And I used to wonder about Puritan John Milton being the guest of a car-
dinal in Rome, she [Marguerite] thought. In this land where everything
is accomodated. Where nothing is resolved because it's all an unfolding
spiral.

—Helen Barolini, *Umbertina*

Representation of that which is Italian in Italian/American culture
seems, at times, to be contradictory within the artistic world of Italian
America. Today, Italian Americans can easily boast of the glories of
Rome and be proud of the grand philosophical, literary, and artistic her-
itages of other cities, such as Naples, Florence, Turin, Milan, and Venice,
to name a few of the famous intellectual centers of Italy throughout the
centuries. However, a large number of their ancestors came to the
United States as an escape from insufferable poverty and socio-political
oppression in Italy, especially in Southern Italy. In this respect, then,
Southern Italy and the Italian/American sense of Italianness may bring
to the fore contrasting sentiments of pride and shame, attraction and repulsion, and love and resentment. These emotions often surface, at different times and with different levels of intensity, in the blatantly ethnic
literature and films of Italian/American artists.[1]

In *Umbertina*, Barolini presents Italy to the reader in both direct
and indirect ways. The direct way, of course, constitutes the descriptions appearing throughout the novel of the various places in which the
earlier characters lived and later described themselves, or those places
the later characters visited either short-term or long-term. The indirect
presentation of Italy is found in the conversations about Italy, usually
by Italian Americans—self-assuring descriptions of a country they may
not even know first-hand, but only heard discussed by their parents or
grand-parents who had emigrated to the United States.

Equally important to remember is that not a single Italy is represented, but, in fact, two Italies, North and South.[2] The representation of these two geographical Italies eventually brings to the fore a number of issues. First, there is the dichotomy between the urban center and country village, the latter locale being the place from which many turn-of-the-century immigrants originated. Second, there is the issue of the ever-present question of the *Mezzogiorno*[3] and all that it entails, including the century-long antagonism between Northern and Southern Italy.[4] Third, there is the issue of class, which figures locally as equally disruptive as any outside force could have been. Finally, in conjunction with the issue of class is that of the Church as a *man*made institution that functions *sui generis* according to exigencies similar to class issues. These issues separately and together constitute to varying degrees those reasons for which certain conditions existed in Italy that eventually forced many to leave their home towns in search of an economically better life. Indeed, as was evident with the majority of the first waves of immigration, economic amelioration was the primary reason for uprooting oneself.

Through the novel's three-part structure, each part recounting the story of a specific woman of a specific generation, Barolini represents Italy at its different stages of the first eighty years of the twentieth century, as well as according to three different perspectives, due to each woman's historical situation (her specific generation) and individual ideology, namely, through Umbertina, Marguerite, and Tina, as we saw in Chapter Three.

Of the dichotomous groups presented by Barolini in *Umbertina*, those of North/South, City/Country and Gentry/Peasants are of primary interest throughout the first large section of the novel, *Part One: Umbertina 1860–1940*. What is intriguing in Barolini's treatment of these dichotomies is that the integrity of the first half of the couplets—North, City, Gentry—is put into question.[5] A young southern woman, Umbertina represents the voice of the southern Italian who feels trapped in an economic situation that offers no solution. Everything seems to be working against her: the political power is in Rome; the overall socio-economic hopes lie in the north; and the local power brokers such as the landowners, mayors, and priests use the peasants for their own survival and socio-economic amelioration.

The North/South question is represented in two ways in this part of the novel. First, as witness to Umbertina's early life in the Calabrian (that is, Southern) village of Castagna, we come to understand the trials and tribulations of leading an existence of poverty without resolution. We also come to understand the reasons why many of these people felt compelled to leave their homeland. The North/South question, however, continues to surface even after Umbertina's emigration to the United States. The social worker Anna Giordani, whose family of "northern Italians . . . were educated and had some money" (p. 66), came to the United States with the 1848 "political immigration" (p. 66). Her presence, as well as the brief appearance of other characters such as Sister Carmela, whom we shall soon meet, continues to remind Umbertina, and Barolini's reader, of the antagonistic relationship between Northern and Southern Italy.

The antagonisms between Rome and the country and between gentry and peasants stand out more conspicuously in this part. Rome is the "*ladro governo* that took bread from the mouths of the poor instead of giving out the lands Garibaldi promised when he told the peasants their day had finally come" (p. 29). The government became the source of their misfortunes just as they suffered from "nature's heavy hand" (p. 29). Rome, the seat of the government, was also where the "land baron, the pope, and now a king lived, all equally indifferent to the fact of [their] existence" (p. 28).[6] Such indifference was also present on the local level with the land barons and priests on the one side and the peasants on the other. A poor man whose home was a "stone hovel" (p. 24), Carlo Nenci, Umbertina's father, worked Baron Mancuso di Valerba's land, a baron who knew absolutely nothing about farming and therefore put his land in the hands of a *fattore*.[7] In return, Nenci and his colaborers, as they thought with bitter humor, "were fortunate because they ate little and so stayed lean and hard" (p. 25). In a similar vein, the village priest Don Antonio wielded his power as a "learned" man over the "ignorant" peasants. In one of his sermons, for instance, he quotes Dante's famous Ulysses episode, "*Fatti non foste a viver come bruti/ma per seguir virtute e conoscenza*" (pp. 23–24), and continues in the following manner:

"These are the words of the great poet, Dante Alighieri, and they mean you were created by God not to live like brutes, like dumb animals, but to attain virtue. You people of the Sila are descendants of the tribe known anciently as the Bruttii. But I tell you, you are no longer Bruttii but Christians," he thundered at them. "No longer heathens beyond God's words, but meant, in the words of the immortal Dante, to hear it and follow it. This is God's intention: that you not live as brutish animals deprived of His word, but come to His Church and follow the Church's holy prescripts for you." (p. 24)

The peasants respond negatively to Don Antonio's sermon.[8] He is "too fine for [them]" just as his "fine words," according to Umbertina's father, should be aimed at "impress[ing] the women," since idle chatter, according to their way of thinking, 1) would not resolve their problems ("It's true we're brutish—his words won't change that"); and 2) was something, we may readily assume, southern Italian men considered more of a female activity.

Yet, while the peasants are not "learned," they are not necessarily "ignorant" of their precarious situation, which they seem to understand all too well. Their anger expresses their frustration not so much with Don Antonio's words but with the actual power structure that forces them to live like the very "dumb animals" Don Antonio condemns. "We're meant to be dumb animals" [they bitterly exclaim]. "Why else would we follow the Church that tells us to feed our fat Don Antonio? But even as animals we're of less value than Don Antonio's chickens or the baron's hunting dogs" (p. 24). Indeed, the difference in quality of life of the two conflicting groups of gentry (Baron Mancuso, Don Antonio) and the peasants (Carlo Nenci) is underscored, here specifically, by Barolini's not too subtle juxtaposition of adjectives in "fat Don Antonio," the "gout[ridden] baron and his "obese" wife, and the "lean and hard" peasants.

More intriguing, however, is Barolini's use of the Ulysses quote. Don Antonio's citation of Dante's Ulysses in order to exhort his flock tells us that Don Antonio "should have stayed in the seminary," as Umbertina's father inveighed; but not in order to stay among the educated, rather to better educate himself. We should remember that Ulysses's words contributed to his own condemnation in the Eighth Circle of Hell. It was with these words that Ulysses defrauded his sailors so that they would follow him into uncharted waters and subsequently to their death.[9] They were asked, in a sense, to do something beyond their control. In a strangely perverted manner, Don Antonio uses Ulysses' words in an analogously fraudulent manner. He also asks his church-goers to do more than they could, showing himself to be totally insensitive to their daily plight of survival, as they "plant wheat . . . , but never eat white bread; cultivate vines, but rarely drink wine; and raise animals, but eat no meat except the tainted flesh of those that die from sickness" (p. 25).

Umbertina, we learn once she emigrated, did not leave this Italy behind her, at least not the Italy of the North/South and Church/peasant dichotomies. Whereas Anna Giordani incarnates the North/South question along with the Church/peasant dichotomy, Sister Carmela represents an amalgamation of these two issues. In explaining her name, Sister Carmela tells Umbertina that Carmela is her religious name because her parents, being from Milan, would not have given her "the name of girls from *bassa Italia*" (p. 92; emphasis textual). Thus, we see that even in the United States, Umbertina must continue to confront the biases of the North, as was already evident with Anna Giordani, and here it is coupled with the presumption of the Church. The difference between how Sister Carmela and Umbertina think is embedded in Barolini's narrative. While Umbertina saw Sister Carmela "teaching the children of the poor" (p. 92), Sister Carmela saw herself "educating the children of the South" (p. 93), so that the specifics of instruction ("teaching") become Carmela's more general cultural enlightenment ("education") and the all-encompassing "children of the poor" become Carmela's more specified "children of the South."

In the second section of *Umbertina, Part Two: Marguerite, 1927–1973*, Italy is presented from two different perspectives, both of which deviate in their own way from how Italy was presented through Umbertina's experiences. It is in this section that the various opposing sentiments in the oxymoronic couplets of pride and shame, attraction and repulsion, and love and resentment are more strongly articulated. While Marguerite, Umbertina's granddaughter, belongs to the third-generation, her parents as second-generation Italian Americans represent characteristics more consonant with the second term of the above-mentioned couplets.[10] We find Marguerite's parents to be in total conflict with all that is Italian and Italian/American. In fact, as we saw earlier, Marguerite learned early on from her parents how un-American it was to be Italian in the United States. We also saw earlier how the sentiments of shame and repulsion toward Italy are perhaps best articulated in Marguerite's father's conversation with his granddaughter, Tina, when they discuss her future as a scholar of Italian culture. Thus, in a manner similar to his in-laws and parents, Sam, familiar only with the Italy of Umbertina's migratory generation, does not see any purpose in dealing with Italy or anything Italian. Italy represented, for him, the Old World from which his parents and their co-immigrants escaped intolerable poverty and political oppression. It remains for his generation, therefore, a place from which to escape both literally and aesthetically, since they knew only 1) the Italy of the barren land South that caused great hardship in their parents' daily life, and 2) the United States' version of Italy as the stereotype perpetuated then and to some extent today,[11] a country of buffoons, gangsters, and womanizers.

Barolini's image of Italy nevertheless changes in this part of the novel. It is primarily through Marguerite's eyes that we see Italy, and, we should add, it is a more recent Italy. No longer the Italy of Carlo Levi's *Cristo si è fermato a Eboli,* here, we find a postwar Italy that has already profited from the economic boom of the 1950s and early 1960s. In addition, Marguerite is married to a Veneto and lives in Rome. And so, along with the issues of the North/South question and class distinction, a third issue raised with Umbertina is here intensified (the woman's dilemma), and a fourth issue is introduced (the Italian temperament).

Class distinction and the North/South question are built into Marguerite's marriage to Alberto, a middle-aged Italian poet who soon becomes well placed in the Italian literary world of publishing and awards. In accusing her of becoming "one of those American Express ladies" (p. 177) early on in their relationship because she was reading Pulci, Ficino, and Poliziano, both issues surface:

> "But Alberto," she protested . . . "it's different for you. These things were part of your background from always. But just think of what my background was—nothing! We don't even know who we are any further than my grandparents, and you've got family trees right back to the thirteenth century. It's only with my parents that reading and writing and speaking correctly began for us. That's the difference between us!"
>
> He understood her resentment because he was a compassionate man, even when he told her in jest, "That's a big difference. It's a good thing your Calabrian grandparents emigrated to America and made it possible for a northern Italian like me to marry you. Not many northerners would let themselves in for marriage with a *terrone.*"
>
> "*Tant pis* for them—you northern intellectuals could use new blood and brains. My grandmother, for one, had native intelligence."
>
> "Then we are a good combination for our children: my beauty and your native Calabrian intelligence. And once we do have children all this cultural mania of yours will evaporate." (p. 178)

To be sure, literacy marks the distinction in class in their conversation. To be able to read and write means to have access to knowledge. To have access to knowledge constitutes a tool for social mobility and the possibility of bettering one's lot. This is precisely what occurred with the offspring of illiterate European immigrants. What then makes this conversation more curious is Alberto's response, in spite of that fact that it is "in jest."[12] For Marguerite, the difference was a question of education: reading and writing. For Alberto, instead, the difference is layered not only by literacy and the lack thereof, but also by regional origin, so that the one, lack of education, is dependent on the other, regional origin.

In one sense, this section may seem to express a love/hate relationship with Italy. Early on, for instance, we find Marguerite seemingly enthralled by how "brilliant [Italians were, as they] darted effortlessly from subject to subject like gorgeous butterflies glittering with wit and daring paradox, never staying long enough to be challenged" (p. 175). Later on, however, through the tirades of some of Alberto's snobbish friends of his literary-cultural circle (Leone Eccli, Clotilde, and Cesare Servi) against literary prizes, we may come to understand Barolini's notion of their brilliance as something else:

> "We didn't invent the literary prize, you know," said Leone. . . . "The French had them first, and even the English and the Americans preceded us. But like everything else we do, *we had to make it more splendid.* Now we have more than three hundred prizes, and they've taken the place of the courts in the duchies and the city-states. . . . [J]urors are like the nobility, and the writers take the place of courtiers vying for patronage. Instead of marriages of alliance and consolidation, there are love affairs according to which husband is on which jury and which wife has to be seduced. *A very Italian phenomenon. . . .* "

> "You can't compare Italian prizes to American ones," said Clotilde, . . . having used Servi and others to pick up a dozen or so prizes for herself. "American writers can live from their work, they don't need prizes, because there they publish a book in editions of ten or fifteen thousand copies. Then there is television, the movies, paperbacks. As with everything else, *it's organized over there. . . .* "

> "You Americans!" said Cesare directing himself toward Marguerite. "Always so practical. Who in Italy would give up *the excitement and pleasure of intriguing and scheming and slandering* to get a million lire in a prize just to earn it honestly? . . . Prizefighting is a way of life in Italy—thrilling, passionate, corrupt, malicious, *a testing of one's cleverness. . . .* What's important is not the book but all the background skill of arranging one's votes, getting to the voters, making important contacts, deploying oneself at the right

receptions and cocktail parties. *Italians have always esteemed cleverness in itself no matter toward what end it's used."* (p. 267–68; emphasis added)

To be sure, one recalls Luigi Barzini's controversial *The Italians*,[13] in
which he discusses two major characteristics of the Italian temperament: the importance of spectacle (= "fare bella figura") and "non farsi
far fesso" (= not having someone make a fool of you), two notions
readily echoed in the words of Leone, Clotilde, and Cesare as we are
told it is not so much the prize as it is the test of one's "cleverness"
through the "excitement and pleasure of intriguing and scheming and
slandering" for a prize the Italians did not invent but made ever "more
splendid"—a veritable "fashion show" (p. 281), as Leone later describes
the Strega Award ceremony.[14]

Through the many people Marguerite meets, the Italian temperament and the woman's dilemma become more prominent themes in this
section. In fact, both themes overlap to the extent that the one seems often to generate the other. What is curious here is that, except for Alberto,
whose seemingly questionable behavior is always explained in differ-
entiating terms of age and culture, the majority of the men Marguerite
meets are quite self-absorbed and gender insensitive. Gillo Gatti, for instance, Marguerite's first Italian lover (married unbeknownst to her),
knew precisely what he wanted. He knew, for instance, which courses
would get him the fellowship that would eventually get him the chair
of English at an Italian university. Moreover, he knew who the special-
ists were in his field and who would help him. Massimo, Marguerite's
later Italian lover, is equally self-absorbed, as winning the literary prize
and getting known abroad as a writer are his main priorities. The roles
of other women Marguerite meets are also subordinate to their men.
Take, for instance, Lalla Fonti, the young wife to the writer, the "Great
Man" Arnaldo, who herself was a writer "perhaps even more so than
the Great Man himself" (p. 187). But it was he, the Great Man, as also
Alberto, and not Lalla or Marguerite, who enjoyed success in both life
and art.

Women in Marguerite's Italy simply did not fare well. Indeed, as
we already saw in the first part of this chapter, notwithstanding Marguerite's vague and undefined goals, Barolini demonstrates how even
Alberto contributed to her gender dilemma. Again, his initial promise,
"I'll make a real human being out of you" (p. 177), is indicative of an
Italian masculine presumption that a woman needs a man for her personal development. Or, when she was truly depressed, he would address her as his "*bambina mia*" telling her that she did love him and was

happy, but only resisted seeing it. Finally, when she asked for divorce, he responded that *she* was tired and that *she*, still upset over the death of their son, should see a psychiatrist once they return to Rome. Marguerite, as stated earlier, was clearly relegated to the "homemaker role," and unhappily so.[15]

Trapped in the traditional female role and thus subordinate to her husband (and lovers), Marguerite was thereby unable to realize any of her desired goals. Indeed, the traditional role sometimes acts, as Gans reminds us, as a "brake on [the female's] aspirations and [more specifically in Marguerite's case] as an accelerator on her frustrations" (p. 216).[16] It is also important to remember that Marguerite's gender dilemma was complicated by the fact that she married an older, conservative Italian who was a defender of the traditional female role and, consequently, of a male-oriented social structure.[17] Thus, these two seemingly distinct issues of the Italian temperament—in this case the male—and gender actually prove to be separate parts of a whole: namely, the female dilemma in Italy.

Marguerite never resolves her gender conflict. Though she remained with Alberto, her affair with Massimo was to be her "bridge to a new reality." Instead, it was *she* who became *his* bridge to a possible literary award; she was his contact to Alberto, then editor of a literary review. She could also spread his fame by translating his prose, and she filled the sexual and emotional void between Massimo and his wife, who had, with the years, become his "domestic," serving and seconding him in everything. Thus, once again Marguerite had become a man's woman, and when Massimo lost the Strega award, Marguerite lost Massimo and, ultimately, her own life, as she chose suicide as a solution to her dilemma.[18]

While for Marguerite, or so she had hoped, Italy was a place where she could define herself, for Tina, Italy—Rome, to be more precise—is much more of an exotic place where she could escape the realities of New York; it is a place where she can "go to the bar for a *cappuccino* [and] read *Gente* or watch the people go by" (p. 300). But Tina also knows she cannot live long-term in Rome, where, as she says, "everything had already been thought of and done," and that New York, instead, was the place of "illimited possibilities" for her (p. 300).

Moreover, for Tina, a member of the fourth generation, Italy is yet again transformed. Because of her desire to (re)discover her roots by making a trip to Umbertina's home town of Castagna, in Calabria, the image of Italy changes once more. While in Marguerite's section of the novel, the South for all practical purposes disappeared from the reader's view—present only as a point of comparison—in *Part Three: Tina, 1950–*, it reappears.

But first, like her mother, she too must deal with the gender issue, as she steals away with the Italian professor, Ferruccio Simongini: 1) believing he truly wants to accompany her to Castagna, when, instead, he was already planning to go south, and 2) dealing with his chauvinist ways, as is evident in the following conversation:

> "It's rather a good thing I have you with me. The women of the southern coasts are not known for their looks, and you, at least, are passable."
>
> She gave him a quizzical look in reply—curious, because of the literal streak in her, about his statements. "Why is that? What's wrong with southern women?"
>
> "The best types are in the mountains. The coastal people have been too mixed and hybridized over the ages by the sea marauders—Turks and Saracens—who invaded these coasts and impregnated the women. About the only thing these women have are large, dark cow-eyes. But that's not for me. I prefer squinty light-green eyes like yours." (p. 376)

Despicable as Ferruccio's ideas are from the viewpoint of gender, they are equally disturbing with regard to the North/South question. Whereas before the problem of the South was presented primarily as a socio-economic question, here it is problematized by the notion of race. As a non-Southerner, Ferruccio reveals himself as, to put it nicely, a racial purist. We see that his racism is aimed at the southern coastal women who, "*mixed and hybridized . . .* by the sea marauders—*Turks and Saracens,*" are no longer, for him, pure Italians. We also see his racism toward southern Italians underscored in his comments about the small resort, "Bagamoyo, which was clean, he said, and well organized because it was run by a German who had stayed behind during the last war" (p. 377).

Barolini directly confronts the issue of the South once Tina and Ferruccio arrive in Castagna.[19] What they find, as Ferruccio anticipates when he tells Tina that "Everything's too late down here; . . . the twentieth century is too late" (p. 377), is a Castagna not too different from the one Umbertina had left behind almost one hundred years earlier:

> *Brullo* was the word for Calabria: burnt like a *crème brulée*, nude, ravaged, scorched. Worse than a lunar landscape, for that is

a natural phenomenon, and what Tina saw was a land despoiled by men and showing its scars. . . .

"Look at this country," she said testily, lashing out at Ferruccio because he, Italian, was accountable, "dry as a bone, bare, parched. Why doesn't someone preach trees to these people?" And she thought of the poplars of her father's Veneto, the cypresses and oaks of Tuscany, the sweet green hills of the Marche. "I'm sick of the official guidebook spiel about the austere beauty of Calabria, and the people living from wild asparagus and wild artichokes. There's nothing growing around here. Why don't they come right out and say, 'This is plundered land'!" (p. 380)

First, we see that the ravaged land of the South is not, as Tina states, due to a "natural phenomenon," but rather pillaged, sacked, and permanently scarred. We also see that Barolini underscores the North/South question in sharing with her reader Tina's mental comparison of "the poplars of her father's Veneto, the cypresses and oaks of Tuscany, [and] the sweet green hills of the Marche" with the "plundered land" of Calabria.

Tina's encounter with Castagna's village priest, the last direct encounter with the South that Barolini affords her reader, offers a curious combination of events. First, the priest tells Tina that people did not always go north or emigrate elsewhere, but that even his own grandfather, a charcoal burner from Carlopoli,[20] had "settled in Castagna and made it good," adding that "it isn't always in America that you can better yourself" (p. 385). The priest's final remark about making it good even in Castagna is, to be sure, a type of reproachment to those, past and present, who considered emigration the only way to better oneself. His admonition, however, does not end here. It continues in his response to Tina's seemingly proud declaration that Umbertina and Serafino had, along with others, emigrated to the United States: "'Yes,' said the priest, 'they never come back. They left because of *miseria* and they forget the others still here in *miseria*'" (p. 386). What is significant about the priest's response is that while Tina had made reference to a completed past event, Umbertina's emigration, the priest brings it into the present. In so doing, he underscores the major reason for leaving—the *miseria*— and quickly adds Umbertina and Serafino to those who continue to leave Castagna, not only never to return but neither to remember those whom they leave behind. Whereas before in the novel the South had been defended by those who were either from elsewhere or descendants of those from the South, here Barolini puts the words directly in the mouth of a Southerner who, had his family emigrated to the United States, would have been a third-generation Italian American like Marguerite.

Tina's final encounter with the South is an indirect one that takes place later when she returns to the United States. Here, Barolini manages to punctuate further still what she had brought to the fore in the Castagna episode, namely, that the South continues to suffer forms of indignation similar to those of the turn of the century. Unbeknownst to her, Tina comes across Umbertina's bedspread, the one she had to sell after her arrival in the United States. Discovering the special exhibit of clothes, trinkets, and other belongings of the early Italian immigrants, she saw the bedspread labeled with the following card: "Origin: Calabria. Owner unknown. Acquired by Anna Giordani in 1886." The "Anna Giordani Collection," as it was called in the Museum of Immigration at the base of the Statue of Liberty (p. 407), consisted of those things Anna Giordani, a northern Italian, had assembled during her years of working with the poor, most of whom, we came to know in the first part of the novel, were southern Italians.

Of the four or five major issues representing Italy that one finds in *Umbertina*, two seem to stand out: the gender issue and the question of the South. Both issues, in fact, precisely because they are also interwined with other issues, not only loom larger than those others, but they indeed seem to frame Barolini's novel. We may see the gender issue, in fact, as the outer set of brackets, whereas the North/South issue figures as an inner set of brackets. *Umbertina* opens with a short prologue of Marguerite in her Italian analyst's office and ends with Tina having resolved her gender issue with Jason and her profession, as well as having come to terms with her ethnic identity; whereas the North/South issue first appears soon after Marguerite's session with her analyst and appears for the last time toward the end of the novel as a catalyst for Tina's ethnic and gender self-reconciliation.

Barolini, in sum, presents a multi-layered image of Italy as she offers her reader 1) a chronological picture spanning more than one hundred years of Italy's social history (1860s–1970s), 2) a socio-literary history of postwar Italy through Marguerite's story, and 3) a portrait of the oppressed in Italy as represented by issues of class, the North/South, and gender, the female plight. Precisely what Barolini, as Italian/American author, may feel about Italy constitutes a discussion in its own right. What we can say is that her narrating voice is, to be sure, sympathetic, if not empathetic, to the issues of gender and class. Yet, on the other hand, one does not really find a conclusive narrative intervention on her part with regard to Italy and its future save the above-mentioned issues of the woman's plight and the *Mezzogiorno*. Perhaps, then, a good way to encapsulate her narrative voices would be to quote from one of the book's characters, Marguerite's Italian teacher, the elderly Matteo De Mariani: "Italy is a great and sad country," De Mariani told her. "I do not hate her."

# 6

# Gianna Patriarca's "Tragic" Thought: Italian Women and Other Tragedies

*Italian Women and Other Tragedies* is a collection of poetry that chronicles an immigrant woman's physical and emotional journies. It is, on the one hand, the story of a woman born in a small town in the province of Frosinone, east of Rome, who as a little girl emigrated with her family to Toronto, Ontario. Yet, Gianna Patriarca's poetry does more than just speak to her narrating *I*'s immigrant experience. At the same time, Patriarca succeeds in chronicling the gender aspect of her narrator's migratory Italian/Canadian existence.[1] In addition, Patriarca's women in *Italian Women and Other Tragedies* represent the entire spectrum of Italian, North Italian/American, and North American women. As she escorts her reader along these personal journies from the province of Frosinone, Italy, to Ontario, Canada, Patriarca introduces her reader to the premigratory women of Ceprano, Frosinone, in "Italian Women," to the postmigratory women of Toronto, Ontario, in her concluding, forward-looking poem "For Gia at Bedtime."

As shall become apparent, the *tragedy* of Patriarca's collection is twofold in nature. It is, on the one hand, a physical/sentimental tragedy of women whose existence, precisely because they are women, is situated in a deprivileged and disenfranchised socio-familial position vis-à-vis their male counterparts. On the other hand, Patriarca's *tragedy* is also epistemological: as a woman in a man's world, she has stepped over the Cartesian threshold of *Cogito ergo sum*. She now thinks; she has constructed an "Andersdenken, un altro pensiero, *il pensiero dell'altro*," as Franco Rella tells us is necessary.[2] In her Cartesian dependence on Reason and thus her discovery of thought—the *other thought* especially—Patriarca has set up her own cognitive process based on her gender specificity. Her semiotic interaction with the world around her, then, can only be one of conflict regardless of any desire for the opposite, precisely because she is *other* of the "pensiero dell'altro" we saw above. It is thus this *other thought* that constitutes Patriarca's epistemological *tragedy*.[3]

In articulating this sense of otherness, Patriarca is also, to para-phrase Aaron, a sort of pioneer spokesperson—Aaron's "first-stage" writer—for the unspoken-for, marginalized Italian/Canadian women of the immigrant generation. Undoubtedly she offers portraits of her co-others with the goal of dislodging and debunking negative stereotypes ensconced in the dominant culture's mind-set. Yet, in so doing, she also creates characters, most specifically the male, possessing some of the very same stereotypes that should be debunked. In this manner, she surely succeeds in humanizing the stereotyped figure, but one might question her general reader's interpretation of "dissipating prejudice." As will become clear, Patriarca does not engage in militant criticism of the perceived restrictions and oppression set forth by the dominant group, and demystification of negative stereotypes is, at best, left for the reader to infer.[4]

The gender *dilemma,* and I use this second term deliberately, opens the collection with Patriarca's first four poems, "Italian Women," "My Birth," "Daughters," and "Paesaggi," where the ethnic/immigrant theme shares the spotlight with the gender issue. Women are, in this promasculinist, bicultural Italian/Canadian world, second-class citizens. Their feelings and desires are shown to be categorically sub-servient to the men's, as Patriarca tells us in "Italian Women":

> these are the women
> who were born to give birth
>
> they breath only
> leftover air
> and speak only
> when deeper voices
> have fallen asleep

Similar dynamics of what may be readily considered second-class citizenry are more specifically underscored in the opening of the above-cited poem. These women's very existence is defined by their reproductive abilities—"born to give birth"—a notion that is punctu-ated by Patriarca's resort to alliteration in the second verse, as well as by the adverb "only," the poem's one true rhyme. Their subservient status to men is further emphazied by their literal position of *afterwards,* that is, first men, then women. We see that not only were they born to give birth, but in spite of such a unique and natural phenomenon that only they can experience, these women are relegated to receiving "leftovers" of the most urgent kind—air—and can speak only when men are not present.

The collection's second poem, "My Birth," brings to the fore the re-strictive, masculinist notion of female *qua* procreator, where females as first-borns, conversely, are "mistakes" by both those who are born as well as those who give birth to them. One-sidedly male, the father, who, according to his *visione del mondo*, figures as the loser in this case, has what he would surely consider the magnanimity to forgive "*even* [her] female birth": "my father is a great martyr / he has forgiven me every-thing / even my female birth." And if there is any solace for these women to find, as did this newborn female, it is possible only among themselves:

> i swear i can still hear the
> only welcoming sounds
> were from my mother
> and she has always been blamed
> for the mistake.

Female bonding between mother and daughter thus constitutes the only possibility of warm feelings; their monogender relationship be-comes the only locus of positive sentiments, while at the same time their status vis-à-vis the male remains firmly situated in second-class citi-zenry. Indeed *one* of the narrating poet's tragedies is her birth; her very existence is twice minimized in the above-cited verses: 1) we find the first-person singular pronoun in lower case; 2) in a similar mode of ex-clusion, the narrating poet's birth cannot be articulated; only its mac-ulinist, value-judging term, *mistake,* can be used. This fact of linguistic evasion on the narrator's part illustrates her exclusion from the male world and further underscores the concept of "pensiero dell'altro" as "conflitto," which, in itself, is another example of the narrator's episte-mological tragedy.

The male (husband/father) is not a happy figure in this collection. Indeed, the same can be said for some other father figures in other Italian/American poetic and prose works.[5] For these men, mothers and homemakers are the only acceptable roles for these women of multiple worlds. In this well-established male world, they are to be good, well-behaved girls before they marry ("Daughters") and well-behaved, faith-ful wives and mothers after they wed ("Paesaggi"). If otherwise, we become witness to violence done to daughters and wives alike. In "Daughters," in fact, we read that the accepted behavior of the new country—staying out late at night—remains totally taboo for the immi-grant father:

> a young Italian woman's
> claim to prostitution
> is any activity past
> the midnight hour
>
> his eyes were coral
> as he rammed his fist
> inside my mouth
> reminding me

Such violence done to daughters clearly escalates as they grow into women and become wives. Patriarca's explicit descriptions of male vi-olence on females continues, in which cases we find that if the woman does not die, she is driven totally insane. "Stories from My Town" is the brief but efficacious and heart-rending description of a husband's vi-cious beating of his wife:

> his hands became fists
> hammering
> like thunder
> her body, her hair
> her arms became one.
> and then silence.
> . . .
> and with one long breath
> he moved away
> leaving her
> to the attending
> vultures.

The husband literally pummels his wife to death. Such a brutal beating is dramatized by a number of stylistic factors. The short verses, for in-stance, add a staccato-like quality to the poem's rhythmic flow; in an equally significant manner, key words such as *hammering, thunder,* and *silence* are situated in a state of isolation or semi-isolation. The ultimate sign of death—*vultures*—closes the poem as a verse unto itself: a sign that clearly underscores 1) the husband's subsequent abandonment of his wife, as she lies dead from his hand, and 2) his identification with the vultures, as both he and the animals clearly appear as the predators or scavengers they truly are.

More dramatic is the case of Nina, of "Nina, la matta," who surely seems to do "crazy" things: she runs out in her underwear; she screams; she pours bags of salt on green grass; she walks on her knees, for hours, the entire length of the church. All this makes the neighbors "think she's crazy" and that her screams are of a "woman gone mad"; "everyone thinks she's mad." But what no one knows is why she acts the way she does:

> the neighbours know nothing
> of the jagged glass
> he tried to shove into her vagina
> as their six-year-old son watched
> they know nothing of her beaten body
> hurled down cellar stairs
> like discarded work shoes.

As in the previous poem, here too, the husband abandons his wife; in the one instance, she was left for the vultures, and here she is reduced to an inanimate object, a pair of "discarded work shoes." Another similarity between both poems is Patriarca's exclusive use of personal pronouns. In no instance does she use the nouns *husband* or *wife*. Given the hierarchy we have seen thus far in the collection, the reader knows by now who the *he* is, for it may seem only *natural*, at this point, as such a technique may indeed aid Patriarca in underscoring an action of this sort as, unfortunately, the expected.

It is, nevertheless, the gut-churning violence that stands out and, though not murderous, equals the previous poem's killing in this husband's abhorrent act of attempted genital mutilation. Along with what we have already seen, this stanza stands out for a number of reasons. First, it is the only stanza in the poem that refers to the husband's action. Second, the husband attempts to mutilate his wife in the presence of his son: a perverted role model, to say the least, of adult male behavior. Third, one may perceive a shift in semantic reference in the English equivalents to the title's Italian adjective *matta*. Lest we forget, the neighbors "*think* she's crazy," they *think* her screams are of a "woman gone mad," and "everyone *thinks* she's mad," the important word being *think*. No one, that is, actually knows why/if she is "crazy." The significance of such uncertainty is that the notion of craziness, or madness, first attributed exclusively to the wife, is suddenly shifted to the husband once we, the reader, come to know of his insane actions of genital mutilation; his madness, we come to realize, is in actuality the source of origin of her insanity. Consequently, any presumed male inculpation of the female is neutralized, and guilt, it becomes apparent, lies where it should, with the male's action(s).

If this one-sided—or better, lopsided—relationship is to change, it seems it can only change dramatically and with finality; if the conversations between daughter and father are to take place, they take place only after his death, as we see in "November 16, 1983":

> my father is dead
> and I have nowhere
> to put this anger
>
> I was sure he would live
> forever
> to continue his battle
> with me and my
> poems.

An equally one-sided conversation appears in "Beautiful Things," where silence is a bittersweet result of her father's death—bitter because she, as adult, cannot "talk to" him; sweet, conversely, because it is also the source of some sort of peace:

> i come, i sit
> i visit with this man
> i could never talk to
> and have long conversations.

But the world does change for these Italian women. We see in "College Street, Toronto," the street that constitutes the heart of the city's Little Italy, that "the Italians are almost all gone . . . [and that ] Bar Italia has a new clientele / women come here now / I come here / I drink espresso and smoke cigarettes." We also see in "Getting Things Right" that the changes that take place are due to an array of reasons that are both external and internal to our narrating female *I*. Indeed, it is her own awareness of self, as it is for any one person to create positive change in her/his life, that helps her "get things right":

> i am
> therefore
> i make no apologies
> woman
> Italian
> overweight, underweight

tall, loud
romantic bore
. . .
i am through
blaming the forces outside
my soul
it is unproductive

In this sense, our female narrator has cut her world into "two half truths"[6] for which she has developed her "altro pensiero," as we saw above. There is the "truth" of men—the old myth of overpowering masculinity—now juxtaposed to the "truth" of women—our female narrator's new myth of woman as she is. Our narrator has, in other words, demythologized the old world of men into which she was born and grew up, only to remythologize her new world of femaleness into which she now moves as a result of her "altro pensiero."[7] As a consequence of such female remythologizing, the *i* that now reappears should be read differently from the previous *i* we encountered. While earlier it was entrenched in the mythical world of masculinity, here it is cradled in the mythical world of femaleness; then it was minisculed to the male *I*, whereas now it reappears as a nondistinguishing marker of the new female myth for which all female *i*s enjoy equal status.

Along with the gender issue that underscores the majority of the poems in this collection, as well as the narrating *I*'s new-found liberation as female, there co-exists a strong sense of understanding, compassion, and empathy for the male as immigrant, stranger, and, ultimately, as in some cases, outcast—be this for internal or external reasons—in this new world without his family and friends of his native land. The same "College Street, Toronto" that chronicles the change of the Italian/Canadian female's social role also alludes to the trials and tribulations of these men who first came alone and lived in basements apartments ("by the light of a forty watt bulb"), scrimping and saving in order to have their familes join them, when finally they could all move literally above ground and into the light.[8]

In a similar manner, both the physical and emotional hardships are recounted in Patriarca's collection. Early on, we find an empathetic testament to the father's broken spirit, afflicted by thirty years of being elsewhere, as her use and juxtaposition of certain words punctuate the immigrant's dilemma. Indeed, the adjective for the present, *foreign,* is now synonymous with *old* and conjures up notions of futility and despair; whereas the adjective for the past, *young,* is synonymous with *new* and conversely conjures up the notion of possibility and hope. But, in the end, all hope is lost ("rotted"), as the immigrant does not, perhaps *cannot*, return to his native land:

> but for thirty years now
> he's slept in a foreign bed
> that has curved his spine
>
> the corn husks of his young bed
> have rotted in a cradle
>
> if he could return
> to smell the earth
> his father left him
> he would understand

All this because the "return," as we are told ("Returning"), is "the other dream," for which "other" is another form of impossibility for these old immigrants who no longer "discuss the distance anymore" since for them it is no longer a reality. The "distance" that these immigrants no longer discuss represents indeed the very difference between them and the new world in which they live. They do not "discuss the difference" precisely because they have not developed that "altro pensiero," as has instead our female narrator.

The immigrant's life of long ago is, as we see, a bitter-sweet experience. To be sure, Patriarca could not offer a better description of the immigrant worker's plight than that which she presents in "Dolce-Amaro," a tribute to her father's experience of close to thirty years "under the white weight / of endless Januarys":

> this country has taken everything
> his health, his language
> the respect of his modern children
> the love of his angry wife.
>
> in some forgotten lifetime
> he was a young, dark-haired man
> in a ship packed with young
> dark-haired men
> floating uncomfortably towards
> a dream they didn't want to bury
> with the still young bones
> of mothers and fathers
> among the ruins of a postwar Italy.

The result of the hard voyage and the clash of two diametrically different worlds has turned the immigrant's life topsey-turvy. His entire well
being, which we assume existed to some extent before his voyage, is can-
celled out, as his "health" and "language" have been taken from him. In
addition, the profound rupture between him and his family is articulated by Patriarca's keen use of adjectives—as seen earlier with *foreign*
and *young*—such as *modern* and *angry*, where *modern* may also signal
*change*, and *angry* may also underscore the frustration brought about by
the men and women no longer knowing or understanding one another.
To be sure, Patriarca's compassion and understanding for these men and
their trials and tribulations continue, as their dream was just that, a
dream that "did not come easily / the golden paved North America /
wasn't paved at all." For "there was the smell of group sweat / cheap
meals seasoned with resentment / by the wives of aspiring landlords."
This is not unfamiliar imagery for those knowledgeable of the immigrants' plight, be they Italian, Hispanic, Irish, Jewish, or of any other eth-
nic/racial group, or, for that matter, of any one time of immigration to
North America. For those conversant with Italian/American literature,
Pietro di Donato's classic *Christ in Concrete* (1939) comes to mind as we
find out that not only did the dream end early for our narrator's father,
but there was no true concern from either employer or state:[9]

> for my father
> the dream ended early
> when his knees were crushed
> by the weight of steel
> along some railroad line
> he was thirty-one
> there was no insurance then
> and little interest
> for the benefits of the immigrant man.
>
> he bends easily at fifty-seven
> walks with a cane
> rarely opens his lifeless eyes
>
> the government sends him
> fifty-one dollars a month
> in recognition.

Not all is tragic in *Italian Women and Other Tragedies*. The last five
poems, especially, communicate more positive feelings than what one
finds in the earlier poems. "Compleanno" speaks of the sweet nostalgia

for the past which is filled with those actions and things she desired but, for whatever reason, could not have:

> i want a ripe fig
> i want to steal a persimmon
> . . .
> my mouth smeared orange
> from the sweet flesh of
> the forbidden fruit.

It is a past steeped, more specifically, in the author's world of femininity, a world that has its roots in the matrilineal world of her Italian heritage. It is important to underscore, I would contend, that Patriarca's nostalgia is based on a reverie and reminiscence that hark back to her interactions with her female counterparts. In this sense, then, she pays homage to her sister women through such nostalgia.[10] The significance of this reverie for the narrating poet's peace of mind is most evident at the end of "Mary," a poem that precedes "Compleanno":

> I visit often
> to hold my new nephew
> and to reminisce
> of the days when we were
> nieces
> and all the living rooms
> were open spaces.

We see the gender issue underscored by the juxtaposition of the two nouns, *nephew* and *nieces*, as this second term now stands alone, a verse unto itself. In like fashion, "grandmother" and "mamma" constitute the desirables in the narrating poet's reverie/wishful thinking in "Compleanno":

> i want to run my hand through
> the rosemary bush by the gate
> where my grandmother's iris grows
> to sit by the stone wall
> waiting for mamma
> as she pedals back from town

Peace and serenity of the present, along with hope for good things in the future, fill the remaining few pages of the collection in poems such as "Beautiful Things," "Grace Street Summer," and "For Gia at Bedtime." The narrating poet's sense of peace and tranquillity originate, in "Beautiful Things," from the absence of the punishing male figure we saw earlier. The beautiful things are now those things that before were eschewed. More precisely, and more poignantly, I would add, we find in this poem, for lack of a better term, the second half of a type of chiasmus. First, whereas the birth of a female child was before considered a negative, provoking rage and violence in the male father figure, here the female child's birth becomes one of those "brave, beautiful things." It is, in fact, beyond description; these beautiful things "do not need words they are." Second, the silence previously imposed on the females, mother and child alike, is now shifted onto the male father figure. In addition, the silence that then exercised a negative function on the female now has a positive quality to it, as it affords the narrating poet her own sense of peace and calm at her father's tomb. The previous, violent male figure is now gone, and in the poem's closing stanza one may perceive an ambiguity, perhaps even multilayered, in a simultaneous reference to both the past and the present:

> i come, i sit
> i visit with this man
> i could never talk to
> and have long conversations.

The ambiguity lies in the final two verses in that they may refer to an habitual action of the narrating poet's past, that which she was never able to do. On the other hand, these verses may also refer to her present situation, sitting there in front of her father's tomb, no longer with the possibility to speak with her father. Or, finally, these verses may refer to both the past in the one verse and the present in the other; namely, the third verse ("i could never talk to") figures as a relative clause with an adjectival function that describes the man—that the man, with whom she was never able to speak and who is now silent, is the one with whom she now has long conversations.

The positive aspect of silence seen in the previous poem is now underscored in "First Snow," where "silence" appears at the end of verse one, set in a position that anticipates and illustrates its synonymy with "peace," at the end of verse two. The silence and peace that open this poem are possible, we see later, only because the narrating *I*, adult woman with husband and child, now looks forward:

> alone with thoughts that smile
> in my head
> the coming of Christmas
> it is my favourite time
> the joy of family at its best
> the celebration of love
> of this one Canadian thing
> i crave
> the beauty and silence of the
> first snow

The current, as well as future, situation that she envisions is different from her own, when she was a child. The "joy of family" and the "celebration of love" are, as we saw in earlier poems, the two things our narrating *I* did not experience as a child. Then, certain experiences, one could infer, were due to a certain Italian aspect of her background; here, conversely, we see that the negative has been supplanted by a positive, the "first snow," "this one Canadian thing" that, metaphorically speaking, wipes out all that there was, offering up a type of tabula rasa for that which can be.

"Grace Street Summer" and "For Gia at Bedtime," the final two poems in the collection, lay the groundwork for what could come. In these two poems the reader gets a good hint at what could be written on our metaphorical tabula rasa. The summer night of the first poem is one of great harmony, not only for "his wife's voice in harmony" with "Calabrian songs" but for the entire family that is a combination of Italian and Canadian that results in the new Italian/Canadian family, dramatically different from that which, as we previously saw, the narrating *I* had to endure as a child and young woman.

All the negative is ultimately neutralized in the collection's final poem, "For Gia at Bedtime," as the poem itself, as ending, is now in complete counterdistinction to the collection's opening poem. The women's subservience to men, the resultant second-class citizenry, and their literal position of *afterwards*—first men, then women—of the opening poem are all obliterated by the time we get to this final poem. "For Gia at Bedtime," as well as the little girl herself, represent all that which is now possible. The limited existence of the women of the first poem is cast aside and replaced by a sense of unlimited possibilities:

> she smells of something so beautiful
> it has no name

> her face is the passion fruit flower
> i held in my hand as a child
> and never let go
> she brings back all the evenings
> of spring in the farmhouse
> she gives her smile freely
> without conditions
> she loves the size of my body.

These possibilites indeed constitute a multitude of positive aspects now open to the newer generation that the older generation could not experience. The notion of unlimited possibilities frames this first sentence, the poem's opening verses, from two viewpoints. First, in a more general sense, the namelessness of that something beautiful she represents figures as another metaphor of the tabula rasa on which she, Gia, can now inscribe that which she desires, the possibility of possibilities. Second, the verse "without conditions" finds itself ambiguously situated in that it can modify either the previous or subsequent verse, if not both, so that the unconditional freedom of her smile is accompanied by her unconditional love for her mother's body ("overweight, underweight / tall, loud" ["Getting Things Right"]).

These two viewpoints may readily figure as the outer brackets of a frame that enclose and, to a certain degree, make a connection to the narrating poet's past hopes ("passion fruit flower / i / . . . never let go," "all the evenings of / spring in the farmhouse"). In this sense, Gia is also that connection to the past that is, seen from the narrating I's perspective, a hopeful look to the future.[11] In looking back at the first poem, whereas the women were at that time in a literal position of *afterwards*, here Gia represents both a recuperation for her narrating *I* mother and more significantly a literal and metaphorical position of *forward*—all that which is *in potentia*. As that "something so beautiful / that has no name," Gia is also one of those previously seen "brave, beautiful things" that are beyond description and, consequently, "do not need words they are."

In closing this chapter, I would remind the reader, in accordance with Aaron's description, that personal experiences indeed comprise "the very stuff of [Patriarca's] literary material." She writes equally about what she *thinks* and what she *experiences* in her surroundings. Her art, then, records her experiential feelings more than her analytical thoughts. We do not have any militant denouncement of either the ethnic or gender dilemma. Indeed, it is the reader's task to infer such things: her ethnic and gender experiences of the more visceral kind serve more as the foundation of his/her literary signification.

This said, Patriarca's creativity transcends the story she wants to tell. Along with what she wants to say, her creative originality is equally rooted in how she says what she says. Patriarca's language is, on the surface, straightforward, which, along with its recall of realistic narrative prose, has an artistic function. It adds a certain realistic tone to Patriarca's frequent narrative technique of non linearity. Within a framework of seemingly direct language combined with her use of gut-wrenching imagery, Patriarca succeeds in portraying problematic situations of human interactions, specifically, gender issues and family relationships. Whereas narration, in both prose and poetry, tends to be more descriptive than expressive, Patriarca's narration maintains its descriptive component while adding an explicitly expressive one. Namely, form and content become intricately engaged so that the one is always dependent on the existence of the other; the work of art cannot stand alone, as *ars gratia artis* is not consonant with Patriarca's poetics. Something of which she is well aware is the intricate relationship of art and life:

> i think of poems i might write
> but there is no image
> for this moment
> for who she is
> my only daughter
> my prayer
> the greatest poem of my life.

The result is an intensely emotional, quasi–visual work of art—in this case, poetry—that engages the reader in its communicative act: the reader, that is, becomes a coparticipant in the collection's point of view and signifying act and therefore experiences the narrator's emotional *iter.*

# 7

# Italian/American Writer or Italian Poet Abroad?: Luigi Fontanella's Poetic Voyage

Incendio non vero
è quello ch'io scrivo,
non vero seppure è per dolo.
Àn tutte le cose la polizia,
anche la poesia.

—Aldo Palazzeschi, "L'incendiario"

Certo è un azzardo un po' forte,
scrivere delle cose così,
che ci son professori oggidì
a tutte le porte.

—Aldo Palazzeschi, "E lasciatemi divertire"

## Some Preliminary Comments

In this explorative chapter, I would like to offer a few general observations on the notion of Italian writing in the United States vis-à-vis what is traditionally considered to be Italian/American writing. I shall do so by using certain texts from the Italian poetry of Luigi Fontanella, thus offering my own reading of a major part of his work in verse. Included in my analysis are *Simulazione di reato* (Manduria: Lacaita, 1979), *Stella Saturnina* (Rome: Il ventaglio, 1989), and *Round Trip* (Udine: Campanotto Editore, 1991).

It might indeed prove fruitful were we to expand our notions and begin to think of ethnic literature, however we define its specificities and peculiarities vis-à-vis the various ethnic groups,[1] as an ongoing phenomenon transmuting itself insofar as there are always new groups and individuals who will continually reconstitute the ethnic/*other* writer. As it stands today, we may surely speak in terms of at least three

general categories of ethnic writers prevalent today in the United States:
1) along with the European immigrant writers of the great wave of immigration, some of whom may still be alive and writing today, I would
include their contemporary African/American, Native/American, and
Hispanic/American writers who, after more than a century of social,
economic, and cultural suppression of the 1800s, began to engage in
artistic invention and, in so doing, imbued their creative works with
their ethnoculturally specific mind-set; 2) the (grand)sons and
(grand)daughters of the immigrants of the first half of this century, who
eventually rediscover or reinvent their ethnicity, along with younger
members of other United States racial groups; and 3) a new group of
writers, analogous to the United States Spanish-writing author,[2] who,
having arrived in the United States after the economic boom of the
1950s,[3] resides in the United States and writes in the language of his/her
country of origin.

Indeed, with regard to the Italian writer in the United States of this
third category, Paolo Valesio offers a working paradigm for a greater understanding of this writer in his substantive essay, "The Writer Between
Two Worlds: The Italian Writer in the United States."[4] This writer, according to Valesio, "dialogue[s] with the English language–and–culture
that surrounds [him] . . . [with the hopes of being] heard a little better
(p. 272)."[5] To be sure, because of language plurality—standard Italian,
Italian dialect, and United States English—and the ideological cluster of
the United States, this writer surely constitutes one of several types of
writers that may fall under the general category of Italian/American
writer. They range from the immigrant writer of Italian language to the
United States-born writer of Italian descent who writes in English; and
in between, of course, one may surely find the many variations of these
two extremes. Hence, my use of the term Italian/American writer
should imply, accordingly, any and all of these types of writers.

In Chapter One I called into question those works of art that do not
*explicitly* treat Italian/American subject matter, though they seem to exude a certain ethnic Italian/American quality, even if we cannot readily
define it. I suggested subsequently that we expand our own reading
strategy of Italian/American art forms in order to accommodate other
possible, successful reading strategies. With regard to Italian/American
literature we should thus consider it a series of on-going written enterprises which establish a repertoire of signs, at times *sui generis,* and
therefore create verbal variations (visual in the case of film, painting,
sculpture, and drama) that represent different versions that are dependent, of course, on one's generation, gender, and socio-economic condition. Turning now to the Italian-language writer, having established

such a working paradigm, I would now also add language to this working definition—that is, Italian, English, or some conscious maccheronic combination thereof—of what can be perceived as the Italian/American interpretant. As I already stated in Chapter One, the Italian/American experience may indeed be manifested in any art form in a number of ways and at varying degrees, for which one may readily speak of the variegated representations of the Italian/American ethos in literature, for example, in the same fashion in which Daniel Aaron spoke of the "hyphenate writer," whether that literature is written in English, standard Italian, Italian dialect, or some combination thereof.

## Fontanella's Poetic Voyage

Language in its many manifestations, including Italian, English, on rare occasions French, and experimentation especially in the first, lies at the base of Fontanella's poetry. If one were to speak of an Italian influence, names such as Palazzeschi and Gozzano or Montale and Zanzotto are a few that come to mind. Further still, one might also think of the historical avant gardes as other possible intertexts to Fontanella's sign-producing repertoire.[6] Whoever these writers may be, the one common denominator is language manipulation, the poet's desire to deviate from the norm and re-invest his/her language with a valence that is not always in concert with that of the dominant culture. Luigi Fontanella engages in such activity, and in so doing, he *has his fun,* as one of his predecessors, Palazzeschi, would happily say. Fontanella, to express it in his national language, *si diverte,* and, I would hasten to add, he also, polysemically speaking, *diverte!*

Fontanella's morphic experimentation constitutes a good part of his poetic diversion (*divertimento*). In this regard, he constantly creates new words through combination, contamination, and pure invention. Indeed, a significant part of his experimentation is both Gozzano-like and Palazzeschian in tone. If he emulates or apes others (or borrows from other languages), as did Gozzano, he does so in a totally inventive way. If he creates a playful tone, it recalls the early poetry of Palazzeschi. And if he creates *ex nihilo* (if this is still possible for any artist today), he reminds us more of the morphic and semantic machinations of Zanzotto.

In *Simulazione di reato* (1979) we find a variety of noun-adjective and noun-noun combinations (some plausible and others not), forming a type of language contamination or borrowings, especially from English (such as titles of poems), and some inventions of other words created at (?) and for (!) the moment:

quantocaldo qui vicino

. . .

il treno che gira che fischia suonicoriandoli ("Play-ground")
Bleeker street quantacarne di macello ("Bleeker street")
carcinomaverbosologizzazione ("A certa 'avanguardia' italiana")

To be sure, the first two examples demonstrate the expected and
playful—yes, pun intended vis-à-vis "Play-ground"—word-play Fontanella's poetry readily offers. But Fontanella goes further. His *suonicoriandoli*, two nouns, each one easily functional also as an adjective,
signal both the tactile and audible qualities of language. Fontanella's
poetry, as this poem may surely imply, is a "playground" in its own
sense, in a serious *sense* indeed. But it is a *sense* that is based on oppo-
sites coming together (for example, English titles of Italian poetry at
times peppered with English words) yet not always attracting. As he
says in "Bleeker street":

> Bleeker street quantacarne di macello
> urla di colori notte sinestetica che da sola
> può racchiudere ere da manuali

Like the "notte sinestetica che da sola / può racchiudere," so too
is Fontanella's poetry chock full of elements pertaining to different sensorial spheres which his reader must now process in his/her act of signification. Indeed, Fontanella's reader, similar to the one Calvino had
proposed decades earlier, relies on a form of semiosis which places
him/her in an interpretive position of *superiority* vis-à-vis the author, as
we saw earlier.[7] In "Whom Do We Write For" Calvino tells us that the
writer . . . be ready "to assume a reader who does not yet exist, or a
change in the reader" (p. 82), a reader who would be "*more cultured than
the writer himself*" (p. 85; Calvino's emphasis).[8] In fact, on certain occasions, Fontanella actually leaves space for his reader to fill. When his poems end with punctuation, a good number of them do not end with the
expected period. Rather, the final point of punctuation is at times a
colon, an obvious signal of continuation which thus creates the prover-
bial, constitutive blank, concrete or imaginary, for the reader to fill.[9]

Fontanella's *divertimento* (diversion/fun) becomes more prevalent
as his reader progresses through this and most other volumes he has
published thus far. Indeed, "A certa 'avanguardia' italiana" serves as a
plausible manifesto in verse of Fontanella's *diversion*ary *ars poetica*:

> L'osservazione non basta la critica
> l'analisi il giudizio non basta
> non basta l'applicazione lo studio
> la citazione opportuna (perfino qui
> il bisogno dei padri) non basta
> la brava frase metafrase
> intellettuale cerebrale paranale
> finale di partita metafora girochiuso
> segmenti virgolette strapuntini di parole
> sema rema battuta a vuoto
> carcinomaverbosologizzazione.

Fontanella's disenchantment, to say the least, with the academic and non–academic establishments (in the latter case, more precisely, the empowered, non–canonical canon-makers) is clearly manifested in this poem and those immediately following in this same section. For it becomes quite clear that the "certa 'avanguardia'" is by no means, for Fontanella, an avant–garde. Throughout the poem Fontanella, in what is clearly an "angry" period, tells his reader what the "certi professors" "senzamore" ("A certi professors") can not obtain ("buoniversi"), through their various formulae, as listed in the above-cited poem, or their "linguistica" aggressivity, as he states in "Postilla ultima," directed to Adriano Spatola. Indeed, Fontanella's disdain for the so-called avant–garde manifests itself in the series of "paranale" what-nots that culminate in the final verse/word of the poem, "carcinomaverbosologizzazione"—an underscoring of what the poet perceives as the unnecessarily wordy ("verboso") cancer ("carcinoma") that has overwhelmed the act of verse writing ("logizzazione").

Indeed, the title itself ("A certa 'avanguardia' italiana") provokes uneasiness for a number of reasons. First, the lack of an indefinite article may signal a shift in meaning of the initial adjective, *certa,* from that of a specific avant–garde to any, that is, unspecific and therefore insignificant avant-garde, as he states in "A certi professors":

> *imbecilli* di fine accademia tentativi
> di persistenza nel vostromondo ovattato e senzamore
> . . .
> quanto *marcio fraudolento* panegirici
> copiosi tra voi *pellivecchie al neon*
> eppure *morti* vi muovete (emphasis added)

Second, in 1979, after the end of the second Italian avant–garde and on the threshold of what we have come to know as the postmodern condition, what kind of "avanguardia" can we expect? Third, we are forced to ask what kind of Italian avant–garde? Indeed, we may not receive a clear-cut, precise answer. Yet we do know it is a "certa . . . italiana," which, given the general circumstances that contributed to Fontanella's poetry—his own migration to the United States and his decision to live in two different countries, since he constantly travels between the two— we may be inclined to substitute the nebulous *certa* with a more precise adjective: perhaps *American*. In his own way, then, in a manner similar to what Valesio describes in his essay, Fontanella sets the stage for what we may now consider a *sui generis* Italian/American *ars poetica*. Lest we forget that the first section of this collection, though short, is entitled "Quale America," and the poem currently under analysis opens the second section entitled "Lettere nuove"—"nuove," to be sure, in every *sense* of the word.

Divided into five sections—Quale America, Lettere nuove, Sleeplessness, Simulazione di reato, and Frammenti—*Simulazione di reato* traces a two-year poetic journey in which Fontanella's double existence, both poetic and personal, of Italy and the United States indeed dialogues with its other half with the hope of being "heard a little better," as "la seconda realtà [statunitense] ha la funzione di gigantografare la prima [italiana], di mettere in luce i contorni."[10] What is important to keep in mind is that Fontanella can make his trip precisely because "non [si] pon[e] programmi, . . . proced[e] per reazioni" ("Postilla ultima") with his "parola / infingarda matrice d'una storia"—this his "simulazione ('infingarda' = *simulatrice malizioza* [?] aimed at the empowered anti/canon-makers) di reato ('reazione' = *azione anti~~giuridica~~poetica* [?] because he disdains everything that smacks of 'programmi')." But Fontanella's "rabbie" (the source of his "reato") eventually subside, and his lyrical voyage continues with the assurance that "rimanga intanto una prima elementare verità / certezza esistenziale: libertà" ("Richiesta di Verifica" 3). His is both a "libertà di vivere" as well as a "libertà di poetare," and his "viaggio" is not "a ritroso" with a "rapporto monovalente" ("Metastabile" 6). To be sure, now free of the "certi professors," Fontanella's poetry transcends the "rapporto *mono*valente" as his "scrittura risulta ogni volta *bi*lenca *bi*naria *bi*forme" (*"Foglio stazione [in treno]"*; emphasis added).

"Stanza e distanza," "Victoria Station," "Lettere e dediche," "Nedelia," "Frammenti," "da 'Round Trip'," "Tre poemetti," and "Stella saturnina" are the sections that comprise Fontanella's next collection, *Stella saturnina* (1989). This volume covers a trajectory of seven years

(1979–1986) of poetry written both in Italy and the United States, a lyrical documentation of an errant existence. Not as prevalent nor as intense as in *Simulazione di reato,* word-play and language manipulation (for example, word combinations such as "Cosaparola" [50], "chiusovetro" [65], and "falsodistratto" [110]) are also present here. One also finds Fontanella's penchant for the *a*structured sentence, seemingly illogical connections, and sporadic punctuation, not to speak of his admitted "sporadici segni" (p. 27).

Yet, *Stella saturnina* is also a volume of a much more admittedly self-reflexive poet who opens his collection with an immediate reference to his *poetare*: "ovattato è tutto e io metto parole / ai gesti lenti di ciò che appare e scompare / tutto è meraviglia e passaggio." And as the poet starts out on his personal poetic voyage of "meraviglia e passaggio," the anger of his previous collection is mollified. Here, he demonstrates a certain maturity as artist and individual with his calm acceptance of the uncertainty ("ciò che *appare* e *scompare*"; emphasis added) of his dual existence: "Di questo breve sogno / ritrovo, precisi, due momenti / d'un identico / e diverso divenire."

Whereas in his previous volume Fontanella was less direct in speaking of his poetry, here he candidly describes his writing as an ongoing, slow, and at times difficult process of verse writing with its occasional stalls: "Progressione e coagulo istantaneo della mia poesia / . . . / che il testo matura lento e placido / verso la nuova figura, / brano a brano dissolvendo / l'edificio del suo mondo precedente" (p. 27). And while the anger is gone, his awareness of an aesthetic discord with the establishment is present, as evident both above and below. Diversion is still the desired procedure—"Prodigio del *gioco* la mia *faziosa* poesia / *forma dissacrata asimmetria*" (p. 28; emphasis added)—and meaning remains ever so unsure, still *in potentia,* as he states in the poem, "Diversificazione," a most telling title, given the poet's penchant for word-play. Read as one word, the title translates as "diversification"— *variation* on a theme if not variation of style. From the point of view of self-reflexivity, we might also read the title as two words, "di versificazione," concerning the literal act of verse writing. Both readings, I suggest, are valid:[11]

Il posto s'affolla ripete all'approccio un *significato*
plurimo mentre scrivi la centunesima lettera
in questa sala d'attesa i segni gli avvisi
sul tavolo già pieno del resto di carte di libri
d'insetti sfuggenti e prendi a leggere
quello che scaraventi subito via. (emphasis added)

Indeed, there is more tension than calm in Fontanella's poetic voyage. But there are occasional moments of repose. The most touching moment of calm appears in the section "Nedelia," "microelegie" for his deceased mother.[12] In seven brief poetic compositions that Manacorda, in his "Prefazione," defines as "gentili *haiku* trapiantati con grande grazia al di qua di un altro oceano" (p. 66), the poet finds his most serene moment of nostalgia:

> Da questa finestra socchiusa,
> un po' mesta,
> ti rivedo, madre,
> come quando mi chiamavi:
> mi volto ti rispondo grido volo
> tra le mille corolle corone.
> E' bello il dormire
> in quest'illusione.

Once Fontanella continues his trip, the collection's penultimate section, "Tre poemetti," reminds his reader of the volume's central theme, a solitary ("Navigazione in solitario"), spiritual and physical ("Interno/Esterno") "viaggio" between two geographical and cultural worlds ("Amerika America Amen"): Italy and the United States. Fontanella's "Congedo, ovvero autobiologia letteraria" closes this volume, but it does not necessarily end his trip.

In 1991, Fontanella returned to his early poetry in the publication of *Round Trip, diario in versi*, a recuperation of earlier verses written entirely "in viaggio" during the period of September, 1982, to June, 1983. As in *Simulazione di reato* and *Stella saturnina*, here too Fontanella engages in an *ars poetica* based on a "forma dissacrata [and an] asimmetria," as he stated in the latter collection. And while it is true that one may discern a Montalian influence in the format of a "diario in versi," as Manacorda stated in his preface to *Stella saturnina*, there is also the influence of the historical avant gardes, both Italian and French, as well as, perhaps, the more recently proclaimed, by some, greatest Italian living poet, Zanzotto.[13] And as this volume comes to an end, so does, at least for the moment, Fontanella's poetry come to a pause.[14] Indeed, the following verses, the closing lines of *Round Trip, diario in versi*, also seem appropriate for this section's closure:

> Finisce oggi ( almeno per quest'anno)
> un *commuting* che mi ha commutato (& consumato) alquanto
> accompagnatomi alla Station per l'ultimo

treno della stagione una girl del corso
(probabilmente preoccupata del voto finale) mentre
attorno a me tutto spappolava in un vano e insano
                              [chiacchiericcio
altrimenti chiamato
*il prurito dei vecchi.*

Just as the "commuting" from Boston to New York has changed and overwhelmed him ("un *commuting* che mi ha commutato [& consumato] alquanto"), so has the existential and intercontinental "commuting" changed and overwhelmed him. The phonemic similarities of "un *commuting* che mi ha commutato [& consumato] alquanto," both in consonance and assonance, underscores the conflagration of the different cultural voices that resonate throughout Fontanella's poetry. In like fashion, the local commute becomes symbolic of the geocultural commute which, here, is efficaciously rendered by the "vano e insano chiacchiericcio"—a most apt description of the agglutination of the varied and diverse voices that now constitute Fontanella's generative intertextual reservoir.

In conclusion, then, *per modo di dire*, one may speak of a poetics that is much more expressive than descriptive. Fontanella's word imagery is not to elicit simply pleasant or unpleasant memories and imagery in his reader's mind. Rather, he attempts to render his reader complicit in an emotional and sensorial state as expressed through his poetry. In this sense, the overwhelming self-reflexivity of Fontanella's poetry seems to place him in a category similar to Giose Rimanelli's synthetic writer, yet he remains surely expressive. This seeming ambiguity of definition is due, I would suggest, to what Paolo Valesio told us in his essay (p. 273): that the writer between two worlds seems to refrain from constructing any direct rapport with the Italian/American community in specifics or the United States society in general. If he does, he engages in generalizations through metaphor and metonymy, as Fontanella has thus far done in his engagement with the United States through his poetry. Indeed it is expression, not description, and metaphor, not verisimilitude, that define Fontanella's poetry. And his reader, in his/her complicity in this polysensorial state, becomes a coparticipant in Fontanella's sign production and signification.

# Part IV
## Further Strategies

# 8

# Italian/American Cultural Studies: Looking Forward

## Part One—Where We Are

In Chapter One, I stated that the trajectory of Italian/American literature is somewhat reflective of the United States mind-set vis-à-vis ethnic studies. Italian immigrants and their Italian/American progeny have considered ethnic difference in terms of the melting-pot attitude and, as a logical consequence, strived for assimilation, if such a beast really ever existed.[1] The question, of course, in this regard is: Who really decides if one assimilates? Is it the individual who strives for assimilation, or is it the phantasmagoric power brokers of the dominant group—the ubiquitously unidentified *They*—that decide when or how the individual has assimilated?[2] This question notwithstanding, be it the end of a modernism or the onslaught of the postmodern, it has become clear that the past two decades have constituted a period of transition, if not all-out change, in this attitude. In intellectual circles today, one no longer thinks in terms of the melting pot, as was evidenced in Chapter One. Instead, the individual ethnic or racial culture and its relationship with the long-standing, mainstream culture paradigm—and not necessarily in negative terms only—has taken precedence and gained greater significance as a argument for discussion.

As stated earlier, with the backdrop of this new attitude of rejecting the melting pot (an obvious metaphor for assimilation) and supplanting it with the notion of Americana as a "kaleidoscopic, socio/cultural mosaic" (an obvious metaphor for multiculturalism) I have re-visited the Italian/American experience with regard to that of other United States ethnic and racial groups. In so doing, it became clear that the population of the United States is indeed similar to a mosaic insofar as our country consists of various bits and pieces, each one unique unto itself. Thus, we saw, this aggregate of different and unique peoples is surely emblematic of a constant flux of changes that manifest themselves as the various peoples change physical and ideological positions, ultimately changing the ideological colors of the national mindset. Therefore, precisely because of such a constant flux of changes, Italian/American intellectuals must continue to reshape their roles, even if so slightly, from that of a raconteur of what took place, a role which may lean more toward nostalgia than analysis, to that of cultural examiner and, eventually, cultural broker.

It is with regard to this new role, something which has already manifested itself in a number of Italian/American intellectuals, that the notions and tools of what we know as cultural studies or multiculturalism can aid us immensely. In general, we may consider cultural studies as that mode of analysis which takes as its focal point of argument, as Stuart Hall tells us, "the changing ways of life of societies and groups and the networks of meanings that individuals and groups use to make sense of and to communicate with each other."[3] What is of primary significance is Hall's insistence on plurality, that is, societies and groups, and interconnectedness, that is, to communicate with each other. Hall's plurality and interconnectedness form an obvious and necessary couplet that resulted from the changing attitude toward the notion of melting pot and the rejection of assimilation that were ultimately supplanted by the many metaphors and similes which readily connote difference and individuality of all groups that constitute the United States population.

But cultural studies must also be "critical" insofar as it must be more than the "mere description of cultural emergents that aims to give voice to the 'experience' of those who have been denied a space to talk," as Mas'ud Zavarzadeh and Donald Morton describe what they distinguish as "dominant" or "experiential cultural studies," which "offers a 'description' of the exotic 'other' and thus provides the bourgeois reader with the pleasure of contact with difference."[4] Instead, for them, critical cultural studies "is not a description but an explanation, not a testimonial but an intervention: it does not simply 'witness' cultural events, but takes a 'position' regarding them" (p. 8).[5] As both Hall and Zavarzadeh and Morton underscore, change is the operative word. For Zavarzadeh and Morton, especially, critical cultural studies should constitute "an articulation of the cultural real that will change the conditions which have blocked those voices from talking" (p. 8).

To digress and consider briefly the topic of "block voices," we might see the Italian American somewhere in an interstitial space. In a general sense, the Italian American has always had a voice; we might hear, *they're all around us!* More significant, however, is their position vis-à-vis what we might call the U.S.A. cultural paradigm; until recently

Italian Americans have often been identified with the superficial, imagistic perception the public has drawn from, for example, a Mario Puzo novel or a Francis Ford Coppola film. This, I would contend, has changed recently, especially with regard to the publishing scene, even at a sort of grass-roots level.[6] On the wake of sociological and historical work done in the 1940s to 1960s by Leonard Covello, Paul Campisi, Frank Femminella, Rudolph Vecoli, and the like,[7] the American Italian Historical Association *Proceedings* have appeared annually since 1966, offering an array of topics from sociology and history to literature and film. A second example is SUNY Stony Brook's own Center for Italian Studies that has in the past decade sponsored conferences and symposia, as well as dedicating some of its publishing efforts to Italian/American culture. New presses and distributors have also contributed to a greater and louder voice: Parentheses Press of San Diego and Fithian Press of Santa Barbara regularly publish creative texts and biographies by Italian Americans. The resurrected *Italian Americana* and the more recently founded *Voices in Italian Americana* constitute two forums for the community of creative writers as well. In addition, Guernica Editions and the newly founded book series *VIA* FOLIOS serve a similar function. All these efforts, as well as others too numerous to mention, contribute to the greater amplification of an Italian/American cultural voice.[8] But more needs to be done.

Turning now to the premise that cultural studies represents, among other things, "the weakening of the traditional boundaries among the disciplines and of the growth of forms of interdisciplinary research that doesn't easily fit . . . within the confines of existing divisions of knowledge" (Hall, p. 11), we may then surely open ourselves up to different modes of analysis that go beyond those "traditional boundaries" of literary study so often concerned with the formalistic and the thematic. Mere rhetoric and signification should not suffice; other critical perspectives should become part of our interpretive arsenal. This is especially true since many contemporary Italian/American writers avail themselves of certain generative tools that were not necessarily popular a decade or two ago, generative tools that have their origin in: 1) different national cultures, if not the *epistemological collision* of different national cultures;[9] 2) critical thinkers becoming creative writers; 3) the influence of other media on the written word; 4) the incorporation of popular cultural forms with those considered more high-brow; or 5) the *high-browization* or glorification of the popular arts such as film, romance narratives, and music videos; and 6) as discussed in parts one and two of this study, the fact that many third- and fourth-generation Italian/American artists may readily engage in a process of "rediscovery" and "re-invention" analogous to the experience of the immigrant or first-generation Italian American.[10]

One such arsenal we may wish to investigate as a source of critical ammunition is that dedicated to the examination of postcolonial literature. As we saw earlier, one voice in what has become a wide field of study among those already well known, such as Edward Said, Fredric Jameson, and, more recently, Homi Bhabha and Tim Brennan, is that of Aijaz Ahmad. In his response to Jameson's essay on national allegory and third-world literature, we saw that Ahmad took issue with what he considered Jameson's limited and reductive assumption that third-world literature revolves primarily around the notion of a national allegory. In an analogous manner, an ethnic literary piece might have to contain certain thematic motifs or adopt specific formalistic structures in order for it to be considered part of that certain ethnic rubric. Otherwise, the work and its author are considered not to belong necessarily to that very same group of *hyphenated* writers.

We already saw in Chapter One, adopting Ahmad's language, that 1) the notion of *ethnic* literature cannot be "constructed as an internally coherent object of theoretical knowledge"; 2) *other* "literary traditions . . . remain . . . [often] unknown to the *American* literary theorist";[11] and 3) perhaps most relevant, "[l]iterary texts are produced in highly differentiated, usually over-determined contexts of competing ideological and cultural clusters, [and each one must] be placed within [that] cluster . . . before it is totalised into a universal category." These three notions, it became clear, constitute a significant ideological framework of cluster specificity within which Italian/American intellectuals could, and indeed should, as we did in chapter one, consider further the notion of Italian/American literature as a validifiable category of United States literature and rethink the significance of the Italian/American writer within the recategorization of the notion of the so-called "hyphenate writer."

In Chapter One we traced the various attempts at defining Italian/American art forms. The one question that remained was: What do we do about those works of art, written and/or visual, that do not *explicitly* treat Italian/American subject matter and yet seem to exude a certain, ethnic Italian/American quality, even if we cannot readily define it? Can we not see the *absence* of any explicit Italian/American sign repertoire, especially in light of documented secondary matter, as a type of Italian/American signifying system *in potentia*? As before, I would still say yes. And in this regard, I would suggest an alternative perspective on reading and categorizing any Italian/American art form.[12] That is, I believe we should stretch our own reading strategy of Italian/American art forms, be they, due to content and/or form, *explicitly* Italian/American or not, in order to accommodate other possible, successful reading strategies.[13] Otherwise, we run the risk of relegating to the dusty storage areas of our libraries the likes of Pietro di Donato, Francis Winwar, Arturo Giovannitti, and the like; and we marginalize *a priori* certain works by contemporary writers such as Tony Ardizzone, Rita Ciresi, Tina DeRosa, Agnes Rossi, Anthony Valerio and Chuck Wachtel.

Recent [re]writings of Italian/American literary history and criticism have transcended a limited concept of Italian/American literature. New publications (literary and critical) have created a need for new definitions and new critical readings, not only of contemporary work but of the works of the past. In addition, these new publications have originated, for the most part, from within an intellectual community of Italian Americans. Origins of such a recent Italian/American self-inventory can be dated back to the first AIHA *Proceedings*, especially those first volumes that were dedicated to an array of topics, both literary and non-literary.[14] In like fashion, Rose Basile Green's 1974 book-length study, *The Italian-American Novel: A Document of the Interaction of Two Cultures* (Fairleigh Dickinson University Press) figures prominently. Over the past twenty-odd years, these volumes constitute a base of knowledge and documentation which should now prove most useful for a further theorization of certain issues. One such successful venture at theorizing the Italian/American experience in literature is an acutely original contribution by Robert Viscusi, *"De vulgari eloquentia*: An Approach to the Language of Italian American Fiction," which remains today equally fresh,[15] followed a few years later by Helen Barolini's best-selling anthology, *The Dream Book: An Anthology of Writing by Italian American Women* (Schocken, 1985).[16] Both Viscusi and Barolini lay the foundation for a self-reflexive Italian/American critical discourse. Viscusi, for instance, looks back to Italy in order to find similarities as well as to distinguish what is Italian from what is Italian/American. He, in fact, tells us: "Italian American eloquence wishes to awaken Italian America to a sense of self . . . and to locate for this mythical nation a secure place that no one can confuse with its homeland or its fabulous landfall" (p. 23). Barolini examines and theorizes the Italian/American situation in a much more gender-grounded discourse. Her discussion of the gender issue vis-à-vis Italian/American literature is both a valid argument in itself and a metaphor for the more general social situation of Italian America. Both of these thinkers, these elder states*persons* of this new critical generation, involve themselves in a self-critique which has paved the way for the rest of us to work in and with a more vast critical arsenal.

Two people of the later generation who have obviously profitted greatly from the lessons of Barolini and Viscusi are Mary Jo Bona and Fred L. Gardaphé. Bona's work has already proven itself indispensable for a rethinking of Italian/American literature. In her essay, "Mari Tomasi's *Like Lesser Gods* and the Making of an Ethnic *Bildungsroman*,"[17] Bona constructs a paradigm for the ethnic novel, here specifically Italian/American, similar but not identical to William Boelhower's paradigm of the immigrant novel. In another essay, "Broken Images, Broken Lives: Carmolina's Journey in Tina De Rosa's *Paper Fish*,"[18] Bona first contextualizes the novel within the broader scheme of Italian/American women writers, and second maps out Tina De Rosa's coding correlations which ultimately lay bare the novel's uniqueness in exploring the ethnic/gender dilemma. In addition to this critical work, one must recognize, as with Barolini, Bona's more personal *impegno* in her anthology of recent Italian/American women's fiction, *The Voices We Carry*.[19]

Whereas Bona operates mostly within and around the literary text, Gardaphé inhabits both the theoretical and textual worlds of Italian/American literature. His threefold Vichian division of the history of Italian/American literature is an excellent updated analogue to Daniel Aaron's three stages of the "hyphenate writer."[20] Gardaphé proposes a culturally "specific methodology" for the greater disambiguation of Italian/American contributions to the United States literary scene. In his essay, discussed in Chapter One, he reminds us of Vico's "three ages and their corresponding cultural products: the Age of Gods in which primitive society records expression in 'poetry' [*vero narratio*], the Age of Heros, in which society records expression in myth, and the Age of Man, in which, through self-reflection, expression is recorded in philosophic prose." These three ages, Gardaphé goes on to tell us, have their parallels in modern and "contemporary [socio-]cultural constructions of realism, modernism, and postmodernism" (p. 24). Ultimately, the evolution of the various literatures of United States ethnic and racial groups can be charted as they "move from the poetic, through the mythic and into the philosophic" (p. 25).

These critics and others have offered alternative perspectives through some of the more recent analytical and interpretive tools of hermeneutics, deconstruction, semiotics, and the like. At this point I would mention Gardaphé's critical book, the first in more than twenty years on Italian/American narrative, *Italian Signs, American Streets. The Evolution of Italian American Narrative* (Duke University Press, 1996). Because of their work we can readily broaden our view of what consititues the Italian/American experience in the arts. I would thus underscore what I first stated in Chapter One: that we reconsider Italian/American literature to be a series of ongoing written enterprises that establish a repertoire of signs, at times *sui generis*, and therefore create verbal variations (visual, in the case of film, painting, sculpture, and drama) that represent different versions of what can be perceived as the Italian/American signified, dependent, of course, on one's generation, gender, socio-economic condition. The Italian/American experience may indeed be manifested in any art form in a number of ways and at varying degrees, for which one may readily speak of the variegated representations of the Italian/American ethos in literature, for example, in the same fashion in which Daniel Aaron spoke of the "hyphenate writer" and Aijaz Ahmad discussed new ways of considering "third-world" literature.

Part Two—Where We Can Go

To return to the notion of cultural studies, we might find that the waters are muddy with regard to their validity and significance to Italian Americana. This is especially true if we look at some of the activities sponsored today in and by the mainstream of Italian/American thinking. By mainstream I mean that majority of the Italian/American population that has gained access to those cultural and economic means that empower such people to invite certain individuals and organize *intellectual* events that discuss the state of affairs of Italian/American culture. Over the years, this mainstream has manifested, in general, an overtly conservative attitude to cultural productions and representations in literature as well as the other arts. For this group, only those cultural productions that clearly inhabit a political *center* are allowed to voice Italian/American concerns. Of course, the other semiotic concern here is that these cultural productions in film, literature, the plastic arts, and video are considered almost entirely through the lens of historical representation, whereas their aesthetic characteristics and valences are rarely taken into consideration. Such a lack of formalistic/aesthetic investigations does not allow for the valuable perforation of any text's surface in order to allow for a penetrating analysis of the text in question. Beyond superficial analysis, such techniques and tones as irony, parody, sarcasm, and the like may readily rise to the surface, thus allowing for an alternative interpretation of the text in question, often dissenting from that put forth by mainstream Italian/American interlocutors.

For this specific point, I have in mind the films of Francis Ford Coppola, Martin Scorsese, and Brian DePalma. It is true, for example, that Coppola's *Godfather* films (1972, 1974, 1992) to a great degree romanticized the figure of the *mafioso*, and thus may be interpreted as a positive *intentio operis/auctoris*.[21] Scorsese's characters, be they those of *Meanstreets* (1973) or *Goodfellas* (1990), however, are clearly, *intentione operis/auctoris*, negative and, in the later film especially, despicable human beings who are unlikely to be brought forth as models to emulate. In a similar vein, I would add that the Italian/American mainstream also manifests a possessive attitude toward its cinematic and literary representations. Again, an alternative semiotics might aid us in *expanding* our hermeneutics and thus see certain films, originally viewed as negative portrayals, as nicely balanced nostalgic representations of a cross-generational Italian/American family. I have in mind Norman Jewison's *Moonstruck*, a film directed by a non-Italian American that originates from a script written by another non-Italian American, John Patrick Shanley, with yet a third non-Italian American, Cher, as its lead character.

To return to these interlocutors and their various and sundry cultural institutions, such as journals and Italian/American Centers and Institutes, both phantom and real, I am referring to a specific event that took place in Washington, D.C., in 1993. During the weekend of the Annual Gala Dinner sponored by the National Italian American Foundation, there was a day-long symposium entitled, "The Disuniting of America: The Plight of the Middle Class. How Cultural Diversity and Political Correctness Affect Italian Americans."[22] One of the participating speakers, Professor John Agresto, then President of St. John's College of Maryland, denied the validity of multiculturalism for Italian Americans. Indeed, Italian Americans often confuse the term *Italian* for *Italian American*, sometimes using the same term, *Italian*, for both Italians in Italy and Italian Americans in the United States. It is precisely this practice of conflating terminology, of not clearly defining one's terms, where Professor Agresto wandered (or was it wondered?). He not only used the term *Italian* for Italian Americans, but in addition it was not clear what he meant by "multiculturalism." In what amounted to a list of no-nos and boo-hoos, Agresto eventually got to the point that, for him, multiculturalism had nothing to offer Italian Americans, because, after all, it is a movement that excludes the great names and successes of Leonardo, Michelangelo, Botticelli—or *Bodakelly* as then pronounced—and the like.[23]

This said, I would like to offer the following suggestions with regard to the construction and maintenance of an Italian/American cultural studies discourse. First and foremost, we Italian Americans must define our terms. In this growing semantic web of multiple discourses, we cannot continue to conflate terminology. As a "theory (albeit vague) about the *foundations* of a culture rather than a practice which subsumes cultural ideas,"[24] multiculturalism figures, within the greater discourse of Italy and the United States, as a United States phenomenon, with Italy as the historical intertext for a better understanding of the Italian/American phenomenon.[25] Thus, when it becomes apparent that Italian Americans are getting the short end of the stick within the greater discourse of U.S.A. multiculturalism, something one may surely argue, we must insist on the inclusion of the likes of Arturo Giovannitti, Francis Winwar, Pietro di Donato, Joseph Tusiani, Helen Barolini, Anthony Valerio, Tony Ardizzone, Daniela Gioseffi, Diane Di Prima, Peter Carravetta, and Rachel Guido deVries, along with the more recent writers who have begun to surface (such as Tony Romano). Among Italian writers in the United States, I would include, among others, Rita Dinale, Luigi Fontanella, and Paolo Valesio.[26] The artistic and literary legacies of Italy, such as Leonardo, Michelangelo, and Botticelli, not to forget Dante and his more recent confreres, are just that, cultural inheritances and influences that have surely shaped in some form or another the historical specificities of that which we examine as Italian/American. These must be taken into account,[27] but I would insist that they are not the major players in the greater sociological landscape that makes up the kaleidoscopic population of the United States. It is the Italian/American experience that must be studied first and foremost. Indeed, for the construction of any cultural studies discourse, historical specificity is of prime importance, as even Hall reminds us (p. 12). Such specificity of each cultural configuration and pattern, then, can be examined with these new analytical and interpretive tools for an eventual reconciliation of the specific group in question with those of the other groups that constitute the greater policultural mosaic of the United States.

Secondly, while it is true that the likes of Botticelli, Michelangelo, and Leonardo are cultural legacies, it is also true that globalization is the buzz word of the nineties, and rightly so. In this vein, I believe it is important to cross borders today geo-intellectually. Programs of an interdisciplinary nature, for example, should be set up to include courses from an array of departments and/or programs, including Italian, Sociology, History, Political Science, and English, that would readily form an undergraduate major which could easily be integrated into a double major. A similar program is also readily feasible on the graduate level. Programs and departments of Comparative Literature can be fertile ground for this type of program, especially in collaboration with American Studies programs.

Globalization of this sort has to be policultural. It should include both a view back to Italy as well as a look to what other United States ethnic and racial groups are doing. Indeed, an integral part of the strategy for success is to work first and foremost with those already at one's own university or college. Such an alliance, for example, with the Italian program especially, becomes fruitful for both Italian and Italian/American studies.[28] Further, I believe that U.S.A. Italian Americans might also benefit from a regularized discourse with Italian Canadians, who, because of a more recent immigration and all of its nuances, seem to maintain a more direct discourse with Italy.

Thirdly, Italian Americans have to come together as one group, inclusive of all Italian Americans, plan a rhetorical strategy, and construct, as Robert Viscusi has so eloquently articulated, a group narrative.[29] This means including even the so-called *blasphemers* of Italian America, such as Francis Ford Coppola, Martin Scorsese, Nancy Savoca, Mario Puzo, Al Pacino, and Robert DeNiro, to name just a few of those who seem to be left on the margins of courtly Italian America by its mainstream interlocutors. Ironically, many organizations and publications remain silent about these figures, yet they willingly list the likes of certain entertainers and business*men* whose professional activities may surely be called into question for their supposed connections to notoriously famous individuals or, in the case of international trade, for their seemingly xenophobic bashing of other countries' industrial prowess while, at the same time, and not always very loudly, they engage in lucrative business dealings with industrial giants of those very countries. But inclusion involves more than the few entertainers, businesspeople, and political figures like those just mentioned. Within the intellectual discourse of Italian Americana, the various voices, no matter how different, must work toward the construction of a self-reflexive, critical discourse between and among ourselves that moves forward toward the eventual construction of an aesthetically and ideologically critical voice that will ultimately dialogue with those other ethnic/racial/sexual voices that exist beyond the confines of Italian America.

This leads us to my fourth suggestion. With regard to these other groups, Italian Americans must begin to speak in terms of us *and* them, not us *against* them. Ethnicity is a socio-political construct, and as such it differentiates only insofar as it points out the major characteristics of one group as compared with those of another. These differences, moreover, may also have corollaries and analogues in certain characteristics of other ethnic groups. Let us not forget that zoology is different from sociology and that one's cellular make-up does not necessarily override one's long-term social and cultural experiences of ethnicity.[30] Italian/American cultural interlocutors must therefore abandon the discourse of binary oppositions—the us *against* them—and adopt, instead, one that also takes into consideration the similarities, of varying degrees and intensities, of experience that Italian Americans and all the other minority and majority ethnic/racial/sexual groups have and continue to encounter. We must learn not to speak in terms of racism or prejudice in the singular, "but of *racisms* [as also prejudices] in the plural."[31] "What is needed," Patrick Gallo tells us as he ends his 1974 study, "is an alliance of whites and Blacks, white-collar and blue-collar workers, based on mutual need and interdependence and hence an alliance of political participation." Namely, the *us and them* mentioned above. "But," Gallo continues, "before this can realistically come to pass, a number of ethnic groups have to develop in-group organization, identity, and unity." And here Viscusi's notion of the "group narrative" comes to mind. Finally, Gallo concludes, "[t]he Italian-Americans may prove to be a vital ingredient in not only forging that alliance but in serving as the cement that will hold our urban centers together" (p. 209).[32]

Such a strategy responds to a necessity of inclusiveness of all groups. For until all groups—the so-called dominant class *and* minorities—are included in a cultural discourse, we run the risk of: 1) maintaining the obvious aesthetic hierarchy of a major literature and numerous minor literatures; 2) remaining stuck within a thematically grounded discourse of nostalgia, for which lietmotifs such as *pizza* and *nonna* continue to possess high aesthetic currency; 3) losing "Italian/American" authors to what some have called either "residual multiculturalism" or "the reductiveness of multiculturalism," both being synonymous with assimilation; and 4) conserving the divisiveness that seems to exist today, precisely because an aesthetic hierarchy is maintained both within and outside of the Italian/American community of creative writers and critical thinkers. With "its focus on the politics of the production of subjectivities rather than on textual operations, [cultural studies] understands 'politics' as access to the material base of [power, knowledge, and resources]" (Zavarzadeh and Morton p. 208). Cultural studies also "insists on the necessity to address [these] central, urgent, and disturbing questions of a society and a culture [in] the most rigorous intellectual way . . . available" (Hall p. 11). It thus "constitutes one of the points of tension and change at the frontiers of intellectual and academic life, pushing for new questions, new models, and new ways of study, testing the fine lines between intellectual rigor and social relevance" (Hall p. 11). For only when all these concerns are addressed and all United States identifiable groups and their differences are foregrounded on equal terms through the exploratory lens of cultural studies—one thing that must take place both within and outside the Italian/American community—can the notion of multiculturalism function effectively as a useful expression of difference,[33] leading ultimately to a more level field of play for critical discourse and intellectual exchange.

# *Notes*

## Preface

1. See his *Italian Americans: Into the Twilight of Ethnicity* (Englewood Cliffs, NJ: Prentice-Hall, 1985).

2. See his *Beyond Ethnicity: Consent and Descent in American Culture* (New York: Oxford University Press, 1988).

3. For those not familiar with C. S. Peirce and his general notions of semiotics, I would point out two helpful books: John K. Sheriff, *The Fate of Meaning: Charles Peirce, Structuralism, and Literature* (Princeton: Princeton University Press, 1989, and Floyd Merrell, *A Peirce Primer* (Toronto: Canadian Scholars Press, 1995).

4. Herbert J. Gans, *The Urban Villagers* (New York: The Free Press, 1963); Joseph Lopreato, *Italian Americans* (New York: Random House, 1970); and Richard Gambino, *Blood of My Blood* (New York: Doubleday, 1974 [Guernica, 1996]). I would, however, distance myself from certain ideological aspects of some of these writers. Richard Gambino, for example, tells us that African Americans are more rhythmic, whereas Italian Americans are more melodious. He would have us believe that such "observations about music and body and language are trivial." On the contrary, such observations indeed underscore a long-lived stereotype we should eschew. See his *Blood of My Blood:* especially pp. 331–33.

5. I would point out here parenthetically that the basic tenet of Sollors's notion of consent and descent is, to be sure, implied if not already articulated, albeit differently, both in Aaron's notion of his three stages of the hyphenated writer and in Basile Green's analogous phenomenon of what she sees within the history of Italian/American narrative, when she discussed her four stages of "the need for assimilation," "revulsion," "counterrevulsion," and "rooting" (see her *The Italian-American Novel: A Document of the Interaction of Two Cultures* (Madison, NJ: Fairleigh Dickinson University Press, 1974), especially chapters 4–7).

6. Francesco Loriggio's recent collection of essays dealing with both the Italian American and Italian Canadian implies such a conflation of groups. See his *Literary History and Social Pluralism: The Literature of the Italian Emigration,* ed. Francesco Loriggio (Toronto: Guernica Editions, 1996).

7. Paolo Valesio, "The Writer Between Two Worlds: The Italian Writer in the United States," *DIFFERENTIA review of italian thought* 3/4 (Spring/Autumn 1989): 259–76, and "Conclusione: I fuochi della tribú," *Poesaggio,* eds. Peter Carravetta and Paolo Valesio (Treviso: Pagus, 1993), pp. 255–90; Peter Carravetta, "Introduzione: Poesaggio," *Poessaggio,* pp. 9–26; Paolo Giordano, "Emigrants, Expatriates and/or Exiles: Italian Literature in the United States," *Beyond the Margin: Readings in Italian Americana,* eds. Paolo A. Giordano and Anthony Julian Tamburri (Madison, NJ: Fairleigh Dickinson University Press, 1997), pp. 221–38.

8. Here, I would underscore William Boelhower's warning not to fall into the same trap of the essentialist monoculturalists (see his *Through a Glass Darkly: Ethnic Semiosis in American Literature* (New York: Oxford University Press, 1987 [Helvetia, 1984]) p. 20).

9. For a conservative reaction to my *To Hyphenate or Not to Hyphenate,* see Franco Ricci, "Disenfranchisement, or 'Your Life or Your Life'," in *The Flight of Ulysses. Studies in Honor of Emmanuel Hatzantonis,* ed. Augustus A. Mastri. AdI. Studi & Testi 1 (Chapel Hill, NC: Annali d'italianistica, 1997) pp. 348–59.

For discussions on alternatives to the usual hyphenated term, "Italian-American," see the following two cogent essays: Ben Lawton, "What is 'ItalianAmerican' Cinema?" *Voices in Italian Americana* 6.1 (1995): 27–51, and Luigi Fontanella, "Poeti Emigrati Ed Emigranti Poeti negli Stati Uniti," *Italica* (forthcoming).

## Acknowledgments

1. It was Paolo Giordano who first invited me to participate in an Italian/American seminar at the 1981 MLA convention; there I spoke about Helen Barolini's *Umbertina,* which was first introduced to me by Teodolina Barolini.

## 1. In (Re)cognition of the Italian/American Writer

1. Of numerous historical cases, I have in mind the egregious examples of Native Americans and African Americans.

2. I use the adjective *other* in this essay as an umbrella term to indicate that which either has not yet been canonized, that is, considered a valid category, by the dominant culture (read, for instance, MLA) or, if already accepted, has been so in a seemingly conditional and a somewhat sporadic manner. Namely, when it is a matter of convenience on the part of the dominant culture.

As this book goes to press, the MLA has accepted a proposal for an Italian/American discussion group to begin its five-year stint with the 1998 annual convention.

3. This is also true for the more popular press. In a Gannett News Service daily, *Journal and Courier* (Lafayette, IN), DeWayne Wickham, a national columnist for the Gannett News Service, wrote in favor of using the metaphor of "stew" rather than "melting pot" in describing the racial/ethnic composition of the United States. See his, "U. S. is stew, not a melting pot" (11 March 1992).

4. See my *To Hyphenate or Not To Hyphenate?* p. 48.

5. See Aijaz Ahmad's response, "Jameson's Rhetoric of Otherness and the 'National Allegory,'" *Social Text* 17 (1987): 4; now in *In Theory* (New York: Verso Press, 1992).

6. Because of nuances, subtleties, and semantic and grammatical differences between the various English languages spoken throughout the world, I believe it is necessary to recognize these different languages. And since *American*, as adjective, can refer to any one of the many geographical and cultural zones of the Americas, for the sake of convenience and economy, I shall refer to United States English in the following pages as, simply, English.

7. While there does not yet exist an exhaustive study on the various categories of the Italian/American writer, Flaminio Di Biagi has offered us a valiant first step in that direction. See his "A Reconsideration: Italian American Writers: Notes for a Wider Consideration," *MELUS* 14.3/4 (1987): 141–51.
Also, with regard to the Italian writer in the United States, I would remind the reader of Paolo Valesio's substantive essay, "The Writer Between Two Worlds: The Italian Writer in the United States," *Differentia* 3/4 (Spring/Autumn 1989): 259–76. Gustavo Pérez Firmat, in an analogous manner, takes the matter one step further and offers an equally cogent exegesis of the bilingual writer—in his case the Cuban American—who, in adopting both languages (at times separately, at other times together in the same text), occupies what he considers the "space between" (p. 21); see his "Spic Chic: Spanglish as Equipment for Living," *The Caribbean Review* 15.3 (Winter 1987): 20ff.

8. In stating such, I do not intend to ignore the bilingual Italian/American writer: s/he who operates in both linguistic melieus. Hence, the absence of Joseph Tusiani in this essay; and possible topics of discussion in any further versions of this type of study may also indeed include the works in English by someone like Mario Fratti, Peter Carravetta, and/or Lucia Capria Hammond.

9. Jean-François Lyotard, *The Postmodern Condition: A Report on Knowledge*, trans. Geoff Bennington and Brian Massumi with a foreword by Fredric Jameson (Minneapolis: University of Minnesota Press, 1984) p. xiv.
An acute rehearsal of a "postmodern" critical analysis specifically focused on Italian/American literature can be found in Fred L. Gardaphé's excellent essay, "Visibility or Invisibility: The Postmodern Prerogative in the Italian/American Narrative," *Almanacco*, Vol. II, No. 1 (1992): 24–33.

10. With regard to a discussion on the general notion of canon, I leave that for another setting which allows more space for such an encompassing argument. For more on the notion of canons, see *Canons*, ed. Robert von Hallberg (Chicago: University of Chicago Press, 1984), especially Charles Altieri, "An Idea and Ideal of a Literary Canon," and Richard Ohmann, "The Shaping of a Canon: U.S. Fiction, 1960–1975": 41–64, 377–402.

11. See his "Moments in Italian-American Cinema: From *Little Caesar* to Coppola and Scorsese," *From the Margin: Writings in Italian Americana*, eds. Anthony Julian Tamburri, Paolo A. Giordano, and Fred L. Gardaphé (West Lafayette: Purdue University Press, 1991) p. 374.

12. He then continues to say that "in such writing Italian-American experiences and values are delineated in dramatic interaction with the mainstream culture." See his review of *Delano in America & Other Early Poems*, by John J. Soldo, *Italian Americana* 1.1 (1974) 124–25.

13. One problem with definitions of this sort is that they exclude any discourse on the analogous notion of, for example, the "hyphenate" filmmaker. I refer to Daniel Aaron's "The Hyphenate Writer and American Letters," *Smith Alumnae Quarterly* (July 1964): 213–17; later revised in *Rivista di Studi Anglo-Americani* 3.4–5 (1984–85): 11–28.

14. Dana Gioia, "What Is Italian-American Poetry?" in *Poetry Pilot* (December 1991): 3–10.

15. One may also take issue with Gioia's revisionist history of Italian/American poetry dating back to Lorenzo Da Ponte, or his statements on Italian language that *"Toscano* [is] the standard literary dialect of written Italian."* Da Ponte was an Italian who, as an adult socialized in Italy, came to the United States under questionable circumstances and, as the first Italian professor in North America, became a member of a privileged class. This, I would contend, is quite different from that Italian/American literature one finds rearing its head at the beginning of the twentieth century. With regard to the *questione della lingua*, I would only point out that Italian is a national language which has evolved over the centuries, influenced heavily by its many dialects, *fiorentino* included. But there is not really any one dialect today that is considered the nucleus of standard Italian.

16. What is important to keep in mind is that one can perceive different degrees of ethnicity in literature, film, or any other art form, as Aaron already did with his "hyphenate writer."

17. Origins of recent Italian/American self-inventory can be dated back to Rose Basile Green's 1974 book-length study *The Italian-American Novel: A Document of the Interaction of Two Cultures* (Madison, NJ: Fairleigh Dickinson University Press). Since then, the field of Italian/American criticism has emerged sporadically in conference proceedings and, more specifically, in an acutely

original contribution by Robert Viscusi ("*De vulgari eloquentia*: An Approach to the Language of Italian American Fiction," *Yale Italian Studies*, Vol. I, No. 3 [1981]: 21–38) and in Helen Barolini's best-selling anthology, *The Dream Book: An Anthology of Writing by Italian American Women* (Schocken, 1985). The recent publication of the above-mentioned *From the Margin: Writings in Italian Americana*, the establishment of journals such as *la bella figura* and *VIA: Voices in Italian Americana*, and the resumption of the journal *Italian Americana* further represent the rise of an indigenous interest in the critical study of Italian/American culture. Moreover, in this category, there is Fred L. Gardaphé's book-length study, *Italian Signs, American Streets* (Duke University Press, 1996).

In addition, the fall 1987 (1989) issue of *MELUS* was devoted to Italian/American literature and film, and the *South Atlantic Quarterly* dedicated an entire issue to the work of Don DeLillo. These are but two examples of interest in Italian/American cultural studies by non-Italian/American scholarly organizations. Finally, there are the special issues of *Differentia* 6/7 (Spring/Fall 1994) and *Canadian Journal of Italian Studies* Vol. XIX, No. 53 (1996).

18. See his "The Hyphenate Writer and American Letters." Here, I quote from the original version.

19. Aaron is not alone in discerning this multi-stage phenomenon in the ethnic writer. Ten years after Aaron's original version, Rose Basile Green spoke to an analogous phenomenon within the history of Italian/American narrative; then she discussed her four stages of "the need for assimilation," "revulsion," "counterrevulsion," and "rooting" (see her *The Italian-American Novel: A Document of the Interaction of Two Cultures*, especially chapters 4–7).

As I have already rehearsed elsewhere (*To Hyphenate or Not To Hyphenate?*), I would contend that there are cases where a grammar rule/usage may connote an inherent prejudice, no matter how slight. Besides the hyphen, another example that comes to mind is the usage of the male pronoun for the impersonal, whereas all of its alternatives, such as *s/he, she/he*, or *he/she*, are shunned.

20. In order to avoid repetitive textual citations, I should point out that Aaron's description of these three stages is found on page 214.

I would also point out that Daniel Aaron's three stages of the hyphenate writer have their analogs in the different generations that Joseph Lopreato (*Italian Americans* [New York: Random House, 1979]) and Paul Campisi ("Ethnic Family Patterns: The Italian Family in the United States" [*The American Journal of Sociology* 53.6 (May 1948)]) each describe and analyze: "peasant," "first-," "second-," and "third-generation." With regard to this fourth generation— Lopreato's and Campisi's "third generation"—I would state here, briefly, that I see the writer of this generation subsequent to Aaron's "third-stage writer," who eventually returns to his/her ethnicity through the process of re(dis)covery.

21. The danger is, of course, metaphorically speaking, of adding fuel to the fire, since there is no guarantee that such a strategy may convince the dominant culture to abandon its negative preconceptions.

22. There are undoubtedly other considerations regarding Aaron's three categories. He goes on to discuss them further, providing examples from the Jewish and Black contingents of American writers.

23. One caveat with regard to this neat linear classification of writers should not go unnoticed. There undoubtedly exists a clear distinction between the first-stage writer and the third-stage writer. The distinction, however, between the first- and second-stage writer, and especially that between the second- and third-stage writer, may at times seem blurred. In his rewrite, in fact, Aaron himself has recognized this blurring of boundaries, as these "stages cannot be clearly demarcated" (p. 13). This becomes apparent when one discusses works such as Mario Puzo's *The Godfather* or Helen Barolini's *Umbertina*. More significant is the fact that these various stages of hyphenation may actually manifest themselves along the trajectory of one author's literary career. I believe, for instance, that a writer like Helen Barolini manifests, to date, such a phenomenon. Her second novel, *Love in the Middle Ages*, revolves around a love story involving a middle-aged couple, whereas ethnicity and cultural origin serve chiefly as a backdrop. Considering what Aaron states in his rewrite, and what seems to be of common opinion—that the respective experiences of Jews and Italians in the United States were similar in some says (pp. 23–24 especially)—it should appear as no strange coincidence, then, that the ethnic backgrounds of the two main characters of Barolini's second novel are, for the woman, Italian, and, for the man, Jewish.

24. For a cogent example of ethnic signs relegated to the margin—what at first glance may seem to be an absence—see Gardaphé's discussion of DeLillo (pp. 30–31), where he also rehearses his notions of the "visible" and "invisible" Italian/American writers.

25. Again I refer to Gardaphé's analyses of Rimanelli and DeLillo (pp. 28–31), the first the parodist (the "visible"), the second the assimilated (the "invisible").

26. *Principles of Philosophy* in *Collected Papers*, eds., Charles Hartshorne and Paul Weiss, Vol. 1 (Cambridge, MA: Harvard University Press, 1960). Peirce offers numerous versions of his definitions and examples of these three modes of being throughout his writings, especially in this volume.

27. "By a feeling, I mean an instance of that kind of consciousness which involves no analysis, comparison or any process whatsoever, nor consists in whole or in part of any act by which one stretch of consciousness is distinguished from another" (1.306).

28. Secondness, as "the mode of being of one thing which consists in how a second object is" (1.24), provokes a "forcible modification of our ways of thinking [which is] the influence of the world of fact or *experience*" (1.321; emphasis textual).

29. "The third category of elements of phenomena consists of what we call laws when we contemplate them from the outside only, but which when we see both sides of the shield we call thoughts" (1.420).

30. I make this distinction in order not to contradict myself vis-à-vis Peirce's use of the term *real* when he discusses secondness. There, he states: "[T]he real is that which insists upon forcing its way to recognition as *something* other than the mind's creation" (1.325).

31. As an aside, I would merely point out that Gadamer's notion of one's anterior relationship to the subject may also come into play. I shall reserve this, however, for another time and place. See Hans-Georg Gadamer, *Truth and Method* (New York: The Crossroad Publishing Company, 1988) p. 263.

32. Indeed, I would reiterate my contention that, in a similar vein, any number of these stages may even be inferred in a single work of a writer.

33. Michael M. J. Fischer, "Ethnicity and the Post-Modern Arts of Memory," in *Writing Culture: The Poetics and Politics of Ethnography*, ed. James Clifford and George E. Marcus (Berkeley: University of California Press, 1986) p. 195.

34. For more on *italianità*, see Tamburri, Giordano, and Gardaphé, "Introduction," *From the Margin: Writings in Italian Americana*.

35. See his "Cybernetics and Ghosts" and "Whom Do We Write For," in *The Uses of Literature*, tr. Patrick Creagh (New York: Harcourt Brace Jovanovich, 1986). These essays were originally published in 1967 and 1967–68, respectively, and are now available in Italian in Italo Calvino's volume of collected essays, *Una pietra sopra* (Turin: Einaudi, 1980).

36. That is, Calvino foresaw a reader with "epistemological, semantic, practical, and methodological requirements he [would] want to compare [as] examples of symbolic procedures and the construction of logical patterns" ("Whom Do We Write For," pp. 84–85).
Caveat lector: What I have in mind here is that any reader's response in this semiotic process is, to some degree or another, content/context-sensitive.

37. See, for example, V.N. Volosinov, *Marxism and the Philosophy of Language*, trans. Ladislav Matejka and I. R. Titunik (Cambridge, MA: Harvard University Press, 1986): "A sign does not simply exist as a part of reality—it reflects and refracts another reality. Therefore, it may distort that reality or be true to it, or may perceive it from a special point of view, and so forth. Every sign is subject to the criteria of ideological evaluation (i.e., whether it is true, false, correct, fair, good, etc.). The domain of ideology coincides with the domain of signs. They equate with one another. Wherever a sign is present ideology is present also. *Everything ideological possesses semiotic value*" (p. 10).

38. This, for Bakhtin, is dialogized heteroglossia. A work, language, or culture undergoes dialogization "when it becomes relativized, depriviliged, aware

of competing definitions for the same things." Only by "breaking through to its own meaning and own expression across an environment full of alien words and variously evaluating accents, harmonizing with some of the elements in this environment and striking a dissonance with others, is [a word—or for that matter, language, or culture] able, in this dialogized process, to shape its own stylistic profile and tone" (Mikhail M. Bakhtin, *The Dialogic Imagination,* ed. Michael Holquist, trans. Caryl Emerson and Michael Holquist [Austin: University of Texas Press, 1981] p. 258ff).

39. See Paolo A. Giordano, "From Southern Italian Immigrant to Reluctant American: Joseph Tusiani's *Gente Mia and Other Poems,*" in *From the Margin,* p. 317.

40. See his "Song of the Bicentennial (V)," in *Gente Mia and Other Poems* (Stone Park, IL: Italian Cultural Center, 1978).

41. Basile Green expresses an analogous notion in her section on Puzo in *The Italian-American Novel.*

42. In this regard, I would refer the reader to her recent collection of essays, *Chiaroscuro. Essays of Identity.* VIA Folios 11 (West Lafayette, IN: Bordighera, 1997).

43. I first dealt with the gender/ethnic dilemma in *Umbertina* in my "Helen Barolini's *Umbertina*: The Ethnic/Gender Dilemma," in *Italian Americans Celebrate Life: The Arts and Popular Culture,* ed. Paola A. Sensi-Isolani and Anthony Julian Tamburri (Staten Island, NY: The American Italian Historical Association, 1990) pp. 29–44. In addition, as already mentioned, in her later novel, *Love in the Middle Ages,* the subject matter is much more universal insofar as ethnicity and cultural origin are backdrops to a love story involving a middle-aged couple.

44. See Russo's essay, "The Poetics of Gilbert Sorrentino," *Rivista di Studi Anglo-Americani* 3 (1984–85): 281–303.

45. *Vort* 2 (1974): 19. I owe this quote to John Paul Russo, "The Poetics of Gilbert Sorrentino."

46. Again, I refer the reader to John Paul Russo's "The Poetics of Gilbert Sorrentino."

47. Marshall Grossman, "The Violence of the Hyphen in Judeo-Christian," *Social Text* 22 (1989): 115–22.

48. See my *To Hyphenate or Not To Hyphenate?* pp. 43–47.

49. For more on the notions of heteroglossia and dialogism, see Bakhtin, *The Dialogic Imagination,* pp. 426, 428 passim.

50. This is where I would underscore William Boelhower's notion that there is no clear "blueprint," as he calls it, of ethnic categories, and that each sit-

uation is dependent on both the conception and perception of the "ethnic" group in question (p. 20).

51. Lenard J. Davis, *Resisting Novels: Ideology and Fiction* (London: Methuen, 1987) p. 24.

52. Linda Hutcheon, *The Politics of Postmodernism* (New York: Routledge, 1989) p. 49.

## 2. Tony Ardizzone's "Expressive" *Evening News*

1. Tony Ardizzone, *The Evening News* (Athens, GA: University of Georgia Press, 1986). Some of the stories I deal with in this chapter are now included in *Taking It Home. Stories from the Neighborhood* (Champaign-Urbana: University of Illinois Press, 1996).

2. The Flannery O'Connor Award is sponsored by the University of Georgia Press, which has, over the years, unearthed some fine Italian/American writers. Along with Ardizzone, other winners include Salvatore La Puma (1987) and Rita Ciresi (1991).

3. As thin-skinned Italian Americans, I have in mind those persons who see absolutely no thematic value to the works of those like Mario Puzo, Nick Pileggi, Frances Ford Coppola, Nancy Savoca, or Martin Scorsese, for example, because such works, in their opinion, glorify a negative stereotype. This is, to be sure, a curiously superficial reaction by the likes of those who then turn around and call for the biographical rendition, written or visual, of the life of someone like Amedeo Giannini (something which, in fact, is now available from the University of California Press). Not only this, but they call for the preservation of the Italo Balbo monument donated by Mussolini, or extol the "virtues," as they say, of Mussolini's corporate state, or, last but surely not least, invite Italy's leading neo-Fascist, Gianfranco Fini, not to mention Mussolini's own ideologically sympathetic granddaughter, to their annual gala event.

4. Again, I remind the reader that the distinction I point out between these categories is by no means to be perceived as an indication of any sort of hierarchical valence.

5. Indeed, other writers have engaged in direct conversation with their readers over the centuries; one need only think back to Dante. However, given the success and popularity of Italo Calvino's penultimate novel, *If on a winter's night a traveler* (HBJ, 1979), this technique has become increasing identified with him.

6. See Seymour Chatman, *Story and Discourse* (Ithaca: Cornell University Press, 1978) p. 151.

7. For an example of those who, directly or indirectly, classified Italian Americans in this manner, see Bernard Rosen, "Race, Ethnicity and the Achievement Syndrome," *American Sociological Review* 24 (October 1959): 47–60; William Whyte's study also proves unflatteringly race-conscious (see his *Street Corner Society* [Chicago: University of Chicago Press, 1960, 2nd edition]). Such notions notwithstanding, I would point out that while this may seem to be a negative commentary of sociologists early on, today the notion of Italians and Italian Americans as people of color is a more recently positive consideration. See Lucia Chavola Birnbaum's "The History of Sicilians," *Italians and Italian Americans and the Media*, eds. Mary Jo Bona and Anthony Julian Tamburri (Staten Island: AIHA, 1996) pp. 206–15, and Rose Romano's essay, "Coming Out Olive," in Loriggio, *Literary History and Social Pluralism*, pp. 161–75.

8. One need only think back to some of the classic names associated with Italian Americans and Hollywood, such as Rudolph Valentino, Frank Sinatra, Dean Martin.

9. One of the less sensitive figures of the Italian and/or Italian/American father figure is found in Rachel Guido deVries's *Tender Warriors* (Firebrand, 1986). Other figures can be found in the fiction of Helen Barolini's *Umbertina* (Seaview, 1979), in Mario Puzo's *The Godfather* (Putnam, 1969), or in the poetry of Gianna Patriarca's *Italian Women and Other Tragedies* (Guernica, 1994).

10. At this point, it is also important to note that one of Ardizzone's early novels is thematically couched in the metaphor of baseball: *Heart of the Order* (Holt, 1986).

11. Such notions of only hard work and economic success as personal goals and end-alls are reported by some of the earlier voices of Italian/American sociology. See, for example, Joseph Lopreato, *Italian Americans*; Richard Gambino, *Blood of My Blood*; or, especially, Herbert J. Gans, *The Urban Villagers*. We shall see more of this in the first part of the next chapter on Helen Barolini's *Umbertina*.

12. See Mark Shaffer, "Streets of Chicago Yield Faith and Fire," *The Washington Times Magazine* (24 November, 1986).

13. The question of double standards is well documented in various studies on women in Italian, Italian immigrant, and Italian/American communities. For more information, see Chapter Three, note 13 of this study.

14. We shall see a similar situation, in Chapter Three, in Helen Barolini's *Umbertina*, where Umbertina's daughter, Carla, engages in a similar act of self-destruction vis-à-vis the notion of double standards and its negative effects on women.

15. Throughout the story Peter utters Latin phrases from the liturgy. Be they ironic or not, they serve to keep alive and underscore old-world ways. In fact, one may see this connection both in form and substance. Latin as form is reminiscent

of the old-world ways of the church. However, the positioning of these phrases may also underscore a point of the story. In this regard, I would point to the end of the story where, after the three seem to be heading back to some old form of family structure, Peter utters: "Sicut erat in principio, et nunc, et semper: et saecula saeculorum," where the subject of *erat* could easily now be *family*.

16. For a sense of arbitrariness to which I allude here, I have in mind, specifically, Peirce's definition of sign, which states: "A sign or *representamen*, is something which stands to somebody for something in some respect or capacity. It addresses somebody, that is creates in the mind of that person an equivalent sign, or perhaps a more developed sign. That sign which it creates I call the *interpretant* of the first sign. The sign stands for something, its *object*. It stands for that object, not in all respects, but in reference to a sort of idea, which I have sometimes called the *ground* of the representamen" (2.228). Another definition that Peirce offered during the same period refers to a sign as "anything which determines something else (*interpretant*) to refer to an object to which itself refers (its *object*) in the same way, the interpretant becoming in turn a sign, and so *ad infinitum*" (2.303).

17. What is significant here is that the so-called sons and grandsons of the people Nonna once knew are really the newly arrived immigrants, Mexicans. What also becomes significant is that Nonna initially thought of them as different, as they come out of "their strange stores," a type of thinking, we might imagine, similar to what the established non-Italians thought of the newly arrived Italian immigrants in their day.

18. I remind the reader of the titles I mentioned in footnote 9 of this chapter.

19. At the risk of bordering on what some may perceive as the vulgar, I would note parenthetically that we should also not ignore Ardizzone's probable use of metonymy here, as the description of the kiss can readily afford an interpretation of *kiss* as a sign of the act of lovemaking. The preparation to kiss, especially, is reminiscent of the very moment before vaginal penetration. This said, I would also call attention to the pink sofa, at least for this reader, as reminiscent of Aretha Franklin's "Pink Cadillac." The rest I leave to my reader's imagination.

While I feel compelled as a critical reader to point this out, I feel equally obliged to note the subtlety and lightness with which Ardizzone so capably communicates this and other messages, as I have tried to show, throughout his collection.

20. Of the reviews written, just about everyone concurs on this point. In fact, "Nonna" has been anthologized numerous times afterwards.

21. Another ambiguity is in the description of him as "the dark man behind the counter." His ethnicity, though not Italian, is signaled here by the same sign Ardizzone used in other stories to signal previous characters' Italian

ethnicity. Such a use should not come as a surprise since both groups, Mexicans and Italians, share, among other things, a Mediterranean origin.

22. Be it because it is his first book of short stories or be it the subject matter, whatever the case, *The Evening News* has yet to have a full-fledged essay dedicated to it. One of the better reviews, both in length and insight, is by Mark Shaffer, who points out the similarity between Gino's specific world and the rest of Ardizzone's characters. See his "Streets of Chicago Yield Faith and Fire," *The Washington Times Magazine* (24 November, 1986).

23. I borrow this concept from the anonymous review of *The Evening News* in *Booklist* (15 September, 1986).

24. I am aware of the irony involved in my paraphrasing of Booth (*The Rhetoric of Fiction* [Chicago: University of Chicago Press, 1960]). But it is true that we, in our poststructuralist theoretical mind-frame, must not forget where the foundations of some of our new ideas lie. Our debt is too big to ignore.

25. Jim Spencer, "N. Sider's Tales of Urban Life," *Chicago Tribune* (13 January, 1987), Section 5: 3. Another reviewer suggests that Ardizzone become "a free agent from his past" (Mary Elizabeth Courtney, "Making Games of Allegories" *Columbus Dispatch* [19 October, 1986]). It is his attachment to his past that indeed has made Ardizzone the Italian/American writer he is. Humor, as Courtney would have it, is not necessarily a requirement, it is a choice of style, technique, and rhetoric.

## 3. Helen Barolini's "Comparative" *Umbertina*

1. In comparing the Jewish immigrant's assimilation process to the Italian's, Riesman stated: "As the Italian immigrant has to go through a gastronomically bleached and bland period before he can publicly eat garlic and spaghetti, so the Jewish immigrant must also become Americanized before he can comfortably take pride in his ethnic cuisine, idiom, and gesture" (David Riesman, "Introduction," *Commentary on the American Scene: Portraits of Jewish Life in America,* ed. Elliot E. Cohen [New York: Alfred A. Knopf, 1953] p. xv).

2. Both Joseph Lopreato and Paul Campisi ("Ethnic Family Patterns: The Italian Family in the United States," *The American Journal of Sociology* 53:6 [May 1948]: 443–49) use similar tags in distinguishing the various Italian/American generations: "peasant," "first-," and so on. The common practice among sociologists, however, is to use a slightly different set of tags. Thus, Lopreato's and Campisi's "peasant" family corresponds to the more widely used "first-generation" family; their "first-," "second-," and "third-generation" families correspond to the more popular "second-," "third-," and "fourth-generation" families. In this essay I have opted for the more commonly used set of tags, which are also those Barolini occasionally adopts throughout her novel.

3. We can find those Italian Americans with the seemingly insignificant desire to Americanize their names: Giacomo and Benedetto soon want to be called Jake and Ben. We also encounter the more enterprising "status climber" who makes attempts at all sorts of endeavors that the previous generation cannot understand: such is the case with Paolo, soon to become Paul, who, "filled with ambitions for himself that had nothing to do with the kind of hard work and drudgery the rest of the family engaged in" and believing himself "too smart to waste his time around two-bit family stores" (pp. 123–24), suddenly finds himself without a home since he refuses to do his part in the family business.

4. I quote from the original printing of *Umbertina* (New York: Seaview Books, 1979). Since then, the novel has been reprinted on two other occasions. In 1980, a Bantam Paperback edition appeared; in 1989, Ayers Company Publishers, Inc., of Salem, NH, produced a "Reprint Edition" of the 1979 printing.

5. See Richard Gambino, *Blood of My Blood*, p. 130.

6. Herbert J. Gans, *The Urban Villagers*, p. 129.

7. We have already seen this notion expressed by her father in his conversation with Tina.

8. At other points during her story, we can find Tina comparing the two different countries, as well as herself in each place. For example:

> Her sense of illimitable possibilities awaiting her could not stop at the softness and languor of Rome, beneath which, she knew, there were deadly poisons of unrest and discontent. Rome is too old, she thought; nothing matters anymore. In New York everything does. In New York she felt competitiveness throbbing in the air and became frenetic because of so much going on, because of the sense of space to fill. In Rome she was squelched by the sense of time: Everything had already been thought of and done—it was time to rest and savor. (p. 300)

To her future husband, Jason, she later described herself in the following manner:

> "I'm two different people, Jason. The Italian part, when I get back to Rome, likes civilized comforts: eating well, having Giovanna go out and do the shopping and prepare the *caffè-latte* for me each morning while I sleep. Here I like to get all dressed up and go shopping and have Mauro cut my hair. I dress in blankets and clogs when I'm in the States and sometimes don't comb my hair for days. I drive my grandmother in Gloversville crazy when I go see her because she says I'm a hippy. But in Rome I'm purely a sybarite." (p. 323)

9. Also significant here is her father's educational background. While it is true that he too was very much part of the Old World, he held a university degree, and Tina initially identified intellectually with his side of her heritage.

10. Umbertina became a sort of past idol for Tina, and only after she makes a trip back to Umbertina's native village in Italy does she begin to understand truly the hardships that all her relatives who came before her, the women especially, had encountered.

11. After Tina's conversation with her grandfather, when he objected to her choice of Italian as a field of study, she demonstrates a good deal of understanding with regard to his ethnic dilemma. She thought:

> What was wrong with the immigrant's children that left them so distrustful of their *italianità*? It was, she knew, the burden of the second generation, who had been forced too swiftly to tear the Old World from themselves and put on the new. They were the sons and daughters ashamed of their illiterate, dialect-speaking forebears—the goatherds and peasants and fishermen who came over to work and survive and give these very children, the estranged ones, America. Tina was torn between compassion and indignation: She understood him, why couldn't he understand her? (p. 398)

12. Marguerite is surely the most complex of all the characters in the novel. Indeed, an analysis of her character vis-à-vis the patriarchal society in which she was raised would make for an interesting study in itself, which warrants more time and space than what can be afforded in this chapter. This notwithstanding, it should not be ignored that her lack of vision most surely stems, at least in part, from her ethnic and gender dilemma.

13. For more on the Italian peasant woman in Italy, see Charlotte Gowers Chapman, *Milocca, A Sicilian Village* (Cambridge, MA: Schenkan, 1971) and Ann Cornelison, *Women of the Shadows* (New York: Vantage Books, 1977). For more on the Italian immigrant woman in America, see Valentine Rossilli Winsey, "The Italian American Woman Who Arrived in the United States Before World War I," *Studies in Italian American Social History*, ed. Francesco Cordasco (New Jersey: Rowman and Littlefield, 1975), Virginia Yans-McLaughlin, *Family and Community. Italian Immigrants in Buffalo, 1880–1930* (Ithaca: Cornell, 1977), and Betty Boyd Caroli, Robert F. Harney, and Lydio F. Tomasi, eds. *The Italian Immigrant Woman in North America* (Toronto: The Multicultural History Society of Ontario, 1978).

14. Tina herself soon begins to understand how her father had led Marguerite from her own aspirations, and that he had never seen his wife as a woman:

> There was never time, Tina remembered her mother saying, to live as artists, the two of them. The babies and moving absorbed Marguerite and soon her vision of herself swerved. Alberto relied on words as Marguerite did on her feelings for truth. When he told her that she should be happy with things as they were—with her successful husband, her beautiful home, her fine daughters—and not pine after what was lost or the illusion

of her fulfillment, she tried to examine why her feelings mistrusted him. It was not what he had said before. (p. 333)

And: "Tina knew her father's disappointments; she knew he had suffered from her mother's unhappiness and restlessness; *'la mamma è bambina,' 'la mamma è difficile,'* he used to write to her in college, showing how protective he had to be, and all the time he was dead wrong—her mother wasn't a child, her mother was a woman" (p. 405). Sensitive and gentle as he may have believed to have been, it becomes clear that Alberto was always trying to relegate his wife to the homemaker role.

15. Harriet Perry, "The Metonymic Definition of Female and the Concept of Honour Among Italian Immigrant Families in Toronto," in *The Italian Immigrant Woman in North America*, p. 223.

16. Again, we see that Alberto had reneged on his initial promise that they would live together as artists: proposing, Alberto said they would learn each other's language and grow to be artists together, although it would be wise, he thought, if they started a family soon.

17. As we shall see in Tina's story, abortion figures as a violation of both the female's body and psyche.

18. Barbara Hayler, "Abortion," *Signs: Journal of Women in Cultural and Society* 5:2 (1979): 332.

19. Mary Daly, *Gyn/ecology: The Metaethics of Radical Feminism* (Boston: Beacon Press, 1978) p. 245.

20. At the same time, she also reconciles with Jason, thereby prospering personally also.

21. See Rose Basile Green, "The Italian Immigrant Woman in American Literature," in *The Italian Immigrant Woman in North America*, p. 342.

## 4. Giose Rimanelli's "Synthetic" *Benedetta in Guysterland*

1. Giose Rimanelli, *Benedetta in Guysterland. A Liquid Novel,* preface by Fred L. Gardaphé (Montréal, Quebec, and Cheektowaga, NY: Guernica Editions, Inc., 1993). Unless otherwise stated, all translations of secondary texts from the Italian are mine.

2. This poem was originally included in Palazzeschi's *L'incendiario* (1910). Translation: Surely it is a risk to bare, / to write things in such a way, / since there are professors today, / everywhere ("And Let Me Have My Fun" [*The Arsonist* (1910)]).

3. As we saw in Chapter One, Michael M. J. Fischer tells us that "ethnicity is something reinvented and reinterpreted in each generation by each

individual," which, in the end, is a way of "finding a voice or style that does not violate one's *several components of identity*" constituting the specificities of each individual. Thus, ethnicity—and more specifically in this case, one's *Italian-ness*—is redefined and reinterpreted on the basis of each individual's time and place, and is therefore always new and different with respect to his/her own historical specificities vis-à-vis the dominant culture ("Ethnicity and the Post-Modern Arts of Memory," p. 195; my emphasis).

4. I shall use *Guysterland* as an abbreviated form of *Benedetta in Guyster-land. A Liquid Novel.*

5. I refer to Maria Corti's essay, "Testi or microtesti? I racconti di Marco-valdo di Italo Calvino" (*Strumenti critici* 27 [June 1975]: 182–93), where she de-fines the macrotext as follows: "Una raccolta di racconti può essere un semplice insieme di testi or *configurarsi essa stessa come un macrotesto*; nel secondo caso ogni racconto è una ministruttura che si articola entro una macrostruttura, donde il carattere funzionale e 'informativo' della raccolta; nel primo caso la definizione di una raccolta come insieme di testi è soltanto tautologica" (p. 182; emphasis added. Translation: A collection of stories can be a simple gathering of texts or it can take the form of a macrotext; in the second case every story is a ministructure that defines itself within the macrotext, whence the collection's functional and "informative" character; in the first case the definition of a col-lection as a gathering of texts is merely repetitive.).

6. For clarity's sake, I shall use the term *novel*, for now, to refer to the mi-crotext "Benedetta in Guysterland," whereas the term *book*, as has already been used, refers to the overall collection of texts, Gardaphé's and Rimanelli's.

7. I shall reserve my comments on the "Appendix" for another setting, since they include different voices of actual, different people. However, I would state here, for my reader's benefit and curiosity, that Rimanelli not only admits again to his deliberate sacking of all sorts of works of art originating out of west-ern civilization's tradition and its popular culture, but he offers a bibliography of the sources in Appendix 3 and annotates his first chapter, identifying all the sources, in Appendix 4.

8. In a sense, this microtext, as therefore the entire book, throws the reader *in medias res.* The opening words—"Just after finishing *this*, I went out in the open . . . " (p. 27; emphasis added)—make reference to a previous act/thing, that being the act of writing and/or the actual finished product. This beginning, however, I would contend, also adds a personal touch in that it simulates an ex-change between author and reader, as if the author were handing the book over to the reader.

9. I use the label "Benedetta in Guysterland," that which I have already used to describe one of Rimanelli's three microtexts, as it is clear that Rimanelli is here distinguishing between the text of the "For-a-word" and the fictive text "Benedetta in Guysterland."

Also, with regard to possible Italian intertexts in Guido Gustavo Gozzano's and Aldo Palazzeschi's poetry, I would point out that Gozzano's borrowings from other European poets are well known and have been studied and examined by a number of Italian critics. Similarly, Palazzeschi also spoke in terms of other poets' work, though differently. In describing his "strofe bisbetiche," he states: "Sapete cosa sono? / Sono robe avanzate, / non sono grullerie, / sono la . . . spazzatura / delle altre poesie" ("E lasciatemi divertire"; translation: Do you know what they are? / They're leftover things, / they're not silly acts, / they're the . . . garbage / of other poetry [And Let Me Have My Fun]). In his Appendix 15, Luigi Ballerini makes a parenthetical allusion to both Gozzano and Palazzeschi.

10. With regard to Rimanelli's For-a-word I would offer two possible readings of its orthography. First, it may signal the space in which Rimanelli wants to offer some information to his reader for his/her semiotic encounter with the text[s]. Thus, he has space *for a word*. From another point of view, instead, one might read Rimanelli's For-a-word as a type of signal of his bicultural status. Considering the strong parodic element in *Guysterland*, as well as in other works of his, For-a-word may signal graphically an Italian pronunciation of the English word *for[e]word*.

11. The gender issue in *Benedetta in Guysterland* deserves its own space and time, more than what can be examined in this chapter. Briefly, nevertheless, I believe that Rimanelli is more concerned with the specific role of the female and the question of sexual liberation as we knew it in the 1970s, rather than with the general issue of gender as we know it today. Whatever the case, the female characters in Rimanelli's novel remain, or so it seems, on an even par with the male characters. If anything, the male characters cut a less impressive figure.

12. From the New Americanist perspective, Fred L. Gardaphé, deals with *Benedetta in Guysterland* in his penetrating book-length study, *Italian Signs, American Streets* more than he does in his preface to Rimanelli's book. Gardaphé offers an excellent analysis of Rimanelli's socio-cultural parody that lies at the base of *Benedetta in Guysterland*.

13. Again I refer the reader to Gardaphé's preface to *Benedetta in Guysterland. A Liquid Novel* and his chapter dedicated to Rimanelli in *Italian Signs, American Streets*.

14. To the 1990s English-reading public, who may or may not know Italian, as sign, *La Gaia Scienza* may conjure up least two possible interpretants. To her/him who knows no Italian, the visual sign itself may recall for the reader the English title of Friedrich Nietzsche's *Die Fröhliche Wissenschaft, The Gay Science*. For the Italian speaker, instead, the Club's name may conjure up, in addition to Nietzsche's work, Giambattista Vico's *La Nuova Scienza*, a philosopher Rimanelli knows well (see his autobiographical account of his intellectual encounter with Vico, "Sensi diritti: Vico, Vichismo, Vicoli," *Misure critiche* 21.80–81 [July-December 1991]: 121–34.). The above-mentioned works of these two

philosophers may surely figure as possible influences, be it here or elsewhere in Rimanelli's *opera*. But that is for another setting.

I would close this digressive note with one other point. As a *phonetic* sign, *gaia* recalls the very title of the book, especially Rimanelli's idiosyncratic sign *guyster* for gangster—lest we ignore other possible interpretants of guysters!

15. There are other issues that raise eyebrows and problematize interpretation in Benedetta's story: change in time sequence; the switching from Benedetta's first-person narrative to a rare occurrence or two of Benedetta being referred to in the third person; occasional occurrences of free indirect discourse (FID); and, a type of distortion of FID, occasional opinions/ thoughts of other characters appearing without dialogue markers or tags of some sort such as quotation marks or, for example, "he said" or "she responded."

16. For any reader's [re]construction of meaning, I have in mind a plethora of notions ranging from Peircean/Econian semiotics to Gadamerian hermeneutics, with a good dose of Barthesian semiology and Iserian reader response. For more on these notions, see: Charles Sanders Peirce, *Principles of Philosophy* in *Collected Papers*, eds. Charles Hartshorne and Paul Weiss, Vol. 1 (Cambridge, MA: Harvard University Press, 1960); Umberto Eco, *The Role of the Reader: Explorations in the Semiotics of Texts* (Bloomington: Indiana University Press, 1979); Hans-Georg Gadamer, *Truth and Method* (New York: The Crossroad Publishing Company, 1988); Roland Barthes, *S/Z*, trans. Richard Miller (New York: Hill and Wang, 1975); and Wolfgang Iser, especially his *The Act of Reading. A Theory of Aesthetic Response* (Baltimore: Johns Hopkins University Press, 1978).

17. I cite from the English version in *The Uses of Literature*, trans., Patrick Creagh (New York: Harcourt Brace Jovanovich, 1986). In Italian, this essay is included in Calvino's larger collection of essays, *Una pietra sopra* (Torino: Einaudi, 1980).

18. Indeed, here, Calvino echoes notions similar to his ideological confrere, Roland Barthes. One need only think back to the French critic's notion of the death of the author ("The Death of the Author," *Image Music Text*, trans. Stephen Heath [New York: Hill and Wang, 1974], pp. 142–48) and his concept of text divided into the categories of readerly and writerly (see his *S/Z*).

19. This notion of textual signification is underscored by Gadamer when he states: "The real meaning of a text, as it speaks to the interpreter, does not depend on the contingencies of the author and whom he originally wrote for. It certainly is not identical with them, for it is always partly determined also by the historical situation of the interpreter" (p. 263). Gadamer, furthermore, goes on to speak of understanding as "not merely a reproductive, but always a productive attitude as well" (p. 264).

20. My reference to Palazzeschi concerns the closing of "E lasciatemi divertire." The final verses are: "Infine io ò pienamente ragione, / i tempi sono molto cambiati, / gli uomini non dimandano / più nulla dai poeti, / e lasciatemi divertire" (translation: In the end I am completely right, / times have certainly

changed, / people no longer ask, anymore, / anything from poets, / and so let me have my fun).

21. At this point, I should offer my reader some highlights of Rimanelli's literary career. His first novel, *Tiro al piccione*, was published by Mondadori (1953), one of Italy's major publishing houses, then and now; very well received in Italy, it was soon translated into English and published by Random House (1954) as *The Day of the Lion*. In that same year, Mondadori published his second novel *Peccato originale*. Other works include: novels, *Una posizione sociale* (Florence: Vallacchi, 1959), *Graffiti* (Isernia: Marinelli, 1977), and most recently, *Detroit Blues* (Montreal: Soleil, 1996); a one-act play, *The French Horn* (New York: Actor's Studio, 1960), three plays, *Tè in casa Picasso, Il corno francese, Lares,* in *Dramma* (1961); an anthology, *Modern Canadian Stories* (Toronto, 1966); critical and autobiographical essays, *Biglietto di terza* (Milan: Mondadori, 1958), *Il mestiere del furbo* (Milan: Sugar, 1959), *Tragica America* (Genova: Immordino, 1968), editor of essays in honor of Thomas Goddard Bergin, *Italian Literature: Roots and Branches* (New Haven: Yale University Press, 1976), *Molise Molise* (Isernia: Marinelli, 1979); *Il tempo nascoste fra le righe* (Isernia: Marinelli, 1986); poetry, *Carmina blabla* (Padova: Rebellato, 1967), *Poems Make Pictures Pictures Make Poems* (New York: Pantheon, 1971), *Arcanò* (Salerno: Edizioni del Sud, 1990), and *Alien Cantica* (New York: Peter Lang, 1993). Most recently, as *A Semiotic of Ethnicity* goes to press, Rimanelli's second novel in English, *Accademia* (Toronto: Guernica, 1997), appeared in print.

22. For more on sign-functions, see Umberto Eco, *A Theory of Semiotics* (Bloomington: Indiana University Press, 1976), pp. 48–62.

23. For more on prejudgments, see Gadamer pp. 234–75.

24. Again, I remind the reader of Volosinov's previously cited notion of ideology and semiotics: "Every sign is subject to the criteria of ideological evaluation. . . . The domain of ideology coincides with the domain of signs. . . . Wherever a sign is present ideology is present also. *Everything ideological possesses semiotic value*" (p. 10; emphasis textual).

25. Here, again, I would refer the reader to Boelhower's notion of ethnic discourse in a postmodern/semiotic context: " . . . ethnocultural construction is itself a possible world among others, a different strategy for creating a world of referents. In this light the ethnic sign functions as a working hypothesis for a possible action. And its range proves limitless exactly because the ethnic verbum has been disencarnated, stripped of its primordial and genealogical uniqueness: which is also why it is epistemologically weak. Only as such can everything imaginable under the sun be transformed into an ethnic sign, into a matter for ethnic semiosis" (p. 133).

26. As we saw in chapter one, this, for Bakhtin, is dialogized heteroglossia. A word, language, or culture undergoes dialogization "when it becomes relatived, de-privileged, aware of competing definitions for the same things" (p. 427).

27. In dealing with the nature of fictions and how we know them, Floyd Merrell states that "certain percepts and concepts constructed within specific contexts are the products of one's *classificatory scheme*" which is eventually "integrated into a *conceptual framework*": that which "entails a world view and knowledge of language and a culture." See his *Pararealities: The Nature of Our Fictions and How We Know Them* (Amsterdam: John Benjamins, 1983), p. 4.

## 5. Looking Back

1. For an excellent example of this phenomenon of contrasting sentiments and contradictions, see Ben Lawton's essay, "America through Italian/American Eyes: Dream or Nightmare?" *From the Margin*.

2. Perhaps even three, were we to include that unique cultural space in the United States, locally labeled in many cities "Little Italy," known also as Italian America. For more on this notion of Italian America, see Robert Viscusi's "*Il caso della casa*: Stories of Houses in Italian America" in *The Family and Community Life of Italian Americans*, ed. Richard Juliani (Staten Island: AIHA, 1983) pp. 1–9, and Fred L. Gardaphé's "My House is not Your House: Jerre Mangione and Italian-American Autobiography," in *Multicultural Autobiography: American Lives*, ed. James Robert Payne (Knoxville: University of Tennessee Press, 1992) pp. 139–77.

3. In Italian "Mezzogiorno" means noon or midday; it is refers to the southern section of a country. In Italy it is a popular synonym for Southern Italy.

4. While Southern Italy may have been the prosperous region of Italy in ancient times, since the Middle Ages it grew increasingly less prosperous, arriving, in the nineteenth century, at a state of widespread poverty among the general population. It is today a land of hot, arid summers and cold, wet winters, with very little adequate farm land. Since the unification of Italy in 1860, promises for a better South were consistently made but never kept. As a result, the South has yet to reach its full economic potential, whereas the North has become both an agricultural and industrial center of prosperity. There are numerous other questions of a more socio-political nature that also need to be examined for a better understanding of the North/South question. For more on this, see Frederic Spotts and Theodore Wiser, *Italy: A Difficult Democracy. A Survey of Italian Politics* (New York: Cambridge University Press, 1986) pp. 222–40.

5. Barolini's situations mirror those in Carlo Levi's *Cristo si è fermato a Eboli* (*Christ Stopped at Eboli*). In both cases the integrity of the first half of the couplet is called into question.

6. Again, one finds a similar situation in Levi's *Cristo si è fermato a Eboli* in which Rome also becomes the source of all evil, where the government is nothing more than one of many "natural" disasters that befall the *peasant* human race.

7. The *fattore* was the landowner's agent and liaison between the landowner and the peasants, who collected from the peasants the major portion of the harvest the land produced.

8. As a caricature of a small-village priest, Don Antonio is a curious Italian/American analogue to Levi's Don Trajella in *Cristo si è fermato a Eboli.*

9. That Ulysses may or may not have sailed this voyage is of little importance here. I consider the Ulysses episode significant as a point of reference for its literary cultural validation of fraud and deceit in *Umbertina.*

10. Differently from Paul Campisi ("Ethnic Family Patterns: The Italian Family in the United States") and Joseph Lopreato (*Italian Americans*), I shall follow the more common practice among sociologists vis-à-vis tags that distinguish the different categories of families such as "peasant," "first-," and so on. The common practice is to label the immigrant generation the "first generation" and so on. This, in fact, is the practice Barolini herself adopts in her narrative in *Umbertina.*

11. What I have in mind is not the type of films we've had from Coppola or Scorsese, directors who, I believe, try to debunk the stereotypes in a dialogue, through their films, with Italian Americans and non-Italian Americans alike. I consider their films different from that type of film or television program that presents a negative image of the Italian or Italian American that is unaccompanied by any form of critical discourse, such as the *Rocky* films of Sylvester Stallone, television characters such as the Fanelli boys, the Torcellis, or even Carla on *Cheers.*

12. I would suggest that Alberto can respond to Marguerite "in jest" for a number of reasons. He is speaking from a position of socio-cultural power as a northern Italian, educated male, while she is the granddaughter of a southern Italian, semi-educated female who emigrated to the United States. To be sure, Marguerite's status as Italian American is another important factor. It allows Alberto to distance himself, in a strange way, from Marguerite's southern Italian origins for the very fact that she is not *Italian*; she is Italian American, an *American*, that is, of *Italian* decent.

13. Luigi Barzini, *The Italians* (New York: Atheneum, 1964), especially Chapters 4 and 9.

14. While Barolini tends to mix fictitious names among the real names of those who constitute the many characters, both primary and secondary, Marguerite meets in her years in Italy, her account of which literary figures Marguerite truly missed helps to underscore her previous criticism of the state of literary affairs in Italy in the 1970s:

Looking about at the people who made up the firmament of sensibility in Italy in their day, Marguerite regretted the missing. Pavese was dead; Vittorini was dead; Ungaretti was dead; Calvino lived in Paris, discredited in Italy for having refused the five million lire of the previous year's Viareggio prize with a telegram to the jury in which he said that the time of such events was definitely over. He had cut through the vanity of literary Italy with all the candor of the child who didn't pretend to see the emperor's clothes, and his honesty was received in a rage. (p. 275)

15. I would remind the reader of Marguerite's desire for a professional career. She once stated to Massimo that she really wanted to be a photographer: "'Why don't you? That's a beautiful thing to do, you know' [Massimo].

'I have a family,' she said. They fell silent. She tried to retrieve things." (p. 229)

16. These antithetical feelings Marguerite experiences with regard to her femaleness are, in a certain sense, analogous to those concerning her Italianness. She finds herself in a confused situation, at times opting for the more traditional role while at other times wanting to break free and be her own person.

17. Again, we see that Alberto had reneged on his initial promise that they would live together as artists: "Proposing, Alberto had said that they would learn each other's language and be artists together, although it would be wise if they started a family soon."

It is important to keep in mind that traditional roles, especially female, were passed on from one generation to the next, and among Italian immigrants it was considered "'normal' [for adolescent females] to expect and to want children when they married" (Harriet Perry, "The Metonymic Definition of Female and the Concept of Honor among Italian Immigrant families in Toronto," p. 223). They were expected to live out their lives as mothers and housewives, and consequently they were relegated to limited personal development as integral individuals.

18. Given the fact that Marguerite's Italy seems to echo very much Barzini's Italy of *The Italians*, dare we see an irony that it is Barzini, in *Umbertina*, who announces, in his "doubly amplified" voice, that the winner of the Strega is Tomaso Campo, not Massimo?

19. While it is true that the South comes up earlier in this section in the brief episode when Tina meets the Italian Americans from Foggia, the encounter has very little to do with the conditions of southern Italy; it is primarily about Tina and her ethnic conflicts and "defense against being merged in the ethnic mess she saw and despised in the States" (p. 315).

20. This is obviously Giosuè, Umbertina's first love whom she had to foresake because of her father's desire to marry her off to Serafino.

## 6. Gianna Patriarca's "Tragic" Thought

1. Indeed, one might wonder about the serendipity of her Italian surname and its semiotic clash with her profeminist thematics.

2. Franco Rella, *Miti e figure del moderno* (Milan: Feltrinelli, 1993, 2nd edition), p. 26; italics textual. Rella goes on to quote Benjamin, that this "pensiero dell'altro," according to the German philosopher, is "il pensiero di ciò che non è stato mai scritto" (p. 26).

3. Here I am using Rella's concept of tragedy in order to localize and particularize a certain relationship between it and Patriarca's cognitive poetic world. Rella, in fact, states: "La tragedia non è la narrazione di eventi luttuosi: è un pensiero. E' il pensiero che fluidifica i confini conosciuti, tra la polis e ciò che è esterno alla polis, tra maschile e femminile, tra umano e divino. E' il pensiero che scopre che il rapporto dell'uomo [sic] con il mondo e con il divino si realizza dentro un conflitto" (p. 15).

4. Again, I remind the reader that the distinction I point out between these categories is by no means to be perceived as possessing any sort of hierarchical valence.

5. While I do not wish to indict the Italian/American male in general, one may nevertheless get the impression that he does not always fare well in literary works by Italian Americans, especially those by women writers. I make this point, albeit *en passant*, because I believe it is a topic to be explored further in its own right. To date, one may look at Mary Jo Bona's work thus far in order to get some idea of the woman's position in Italian/American literature. Along with her essays, there is also her edited anthology, *The Voices We Carry* (Toronto: Guernica, 1994). Indispensable also, of course, is Helen Barolini's earlier anthology, *The Dream Book: An Anthology of Writing by Italian American Women* (New York: Schocken, 1985), which provided us with our first general look at the Italian/American woman writer.

6. I borrow this expression, "due mezze verità," from Rella, who, in turn, cites it from Benjiamin (p. 26).

7. For more on this idea of the "altro pensiero," see Rella (pp. 24–31).

8. To anyone conversant with twentieth-century Italian narrative, the figure of the "peasants" as "beasts of burden" in Carlo Levi's *Christ Stopped at Eboli* comes to mind.

9. For more on Pietro di Donato's novel, see Fred L. Gardaphè's introduction, in *Christ in Concrete* (New York: Signet, 1993). See also the special special issue of the journal *Voices in Italian Americana* (Vol. 2, No. 2 [Spring 1991]) dedicated to Di Donato's work in general.

10. I would state parenthetically that Patriarca's nostalgia is doled out in a healthy dose, whereas too much nostalgia may actually stifle one's feelings and actions. Patriarca's narrating *I* does not fall into the trap of an overbearing nostalgia; the homage she pays other women is such proof.

11. Gia is the third of three women in this narrative collection, each representing experiences of three different Italian/Canadian generations. Such a notion of social progress on gender issues across generations recalls Helen Barolini's poignant Italian/American novel, *Umbertina* (New York: Seaview, 1979), as we saw in chapters three and five herein.

## 7. Italian/American Writer or Italian Poet Abroad?

1. I remind the reader of the general definition I offered in Chapter One, where I stated that for ethnic literature I have in mind that type of writing which deals contextually with customs and behavioral patterns that the North American mind-set may consider different from what it perceives as mainstream. The difference, I might add, may also manifest itself formalistically, that is, the writer may not follow what have become accepted norms and conventions of literary creation, s/he may not produce what the dominant culture considers *good* literature.

2. Again I remind the reader of Gustavo Pérez Firmat's cogent exegesis of the bilingual writer who occupies what Pérez Firmat considers the "space between"; see his "Spic Chic: Spanglish as Equipment for Living" (p. 21).

3. I make this distinction between dates of arrival because I believe the motives for leaving one's country during the great wave of immigration at the end of the nineteenth century to the first half of the twentieth century were different from those of people who decided to migrate to the United States once the economic boom of the 1950s was already well in progress and exhibited a positive effect on those same countries from which others had previously fled.

4. *Differentia* 3/4 (Spring/Autumn 1989): 259–76. Valesio labels this writer the "expatriate" (p. 271), as opposed to the member of the "immigrant" generation to which I refer above in category one.

5. Valesio goes on to specify that this "writer is, rather than nationally based, community based. His or her word always takes off from a community (even if the community may be alive only in memory) and always addresses a community (even if it is only 'a universal audience,' as some scholars of rhetoric call it, referring to possible future readership)" (p. 272). In addition, Valesio continues, the works of the "writer between two worlds in the United States . . . rarely thematize and describe either the Italo-American community or American society in general" (p. 273).

6. Lest we forget that Fontanella's interest in these writers and movements has occupied an integral part of his intellectual career, among his anthologies and book-length studies we find, *"I campi magnetici" di Andre Breton e Philippe Soupault* (Rome: Newton Compton, 1979), *Il surrealismo italiano* (Rome: Bulzoni, 1983), and *La parola aleatoria* (Firenze: Le Lettere, 1992).

For a cogent reading of Fontanella's poetry through 1989, see Manuela Bertone's essay, "La ricerca poetica di Luigi Fontanella: da *Simulazione di reato* (1979) a *Stella saturnina* (1989)," *Otto/novecento* (Jan-Feb), 15.1 (1991): 143–52.

7. See his "Cybernetics and Ghosts" and "Whom Do We Write For."

In "Cybernetics and Ghosts" Calvino considers "the decisive moment of literary life [to be] reading (p. 15), "by which "literature will continue to be a 'place' of privilege within the human consciousness, a way of exercising the potentialities within the system of signs belonging to all societies at all times. The work will continue to be born, to be judged, to be distorted or constantly renewed on contact with the eye of the reader" (p. 16).

8. That is, Calvino foresaw a reader with "epistemological, semantic, practical, and methodological requirements he [would] want to compare [as] examples of symbolic procedures and the construction of logical patterns" (pp. 84–85).

9. Wolfgang Iser deals with the notion of constitutive blanks in his *The Act of Reading* (Baltimore: Johns Hopkins University Press, 1978).

10. Fabio Doplicher, "Prefazione," *Simulazione di reato*, p. 9.

With regard to Fontanella's personal experience with Italy and the United States in his works, see Teresa Maria Lazzaro, "L'essere doppio al di qua e al di là dell'Atlantico: l'esperienza di Luigi Fontanella," *La letteratura dell'emigrazione: gli scrittori di lingua italiana nel mondo*, ed. Jean-Jacques Marchand (Turin: Edizioni della Fondazione Giovanni Agnelli, 1991), pp. 449–58.

11. The ambiguity of this title surely fits well Fontanella's polyvalent word-play. Shall we reread the title, modified as "Diversi / ficazione"? Loosely translated we might read *about doing different/several things.*

12. An equally touching tone often occupies another collection of Fontanella's recent poetry, *Parole per Emma* (Salerno: Edisud, 1991), poems written for his daughter.

13. Zanzotto as possible intertext has already been pointed out by G. Singh in his review of *Round Trip* in *World Literature Today*, Vol. 65, No. 4 (1991): 689–90 ; see also Alessandro Carrera's review in *Canadian Journal of Italian Studies*, Vol. 14, Nos. 44–45 (1991): 77–79.

14. As *A Semiotic of Ethnicity* goes to press, Luigi Fontanella's latest collection of verse, *Ceres* (Cararmanica, 1997), was released; also available in English, *Ceres*, ed. and trans. Laura Stortoni, preface by Rebecca West (Berkeley: Hesperia Press, 1997).

## 8. Italian/American Cultural Studies

1. Along with those I mentioned earlier who deal with experiences of the first and second generations (Gans, *The Urban Villagers*; Lopreato, *Italian Americans*; and Gambino, *Blood of My Blood*), I would add at this point Patrick J. Gallo, *Ethnic Alienation. The Italian-Americans* (Madison, NJ: Fairleigh Dickinson University Press, 1974).

2. This question, of course, deserves its own treatment, and I should not leave my reader hanging. However, I believe the importance of the issue is such that we must pose the question, even though *en passant* as I do here, which, for the time being, leaves the question begged. I would, however, point out that Gallo seems to have dealt with this best in 1974, when he distinguished between "cultural assimilation" (partial) and "structural assimilation" (complete; see Gallo pp. 88–114, especially). In this regard, Michael Fischer has stated that ethnicity "is not simply that parallel processes operate across American ethnic identities, but a sense that these ethnic identities *constitute only a family of resemblances*, that ethnicity cannot be reduced to identical sociological functions, that ethnicity is a process of *interreference between two or more cultural traditions*" (see his "Ethnicity and the Post-Modern Arts of Memory," p. 195; my emphasis).

3. See his essay, "Race, Culture, and Communications: Looking Backward and Forward at Cultural Studies," *Rethinking Marxism* 5.1 (1992): 10–18.

4. See their co-authored study, *Theory, (Post)Modernity Opposition. An "Other" Introduction to Literary and Cultural Theory* (Washington, D.C.: Maisonneuve Press, 1991) p. 8. For Zavarzadeh and Morton, the proponents of the dominant cultural studies include the likes of John Fiske and Constance Penley.

5. I would point out here that Stuart Hall tends to be much more reticent about real (radical?) change, as if to suggest that, *if it happens fine, if not, oh well*. Hall, in fact, seems to limit his vision of change to the academy: "It is the sort of necessary irritant in the shell of academic life that one hopes will . . . produce new pearls of wisdom" (p. 11).

6. Though I would suggest that the same is happening with filmmakers. George Gallo, Nancy Savoca, Alan Alda, Michael Pavone, and Stanley Tucci have changed the relationship between the Italian/American image and its filmic representation.

7. The Center for Migration Studies also deserves a nod of the hat in this regard; it has published a good number of pamphlets and books on Italian Americans.

8. In addition, they have helped, we may assume, in gaining access, for example, to the upper echelon of the MLA for the foundation of an Italian/American discussion group.

9. I have in mind the case of the bicultural and bilingual writer, as I discussed in Chapter Seven. In the analogous case of the Cuban American, Gustavo Pérez Firmat offers a cogent exegesis of the bilingual writer who, in adopting both languages (at times separately, at other times together in the same text), occupies what he considers the "space between" (p. 21); see his "Spic Chic: Spanglish as Equipment for Living."

10. Again, see Fischer on this notion of rediscovering and reinventing one's ethnicity.

11. In this last regard, I would reiterate what I said earlier about Ahmad's use of the adjective. Here, *American* refers to the geopolitical notion of the United States of America, for which, I would contend, the situation of ethnic literatures within the United States is analogous to what Ahmad so adroitly describes in his article on, for lack of a better term, "third-world literature." Thus, we might reconsider Ahmad's *American* within the confines of the geopolitical borders of the United States and thereby reread it as synonymous with *dominant culture.*

12. What is important to keep in mind is that one can perceive different degrees of ethnicity in literature, film, or any other art form, as Aaron already did with his "hyphenate writer."

13. As an example, I refer the reader to my review essay of the short film *Lena's Spaghetti* by Joseph Greco, "What is [not] Italian/American about *Lena's Spaghetti?*", *Voices in Italian Americana* 6.1 (1995): 173–84.

14. AIHA is the acronym for the American Italian Historical Association, founded in 1966 and dedicated to the preservation and study of Italian/American culture and society. Since its inception, AIHA has held yearly conventions and published volumes of selected proceedings.

15. See his *Yale Italian Studies* 1.3 (1981): 21–38. Two other pertinent essays of his include: "Breaking the Silence: Strategic Imperatives for Italian American Culture," *Voices in Italian Americana* 1.1 (1990): 1–13; and "A Literature Considering Itself: The Allegory of Italian America," in *From the Margin: Writings in Italian Americana*, pp. 265–81.

16. Other publications may include the above-mentioned anthology, *From the Margin: Writings in Italian Americana*, the establishment of journals such as *la bella figura* and *VIA: Voices in Italian Americana*, and as mentioned earlier, the resumption of the journal *Italian Americana*, a special issue of *Differentia* (1994), and another of the *Canadian Journal of Italian Studies* (1996).

17. *Voices in Italian Americana* 1.1 (Spring 1990): 15–34.

18. *MELUS* 14.3 (1987 [1990]): 87–106.

19. *The Voices We Carry* (Montreal: Guernica Editions, 1994).

20. Fred L. Gardaphé, "Visibility or Invisibility."

21. I would hasten to add that I tend to argue otherwise. What is significant here for this type of reading strategy is that I adhere to Umberto Eco's notion of *intentio lectoris* with ample conciliation to *intentio operis*, since any reader's intertextual arsenal must always, to a certain degree, be context sensitive; in some way or another, that is, the reader's decodification must jibe in some way with the text. For more on Eco's notion, see his "*Intentio Lectoris*: The State of the Art," *Differentia, review of italian thought*, Number 2 (Spring 1988): 147–68.

22. I would just add, parenthetically, that NIAF has been very active over the years in the political sphere of Washington, D.C., and in the U.S.A.-wide sphere of the popular media, such as film and television. More recently, NIAF has taken the initiative to become more involved with cultural events and publications and has therefore begun to broaden its scope as not only a watch–dog group for Italian/American antidefamation practices but also as a patron of the arts. I refer to its efforts in helping to support, for example, the semi annual *VIA* (*Voices in Italian Americana*).

23. I mention this non-Italian pronunciation of "Botticelli" not as a criticism or *ad hominem* attack against anyone who does not understand or speak Italian. Rather, I do so in order to underscore my wholehearted agreement with Robert Viscusi that Italian Americans should be not only bicultural but also, and equally important, bilingual in order to understand more fully their cultural legacy that is Italy and the present state of Italian/American affairs in which they find themselves. For more on this notion, see Viscusi's essay, "Breaking the Silence," already mentioned above.

24. Martin Harrison, "On a Poem of Gun Gencer's," in *Multicultural Australia*, eds. J. Delaruelle and Karakostas-Seda (Sydney: Australia Council for the Literature Board, 1985) p. 128.

25. Such a statement, however, is not intended to invalidate a multicultural discourse for Italy and its current experience with African migration. On the contrary, one need only read the recent work of Graziella Parati on African/Italian writers, many of whom still write in their native language and are then translated into Italian. Equally important is Lucia Chiavola Birnbaum's more recent study on black madonnas (*Black Madonnas: Feminism, Religion & Politics in Italy* [Northeastern University Press, 1993]), in which she employs a revisionist stance in examining this phenomenon from a multiculturalist point of view.

26. The classification becomes more complex—*e ben venga!*—were we to include Italian/Canadian writers and thus speak in terms of Italian/North American writers. However, I have opted to limit my analysis and observations to United States writers. For more on Italian/Canadian writers, see Antonio D'Alfonso's *In Italics* (Toronto: Guernia, 1996) and Pasquale Verdicchio's *Devils in Paradise* (Toronto: Guernica, 1997) and *Bound by Distance* (Madison, NJ: Fairleigh Dickinson University Press, 1997).

In an effort to recognize this type of writer *suspended* between two worlds, *VIA* (*Voices in Italian Americana*) dedicates a regular section to creative writers with their original texts in Italian accompanied by translations by them or translators of their choice.

27. I refer to an essay by Robert Viscusi ("Narrative and Nothing: The Enterprise of Italian American Writing," *Differentia, review of italian thought* 6/7 [1994]) in which the Italian writer Ignazio Silone is used to understand better the ontological plight of the Italian/American immigrant.

28. As mentioned earlier in regard to this type of integration, *Voices in Italian Americana* has already recognized the necessity by dedicating a regular section entitled *Italian Writing in the United States.*

29. See his excellent essay, "Breaking the Silence."

30. For more on this idea in general, see Ernest Renan, "What is a Nation?" in *Nation and Narration,* ed. Homi K. Bhabha (London: Routledge, 1990) pp. 8–22.

For an example of what we should eschew as Italian/American critical thought is Ferdinando Alfonsi's notion of biology *qua* ethnicity (*Dictionary of Italian-American Poets* [New York: Peter Lang, 1989]), that blood "is a force of such inevitableness that it conquers time and space and even individual will" (p. 9). For a response, see my review in *Voices in Italian Americana* 1.2 (1990): 135–37 and Fred L. Gardaphé's review of Alfonsi's bilingual study, *Poesia Italo-americana: saggi e testi/Italian American Poetry: Essays and Texts* in *Italica* 70.2 (1993): 219–21.

For a stimulating read on ethnicity as chiefly representative of cultural, not biological, characteristics, see Tommy L. Lott, "Du Bois on the Invention of Race," *The Philosophical Forum,* Nos. 1–3 (Fall-Spring 1992–93): 166–87.

31. See Hall (p. 11) for more on his notion.

32. And in November, 1997, twenty-three years after Gallo's conclusion, AIHA celebrated its 30th annual conference with this very topic. The conference theme was: "Shades of Black and White: Conflict and Collaboration between Two Communities."

33. For an excellent example of this notion put into effect, see Sneja Gunew, "Denaturalizing Cultural Nationalisms: Multicultural Readings of 'Australia'" in *Nation and Narration,* ed. Homi K. Bhabha (London: Routledge, 1990) pp. 99–112.

# Select Bibliography

Aaron, Daniel. "The Hyphenate Writer and American Letters." *Smith Alumnae Quarterly* (July 1964): 213–17; later revised in *Rivista di Studi Anglo-Americani* 3.4–5 (1984–85): 11–28.

Ahmad, Aijaz. "Jameson's Rhetoric of Otherness and the 'National Allegory'." *Social Text* 17 (1987): 3–25.

Alfonsi, Ferdinando. *Dictionary of Italian-American Poets.* New York: Peter Lang, 1989.

Altieri, Charles. "An Idea and Ideal of a Literary Canon." *Canons.* Robert von Hallberg, ed. Chicago: University of Chicago Press, 1984, pp. 41–64.

Anonymous review of *The Evening News. Booklist,* 15 September 1986.

Ardizzone, Tony. *Taking It Home. Stories from the Neighborhood.* Champaign Urbana: University of Illinois Press, 1996.

———. *The Evening News.* Athens, GA: University of Georgia Press, 1986.

———. *Heart of the Order.* New York: Holt, 1986.

Bakhtin, Mikhail M. *The Dialogic Imagination.* Michael Holquist, ed. Caryl Emerson and Michael Holquist, trans. Austin: University of Texas Press, 1981.

Barolini, Helen. *Chiaroscuro. Essays of Identity.* VIA Folios 11. West Lafayette: Bordighera, 1997.

———. *The Dream Book: An Anthology of Writing by Italian American Women.* New York: Schocken, 1985.

———. *Umbertina.* New York: Seaview 1979.

Barthes, Roland. *S/Z.* Richard Miller, trans. New York: Hill and Wang, 1975.

———. *Image Music Text.* Stephen Heath, trans. New York: Hill and Wang, 1974.

Barzini, Luigi. *The Italians.* New York: Atheneum, 1964.

Basile Green, Rose. "The Italian Immigrant Woman in American Literature." *The Italian Immigrant Woman in North America.* Betty Boyd Caroli, Robert F. Harney, and Lydio F. Tomasi, eds. Toronto: Multicultural History Society of Ontario, 1978.

————. *The Italian-American Novel: A Document of the Interaction of Two Cultures.* Madison, NJ: Fairleigh Dickinson University Press, 1974.

Bertone, Manuela. "La ricerca poetica di Luigi Fontanella: da *Simulazione di reato* (1979) a *Stella saturnina* (1989)." *Otto/novecento* 15.1 (Jan–Feb 1991): 143–52.

Birnbaum, Lucia Chavola. "The History of Sicilians." *Italians and Italian Americans and the Media.* Mary Jo Bona and Anthony Julian Tamburri, eds. Staten Island: AIHA, 1996, pp. 206–15.

Boelhower, William. *Through a Glass Darkly: Ethnic Semiosis in American Literature.* Venice, Italy: Edizioni Helvetia, 1984; by Oxford University Press, 1987.

Bona, Mary Jo. *The Voices We Carry.* Toronto: Guernica, 1994.

————. "Broken Images, Broken Lives: Carmolina's Journey in Tina De Rosa's *Paper Fish.*"*MELUS* 14.3 (1987 [1990]): 87–106.

————. "Mari Tomasi's *Like Lesser Gods* and the Making of an Ethnic *Bildungsroman.*" *Voices in Italian Americana* 1.1 (Spring 1990): 15–34.

Booth, Wayne. *The Rhetoric of Fiction.* Chicago: University of Chicago Press, 1960.

Calvino, Italo. "Cybernetics and Ghosts." *The Uses of Literature.* Patrick Creagh, tr. New York: Harcourt Brace Jovanovich, 1986.

————. "Whom Do We Write For." *The Uses of Literature.* Patrick Creagh, tr. New York: Harcourt Brace Jovanovich, 1986.

————. *If on a winter's night a traveler.* New York: Harcourt Brace Jovanovich, 1979.

Campisi, Paul. "Ethnic Family Patterns: The Italian Family in the United States." *The American Journal of Sociology* 53.6 (May 1948): 443–49.

Carrera, Alessandro. Review of Luigi Fontanella, *Round Trip. Canadian Journal of Italian Studies* 14.44–45 (1991): 77–79.

Casillo, Robert. "Moments in Italian-American Cinema: From *Little Caesar* to Coppola and Scorsese." *From the Margin: Writings in Italian Americana.* Anthony Julian Tamburri, Paolo A. Giordano, and Fred L. Gardaphé, eds. West Lafayette: Purdue University Press, 1991.

Chapman, Charlotte Gowers. *Milocca, A Sicilian Village.* Cambridge, MA: Schenkan, 1971.

Chatman, Seymour. *Story and Discourse.* Ithaca: Cornell University Press, 1978.

Chiavola Birnbaum, Lucia. *Black Madonnas: Feminism, Religion and Politics in Italy.* Northeastern University Press, 1993.

Cornelison, Ann. *Women of the Shadows.* New York: Vantage Books, 1977.

Corti, Maria. "Testi or microtesti? I racconti di Marcovaldo di Italo Calvino." *Strumenti critici* 27 (June 1975): 182–93.

Courtney, Mary Elizabeth. "Making Games of Allegories." *Columbus Dispatch* (19 October, 1986).

D'Alfonso, Antonio. *In Italics.* Toronto: Guernica, 1996.

Daly, Mary. *Gyn/ecology: The Metaethics of Radical Feminism.* Boston: Beacon Press, 1978.

Davis, Lenard J. *Resisting Novels: Ideology and Fiction.* London: Methuen, 1987.

Di Biagi, Flaminio. "A Reconsideration: Italian American Writers: Notes for a Wider Consideration." *MELUS* 14.3–4 (1987): 141–51.

Doplicher, Fabio. "Prefazione." Luigi Fontanella, *Simulazione di reato.* Manduria: Lacaita, 1979.

Eco, Umberto. "*Intentio Lectoris*: The State of the Art." *Differentia, review of italian thought.* 2 (Spring 1988): 147–68.

———. *The Role of the Reader: Explorations in the Semiotics of Texts.* Bloomington: Indiana University Press, 1979.

———. *A Theory of Semiotics.* Bloomington: Indiana University Press, 1976.

Fischer, Michael M. J. "Ethnicity and the Post-Modern Arts of Memory." *Writing Culture. The Poetics and Politics of Ethnography.* James Clifford and George E. Marcus, eds. Berkeley: University of California Press, 1986.

Fontanella, Luigi. *Ceres.* Roma: Cararmanica, 1997.

———. *Ceres.* Trans. and ed. Laura Stortoni, preface by Rebecca West. Berkeley: Hesperia Press, 1997.

———. *Parole per Emma.* Salerno: Edisud, 1991.

———. *Round Trip.* Udine: Campanotto Editore, 1991.

———. *Stella Saturnina.* Rome: Il ventaglio, 1989.

———. *Simulazione di reato.* Manduria: Lacaita, 1979.

Gadamer, Hans-Georg. *Truth and Method.* New York: The Crossroad Publishing Company, 1988.

Gallo, Patrick J. *Ethnic Alienation. The Italian-Americans.* Madison, NJ: Fairleigh Dickinson University Press, 1974.

Gardaphè, Fred L. *Italian Signs, American Streets. The Evolution of Italian American Narrative.* Durham: Duke University Press, 1996.

————. "Introduction." Pietro Di Donato. *Christ in Concrete*. New York: Signet, 1993.

————. Review of Alfonsi's bilingual study, *Poesia Italo-americana: saggi e testi/Italian American Poetry: Essays and Texts*. *Italica* 70.2 (1993): 219–21.

————. "My House is not Your House: Jerre Mangione and Italian-American Autobiography." *Multicultural Autobiography: American Lives*. James Robert Payne, ed. Knoxville: University of Tennessee Press, 1992) pp. 139–77.

————. "Visibility or Invisibility: The Postmodern Prerogative in the Italian/American Narrative." *Almanacco* 2.1 (1992): 24–33.

Gioia, Dana. "What Is Italian-American Poetry?" *Poetry Pilot* (December 1991): 3–10.

Giordano, Paolo A. "From Southern Italian Immigrant to Reluctant American: Joseph Tusiani's *Gente Mia and Other Poems*." *From the Margin: Writings in Italian Americana*. Anthony Julian Tamburri, Paolo A. Giordano, and Fred L. Gardaphé, eds. West Lafayette: Purdue University Press, 1991).

Giordano, Paolo, and Anthony Julian Tamburri, eds. *Beyond the Margin: Readings in Italian Americana*. Madison, NJ: Fairleigh Dickinson University Press, 1998.

————. Special issue on Italian/American Literature and Film. *Canadian Journal of Italian Studies* 19.53 (1996).

Grossman, Marshall. "The Violence of the Hyphen in Judeo-Christian," *Social Text* 22 (1989): 115–22.

Gunew, Sneja. "Denaturalizing Cultural Nationalisms: Multicultural Readings of 'Australia.'" *Nation and Narration*, Homi K. Bhabha, ed. London: Routledge, 1990, 99–112.

Hall, Stuart. "Race, Culture, and Communications: Looking Backward and Forward at Cultural Studies." *Rethinking Marxism* 5.1 (1992): 10–18.

Harrison, Martin. "On a Poem of Gun Gencer's." *Multicultural Australia*. J. Delaruelle and Karakostas-Seda, eds. Sydney: Australia Council for the Literature Board, 1985.

Hayler, Barbara. "Abortion." *Signs: Journal of Women in Cultural and Society* 5:2 (1979).

Hutcheon, Linda. *The Politics of Postmodernism*. New York: Routledge, 1989.

Iser, Wolfgang. *The Act of Reading. A Theory of Aesthetic Response*. Baltimore: Johns Hopkins University Press, 1978.

Lawton, Ben. "America through Italian/American Eyes: Dream or Nightmare?" *From the Margins: Writings in Italian Americana*. Anthony Julian Tamburri,

Paolo A. Giordano, and Fred L. Gardaphé, eds. West Lafayette: Purdue University Press, 1991.

Lazzaro, Teresa Maria. "L'essere doppio al di qua e al di là dell'Atlantico: l'esperienza di Luigi Fontanella," *La letteratura dell'emigrazione: gli scrittori di lingua italiana nel mondo*. Jean-Jacques Marchand, ed. Turin: Edizioni della Fondazione Giovanni Agnelli, 1991, pp. 449–58.

Lentricchia, Frank. Review of John J. Soldo, *Delano in America and Other Early Poems. Italian Americana* 1.1 (1974) 124–25.

Levi, Carlo. *Cristo si è fermato a Eboli*. Torino: Einaudi, 1966.

Lopreato, Joseph. *Italian Americans*. New York: Random House, 1979.

Lott, Tommy L. "Du Bois on the Invention of Race." *The Philosophical Forum*, Nos. 1–3 (Fall-Spring 1992–93): 166–87.

Lyotard, Jean-François. *The Postmodern Condition: A Report on Knowledge*. Geoff Bennington and Brian Massumi, trans. with a foreword by Fredric Jameson. Minneapolis: University of Minnesota Press, 1984.

Merrell, Floyd. *A Peirce Primer*. Toronto: Canadian Scholars Press, 1995.

———. *Pararealities: The Nature of Our Fictions and How We Know Them*. Amsterdam: John Benjamins, 1983.

Ohmann, Richard. "The Shaping of a Canon: U.S. Fiction, 1960–1975." *Canons*. Robert von Hallberg, ed. Chicago: University of Chicago Press, 1984, pp. 377–402.

Palazzeschi, Aldo. *L'incendiario*. Milan: Edizioni Futuriste di 'Poesie', 1910.

Patriarca, Gianna. *Italian Women and Other Tragedies*. Toronto: Guernica, 1994.

Peirce, Charles Sanders. *Principles of Philosophy* in *Collected Papers*. Charles Hartshorne and Paul Weiss, eds. Vol. 1. Cambridge, MA: Harvard University Press, 1960.

Pérez Firmat, Gustavo. "Spic Chic: Spanglish as Equipment for Living." *The Caribbean Review* 15.3 (Winter 1987): 20ff.

Perry, Harriet. "The Metonymic Definition of Female and the Concept of Honour Among Italian Immigrant Families in Toronto." *The Italian Immigrant Woman in North America*. Betty Boyd Caroli, Robert F. Harney and Lydio F. Tomasi, eds. Toronto: Multicultural History Society of Ontario, 1978.

Rella, Franco. *Miti e figure del moderno*. Milan: Feltrinelli, 1993, 2nd edition.

Renan, Ernest. "What is a Nation?" *Nation and Narration*. Homi K. Bhabha, ed. London: Routledge, 1990, pp. 8–22.

Riesman, David. "Introduction." *Commentary on the American Scene: Portraits of Jewish Life in America.* Elliot E. Cohen, ed. New York: Alfred A. Knopf, 1953.

Rimanelli, Giose. *Accademia.* Toronto: Guernica, 1997.

———. *Benedetta in Guysterland. A Liquid Novel.* Montréal: Guernica, 1993.

———. "Sensi diritti: Vico, Vichismo, Vicoli." *Misure critiche* 21.80-81 (July–December 1991): 121–134.

Romano, Rose. "Coming Out Olive." *Literary History and Social Pluralism.* Francesco Loriggio, ed. Toronto: Guernica, 1996.

Rosen, Bernard. "Race, Ethnicity and the Achievement Syndrome." *American Sociological Review* 24 (October 1959): 47–60.

Russo, John Paul. "The Poetics of Gilbert Sorrentino." *Rivista di Studi Anglo-Americani* 3 (1984–85): 281–303.

Scapp, Ron, and Anthony Julian Tamburri, eds. "Special Issue on Italian/American Culture." *Differentia, review of italian thought.* 5 (Spring/Autumn 1994).

Shaffer, Mark. "Streets of Chicago Yield Faith and Fire." *The Washington Times Magazine* (24 November 1986).

Sheriff, John K. *The Fate of Meaning: Charles Peirce, Structuralism and Literature.* Princeton: Princeton University Press, 1989.

Singh, G. Review of Luigi Fontanella. *Round Trip.* World Literature Today* 65.4 (1991): 689–90.

Spencer, Jim. "N. Sider's Tales of Urban Life." *Chicago Tribune* (13 January 1987), Section 5: 3.

Spotts, Frederic, and Theodore Wiser. *Italy: A Difficult Democracy. A Survey of Italian Politics.* New York: Cambridge University Press, 1986.

Tamburri, Anthony Julian. "Gianna Patriarca's 'Tragic' Thought: *Italian Women and Other Tragedies.*" *Canadian Journal of Italian Studies* 19.53 (1996): 184–200.

———. "What is [not] Italian/American about *Lena's Spaghetti?*" *Voices in Italian Americana* 6.1 (1995): 173–84.

———. "In(Re)cognition of the Italian/American Writer: Definitions and Categories." *Differentia. review of italian thought* 6/7 (Spring/Autumn 1994): 9–32.

———. "Rimanelli's *Benedetta in Guysterland*: A 'Liquid' Novel of Questionable Textual Boundaries." *World Literature Today* 68.3 (Summer 1994): 473–78.

———. *To Hyphenate or Not To Hyphenate? The Italian/American Writer as Other American.* Montreal: Guernica, 1991.

————. "*Umbertina*: The Italian/American (Woman's) Experience." *From the Margin: Writings in Italian Americana*. Anthony Julian Tamburri, Paolo A. Giordano, and Fred L. Gardaphé, eds. West Lafayette: Purdue University Press, 1991.

————. Review of Ferdinando Alfonsi. *Dictionary of Italian-American Poets. Voices in Italian Americana* 1.2 (1990): 135–37.

————. "Helen Barolini's *Umbertina*: The Ethnic/Gender Dilemma." *Italian Americans Celebrate Life: The Arts and Popular Culture*. Paola A. Sensi-Isolani and Anthony Julian Tamburri, eds. Staten Island, NY: The American Italian Historical Association, 1990, pp. 29–44.

Tamburri, Anthony Julian, Paolo A. Giordano, and Fred L. Gardaphé, eds. *From the Margin: Writings in Italian Americana*. West Lafayette: Purdue University Press, 1991.

Tusiani, Joseph. "Song of the Bicentennial (V)." *Gente Mia and Other Poems*. Stone Park, IL: Italian Cultural Center, 1978.

Valesio, Paolo. "The Writer Between Two Worlds: The Italian Writer in the United States." *Differentia* 3/4 (Spring/Autumn 1989): 259–76.

Verdicchio, Pasquale. *Bound by Distance*. Madison, NJ: Fairleigh Dickinson University Press, 1997.

————. *Devils in Paradise*. Toronto: Guernica, 1997.

Viscusi, Robert. "Narrative and Nothing: The Enterprise of Italian American Writing." *Differentia, review of italian thought* 6/7 (1994): 77–99.

————. "A Literature Considering Itself: The Allegory of Italian America." *From the Margin: Writings in Italian Americana*. Anthony Julian Tamburri, Paolo A. Giordano, and Fred L. Gardaphé, eds. West Lafayette: Purdue University Press, 1991, pp. 265–81.

————. "Breaking the Silence: Strategic Imperatives for Italian American Culture." *Voices in Italian Americana* 1.1 (1990): 1–13.

————. "*Il caso della casa*: Stories of Houses in Italian America." *The Family and Community Life of Italian Americans*. Richard Juliani, ed. Staten Island: AIHA, 1983, pp. 1–9.

————. "*De vulgari eloquentia*: An Approach to the Language of Italian American Fiction." *Yale Italian Studies* 1.3 (1981): 21–38.

*Voices in Italian Americana* (Vol. 2, No. 2 [Spring 1991]); special issue on Pietro di Donato.

Volosinov, V.N. *Marxism and the Philosophy of Language*. Ladislav Matejka and I.R. Titunik, trans. Cambridge, MA: Harvard University Press, 1986.

Whyte, William. *Street Corner Society.* Chicago: University of Chicago Press, 1960, 2nd edition.

Wickham, Dwayne. "U. S. is stew, not a melting pot." *Journal and Courier* (Lafayette, IN) (11 March 1992).

Winsey, Valentine Rossilli. "The Italian American Woman Who Arrived in the United States Before World War I." *Studies in Italian American Social History.* Francesco Cordasco, ed. New Jersey: Rowman and Littlefield, 1975.

Yans-McLaughlin, Virginia. *Family and Community. Italian Immigrants in Buffalo,* 1880–1930. Ithaca: Cornell University Press, 1977.

Zavarzadeh, Mas'ud, and Donald Morton. *Theory, (Post)Modernity Opposition. An "Other" Introduction to Literary and Cultural Theory.* Washington, D.C.: Maisonneuve Press, 1991.

# Index

Aaron, Daniel, vii, 8–14, 18, 23, 46, 66, 96, 107, 111, 126, 127, 136n. 16, 137n. 19, 137n. 20, 138n. 22, 138n. 23, 159n. 12
abortion, 60–63
Age of Gods, 10
Age of Heroes, 10
Age of Man, 10
Agresto, John, 128
Ahmad, Aijaz, 5–6, 13, 124, 127, 159n. 11
Alba, Richard, vii
Alda, Alan, 158n. 6
Alfoni, Ferdinando, 161n. 30
American Italian Historical Association (AIHA), xi, 123, 125, 159n. 14, 161n. 32
Americanness and Italianness, 52
Anglo/American culture, 6
apathetic individual, 48, 50
Ardizzone, Tony, vii, 14, 23–46, 125, 129, 142n. 10, 143n. 19, 143n. 21, 144n. 25
assimilation, 47; cultural, 158n. 2; structural, 158n. 2
author, 24, 74; and reader, 69; self-consciousness, 25; rendition, 73–74

Bakhtin, Mikhail, 16, 19, 76, 78, 139n. 38
Balbo, Italo, 141n. 3
Ballerini, Luigi, 149n. 9
Barolini, Helen, vii, 17, 40, 47–64, 81–93, 125, 126, 129, 138n. 23, 142n. 9, 142n. 14, 152n. 5, 153n. 14, 155n. 5, 156n. 11
Barolini, Teodolina, 134n. 1

Barthes, Roland, 150n. 18
Barzini, Luigi, 88, 154n. 18
Basile Green, Rose, vii, 125, 133n. 5, 137n. 19, 140n. 41
*Benedetta in Guysterland*, 14, 65–78
Benjamin, Walter, 155n. 2
Bhabha, Homi, 124
bilingual Italian/American writer, 135n. 8
Birnbaum, Lucia Chavola, 142n. 7, 160n. 25
"body-gynocologists," 61
Boelhower, William, viii, 126, 134n. 8, 140n. 50, 151n. 25
Bona, Mary Jo, viii, xi, 126, 155n. 5
Booth, Wayne, 144n. 24
Botticelli, 128, 129
Brennan, Tim, 124

Calvino, Italo, 15, 74, 112, 139n. 36, 141n. 5, 150n. 18, 157n. 7, 157n. 8
Campisi, Paul, 51, 66, 123, 144n. 2, 153n. 10
Canada, 95–108
*Canadian Journal of Italian Studies*, xi
Capra, Frank, 7
Capria Hammond, Lucia, 135n. 8
Carla on *Cheers*, 153n. 11
Carravetta, Peter, viii, xi, 129, 135n. 8
Casillo, Robert, viii, 7
Catholic, beliefs, 50; church, 29; experience, 40; school education, 28
Catholicism, 32–44; Roman, 30
Center for Italian Studies, 123
Center for Migration Studies, 158n. 7
Chatman, Seymour, 25
Cher, 128

*Christ in Concrete,* 103
Church, 61–62, 83–85, 143n. 15
Ciresi, Rita, 125, 141n. 2
class, 92; distinction, 86
Coppola, Francis Ford, 123, 127, 128,
    129, 141n. 3, 153n. 11
Corti, Maria, 67, 148n. 5
Covello, Leonard, 123
*Cristo si è fermato a Eboli* [*Christ
    Stopped at Eboli*], 152n. 6, 153n. 8,
    155n. 8
critical, 122
cultural, assimilation, 158n. 2; dual-
    ism, 37; specificity, 65–66, 67; stud-
    ies, 121–32


D'Alfonso, Antonio, xi
Da Ponte, Lorenzo, 136n. 15
Daly, Mary, 60–61
Dante, 83–84, 129, 141n. 5
Davis, Lenard J., 20
De Mara, Victoria, xi
DeLillo, 138n. 24, 138n. 25
DeNiro, Robert, 130
DePalma, Brian, 127
DeRosa, Tina, 125
deVries, Rachel Guido, 129, 142n. 9
Di Biagi, Flaminio, 135n. 7
di Donato, Pietro, 16, 103, 125, 129
Di Prima, Diane, 129
dialogism, 19, 78, 140n. 49
*Differentia,* xi, 161n. 27
Dinale, Rita, 129
dominant, 122; culture, 5, 8, 15, 17,
    64, 77, 134n. 2; /group, 121–32
double existence, 114
double standards, 33
*The Dream Book: An Anthology of
    Writing by Italian American
    Women,* 155n. 5
dual existence, 115


Eco, Umberto, 150n. 16, 160n. 21
education, 58

emigration, 91
ethnic, denial, 49; dilemma, 16, 146n.
    11, 146n. 12; identity, 53; literature
    (defined), 109, 156n. 1; nostalgia,
    31; re-discovery, 31; signs, 11; stud-
    ies, 3–6
ethnicity, 6, 11, 14, 24–28, 30–32, 46; is
    a socio-political construct, 130;
    mythic writer, 64; (re)invented,
    45–46
ethnogenesis, 66
*Evening News,* 23–46, 144n. 22
"The Evening News," 30–32
"experiential cultural studies," 122
experimentation, 69, 70
"The Eyes of Children," 28, 44


family, "peasant," 47–48; "first-
    [generation]," 47–48; "second-
    [generation]," 47, 48, 49–50;
    "third-[generation]," 47, 49, 51
Fanelli boys, 153n. 11
Fante, John, 16
father figures, 27
Femminella, Frank, 123
Ferlinghetti, Lawrence F., 18
fiction, African/American, 6; Jew-
    ish/American, 6
Fini, Gianfranco, 141n. 3
firstness, 12–14; (defined), 138n. 27
Fischer, Michael M. J., 14, 18, 31,
    147n. 3, 158n. 2
Fiske, John, 158n. 4
Fithian Press, 123
The Flannery O'Connor Award, 23,
    141n. 2
Florida State University Conference
    on Comparative Literature and
    Film, xi
Fontanella, Luigi, viii, 109–17, 129,
    134n. 9, 157n. 6, 157n. 10, 157n. 11,
    157n. 12
food, 44
fore-understanding, 77
*A Fortunate Pilgrim* (1964), 17

framing, 71–72
Franklin, Aretha, 143n. 19
Fratti, Mario, 135n. 8

Gadamer, Hans-Georg, 77, 139n. 31, 150n. 16, 150n. 19
Gadamerian hermeneutics, 150n. 16
Gallo, Patrick, 131, 158n. 2, 158n. 6, 161n. 32
Gambino, Richard, vii, 63, 133n. 4
Gans, Herbert, vii, 63, 89
Gardaphé, Fred, viii, xi, 10–13, 64, 66, 67, 126, 138n. 24, 138n. 25, 139n. 34, 148n. 6, 149n. 12, 161n. 30
gender, 6; dilemma, 39–44, 96–103, 146n. 12; identity, 47; issue, 90
German, 26
Giannini, Amedeo, 141n. 3
Gioia, Dana, 7, 136n. 15
Giordano, Paolo, viii, xi, 134n. 1, 139n. 34
Gioseffi, Daniela, 129
Giovannitti, Arturo, 125, 129
Giunta, Edvige, viii, xi
globalization, 129, 130
*The Godfather*, 17, 138n. 22, 142n. 9; films, 128
*Goodfellas*, 128
Gozzano, Guido Gustavo, 111, 149n. 9
Gozzanoan way, 68
*Gradiva*, viii
grammar rule, 137n. 19
Grossman, Marshall, 18–19
Guernica Editions, xi, 65, 123
gynocide, 61
gynocology, 61

Hall, Stuart, 122, 123, 129, 131, 158n. 5
Hayler, Barbara, 60
*Heart of the Order*, 142n. 10
heteroglossia, 16, 19, 78, 139n. 38, 140n. 49, 151n. 26

Hispanic, 103
Holub, Renate, viii, xi
Hutcheon, Linda, 20
hyphen, 8–10, 18–19, 66
hyphenate writer, 5–6, 8–10, 66, 111, 124, 126, 127, 136n. 16, 159n. 12; stages of, 9
hyphenated, Americans, 23; individual, 66
hyphenation, 17

ideological clusters, 66
ideology, 15–16, 20, 76
immigrant(s), 29, 143n. 17; Italian, 144n. 1; Italian/American, 161n. 27; Jewish, 144n. 1; plight, 103
immigration, 95, 156n. 3
in-grouper, 50
individual, fourth-generation, 52; hyphenated, 66; second-generation, 51; third-generation, 51
intertextual(ity), 69; reservoir, 78
Irish, 103
irony, 71
Italian, fourth-generation, 53; writing in the United States, 109–17
*Italian Americana*, 123
*Italian Americans* (1970), 47
*Italian American Novel: A Document of the Interaction of Two Cultures*, 125
Italian Americans, viii; as people of color, 142n. 7; family, 47; first-generation, 29; male, 27, 155n. 5; thin-skinned, 141n. 3; woman, 47–64
Italian Canadians, viii, 130, 133n. 6
*The Italian Immigrant Woman in North America*, 63
*The Italian Journal*, xi
*Italian Signs, American Streets: The Evolution of Italian American Narrative*, 126
*Italian Women and Other Tragedies*, 40, 95–108, 142n. 9

Italian/American (as adjective), art
forms, 6; literature (defined),
8; sign system, 26; writer
(defined), 6
Italian/Canadian, experience, 95;
generations, 156n. 11; writers,
160n. 26
Italian-American Poetry, 7
ITALIANAMERICAN, ix
*italianità*, 14
*The Italians*, 88, 154n. 18
Italies, North and South, 82–86
Italy, 38, 49, 51, 53, 54, 55, 66, 81–93,
114, 116, 152n. 4, 157n. 10; Southern, 152n. 4

Jameson, Fredric, 124
Jewish, 103
Jewison, Norman, 128

"kaleidoscopic, socio/cultural mo-
saic," 121
Kerouac, Jack F., 18
Kirby, John T., xi

La Puma, Salvatore, 141n. 2
Lawton, Ben, xi, 134n. 9, 152n. 1
Lentricchia, Frank, 7
Leonardo, 128, 129
Levi, Carlo, 152n. 5, 153n. 8, 155n. 8
literature, 5; and film, 6; ethnic, 4–6,
(defined) 109, 156n. 1; postcolonial,
5, 124; "third-world," 127
Lopreato, Joseph, vii, 47, 48, 49–50,
52, 53, 63, 66, 144n. 2, 153n. 10
Loriggio, Francesco, 133n. 6
*Love in the Middle Ages*, 138n. 23,
140n. 43
Lyotard, Jean-François, 6, 18–19, 78

mafia, 71
male, as immigrant outcast, 101–03;
chauvinism, 54; figure, 97, 105; Ital-

ian/American, 155n. 5; violence,
39, 98–100, 105
Manacorda, Giuliano, 116
Martin, Dean, 142n. 8
Masiello, Francine, xi
*Meanstreets*, 128
melting-pot, 4, 121
Merrell, Floyd, 152n. 27
*MELUS*, xi
Mexican(s), 143n. 17, 144n. 21; neigh-
borhood, 44; population, 43
"Mezzogiorno," 152n. 3
Michelangelo, 128, 129
"microtexts," 67
"mind-gynocologists," 61
MLA, 134n. 2, 158n. 8
modernism, 4, 12–13
modernist, 64
Montale, Eugenio, 111
Montalian influence, 116
*Moonstruck*, 128
Morton, Donald, 122, 131, 158n. 4
mosaic, 5, 18
multicultural discourse, 160n. 25
multiculturalism, 121, 122, 132; (de-
fined), 129
Mussolini, Benito, 62–63, 141n. 3
"My Mother's Stories," 28, 45

narrating voices, 68
narrator, 24; female, 70
narration, act of, 24
National Italian American Foundation (NIAF), 128, 160n. 22
national origin, 6
Nietzsche, Friedrich, 149n. 14
"Nonna," 24, 36–44
north/south, dichotomy, 38; question, 90–93
nostalgia, 131; Patriarca's 156n. 10

old world, 85, 145n. 9; concepts, 60;
idea, 51; vs new world, 32–44;
ways, 143n. 15
otherness, 96

Pacino, Al, 130
Palazzeschi, Aldo, 75, 111, 149n. 9,
    150n. 20
Palazzeschian way, 68
Parati, Graziella, 160n. 25
Parentheses Press, 123
parochial school, 51
parody, 71
Patriarca, Gianna, viii; 39, 40, 95–108,
    142n. 9, 155n. 3; nostalgia, 156n. 10
patriarchal society, 146n. 12
Pavone, Michael, 158n. 6
Peirce, Charles Sanders, 12–14, 17,
    139n. 30, 143n. 16, 150n. 16
Peircean/Econian semiotics, 150n. 16
Penley, Constance, 158n. 4
Pérez Firmat, Gustavo, 135n. 7, 156n.
    2, 159n. 9
Pietralunga, Mark, xi
Pileggi, Nick, 141n. 3
"Pink Cadillac," 143n. 19
Poesaggio, viii
postmodern(ism), 4, 6, 12, 77, 135n. 9,
    151n. 25; condition, 114, 121
programs of an interdisciplinary na-
    ture, 129
public school, 51
Puzo, Mario, 17, 123, 130, 138n. 23,
    140n. 41, 141n. 3, 142n. 9

questione della lingua, 136n. 15

race, 6
racism, 90
reader, 15–16, 23, 24, 37, 44, 45, 68,
    70–74, 78, 96, 99, 106, 108, 112,
    139n. 36, 148n. 8; author and, 69;
    interpretive act, 77; modernist, 19;
    postmodernist, 19; process, 75; ren-
    dition, 73–74
reading, 74; task, 107
rebel, 50
Rella, Franco, 155n. 2, 155n. 3, 155n.
    6, 155n. 7

Ricci, Franco, 134n. 9
Riesman, David, 47, 144n. 1
Rimanelli, Giose, vii, 14, 65–78, 117,
    138n. 25, 148n. 6, 148n. 7, 148n. 9,
    149n. 10, 149n. 11, 149n. 14,
    151n. 21
Rocky, 153n. 11
Romano, Rose, 142n. 7
Romano, Tony, 129
Rosen, Bernard, 142n. 7
Rossi, Agnes, 125
Russo, John Paul, viii, 18

Said, Edward, 124
Savoca, Nancy, 130, 141n. 3, 158n. 6
Scorsese, Martin, ix, 7, 127, 128, 130,
    141n. 3, 153n. 11
second stage, 11
secondness, 12–14; (defined), 138n. 28
self-awareness as a storyteller, 45
self-reflexivity, 70
Shanley, John Patrick, 128
sign(s), 16, 77
sign-functions, 76, 77
Silone, Ignazio, 161n. 27
Sinatra, Frank, 142n. 8
slash (/) in place of the
    hyphen (-), viii
sociology, 30
Sollors, Werner, vii, 133n. 5
Sorrentino, Gilbert, 17, 18
the South, 89
Southern Italy, 152n. 4
Spatola, Adriano, 113
Stallone, Sylvester, 153n. 11
"structural assimilation," 158n. 2
SUNY Stony Brook, 123
sweet nostalgia, 103–04

tabula rasa, 106–07
Tamburri, Anthony Julian, 139n. 34
Tender Warriors, 142n. 9
Tesoro, Victor, xi
text (defined), 67; two sides to a,
    73–74

*To Hyphenate or Not to Hyphenate? The Italian/American Writer: An Other American,* xi
Torcellis, 153n. 11
thirdness, 12–14; (defined), 139n. 29
traditional roles, especially female, 154n. 17
truth, 73
Tucci, Stanley, 158n. 6
Tusiani, Joseph, 16, 129, 135n. 8

Ulysses, 153n. 9
*Umbertina* (1979), 17, 40, 47–64, 81–93, 138n. 23, 142n. 9, 142n. 14, 156n. 11

Valentino, Rudolph, 142n. 8
Valerio, Anthony, 125, 129
Valesio, Paolo, viii, 110, 114, 117, 129, 135n. 7, 156n. 4, 156n. 5
Vatican II, 28
Vecoli, Rudolph, 123
Verdicchio, Pasquale, viii, xi
*VIA* FOLIOS, 123
Viano, Maruizio, xi
Vico, Giambattista, 10, 126, 149n. 14
Viscusi, Robert, viii, xi, 125, 126, 130, 131, 160n. 23, 161n. 27
Vitiello, Justin, viii, xi
*Voices in Italian Americana (VIA),* viii, 123, 160n. 22, 161n. 26, 161n. 28
Volosinov, V. N., 151n. 21

Wachtel, Chuck, 125
West, Rebecca, xi

Whyte, William, 142n. 7
Wickham, DeWayne, 135n. 3
Winsey, Valentine Rossilli, 63
Winwar, Francis, 125, 129
woman's dilemma, 88–89
woman's right to self-determination, 61–62
women, 95–108
*World Literature Today,* xi
"World without End," 32
writer, 24, (three possible categories of), 13; bilingual, 159n. 9; bilingual Italian/American, 135n. 8; *comparative,* 13–14, 17, 47–64; three general categories of ethnic, 109–10; *expressive,* 13–14, 23–46; first-stage, 9, 10, 23; "hyphenate," 66, 111, 124, 126, 127, 136n. 16, 159n. 12; Italian/Canadian, 160n. 26; modernist, mythic, 11; postmodernist, philosophic, 11; pre-modernist, poetic, 11; second-stage, 9, 10–11, 63–64; *synthetic,* 13–14, 17, 65–78; third-stage, 9, 11, 66; three possible categories of the Italian/American, 13

Yans-McLaughlin, Virginia, 63

Zanzotto, Andrea, 111, 116, 157n. 13
Zavarzadeh, Mas'ud, 122, 131, 158n. 4